全国高等美术院校建筑与环境艺术设计专业规划教材

专 业 英 语
阅读与提高

武云霞　主编
何晓昕　校审

中国建筑工业出版社

图书在版编目(CIP)数据

专业英语 阅读与提高/武云霞主编．—北京：中国建筑工业出版社，2009

全国高等美术院校建筑与环境艺术设计专业规划教材
ISBN 978-7-112-11258-6

Ⅰ. 专… Ⅱ. 武… Ⅲ. 建筑学-英语-高等学校-教材 Ⅳ. H31

中国版本图书馆 CIP 数据核字(2009)第 155144 号

责任编辑：唐　旭　李东禧
责任设计：董建平
责任校对：梁珊珊　兰曼利

全国高等美术院校建筑与环境艺术设计专业规划教材
专业英语
阅读与提高
武云霞　主编
何晓昕　校审
*
中国建筑工业出版社出版、发行(北京西郊百万庄)
各地新华书店、建筑书店经销
北京天成排版公司制版
北京云浩印刷有限责任公司印刷
*
开本：880×1230 毫米 1/16　印张：9　插页：1　字数：360 千字
2009 年 11 月第一版　2009 年 11 月第一次印刷
定价：38.00 元
ISBN 978-7-112-11258-6
(18521)

版权所有　翻印必究
如有印装质量问题，可寄本社退换
(邮政编码　100037)

全国高等美术院校
建筑与环境艺术设计专业规划教材

总主编单位：
中央美术学院
中国美术学院
西安美术学院
鲁迅美术学院
天津美术学院
四川美术学院
广州美术学院
湖北美术学院
清华大学美术学院
上海大学美术学院
中国建筑工业出版社

总主编：
吕品晶　张惠珍

编委会委员：
马克辛　王海松　吴昊　苏丹　邵建　赵健
黄耘　傅祎　彭军　詹旭军　唐旭　李东禧
（以上所有排名不分先后）

《专业英语　阅读与提高》
本卷主编单位： 上海大学美术学院
　　　　　　　武云霞　主编
　　　　　　　何晓昕　校审

总　序

缘起

《全国高等美术院校建筑与环境艺术设计专业实验教学丛书》已经出版十余册，它们是以不同学校教师为依托的、以实验课程教学内容为基础的教学总结，带有各自鲜明的教学特点，适宜于师生们了解目前国内美术院校建筑与环境艺术设计专业教学的现状，促进教师对富有成效的特色教学进行理论梳理，以利于取长补短，共同进步。目前，这套实验教学丛书还在继续扩展，期望覆盖更多富有各校教学特色的各类课程。同时对那些再版多次的实验丛书，经过原作者的精心整理，逐步提炼出课程的核心内容、原理、方法和价值观编著出版，这成为我们组织编写《全国高等美术院校建筑与环境艺术设计专业规划教材》的基本出发点。

组织

针对美术院校的规划教材，既要对学科的课程内容有所规划，更要对美术院校相应专业办学的价值取向做出规划，建立符合美术院校教学规律、适应时代要求的教材观。规划教材应该是教学经验和基本原理的有机结合，以学生既有的知识与经验为基础，更加贴近学生的真实生活，同时，也要富含、承载与传递科学概念、方法等教育和文化价值。十所美术院校与中国建筑工业出版社在经过多年的合作之后，走到一起，通过组织每年的各种教学研讨会，共同为美术院校建筑与环境艺术设计专业的教材建设做出规划，各个院校的学科带头人们聚在一起，讨论教材的总体构想、教学重点、编写方向和编撰体例，逐渐廓清了规划教材的学术面貌，具有丰富教学经验的一线教师们将成为规划教材的编撰主体。

内容

与《全国高等美术院校建筑与环境艺术设计专业实验教学丛书》以特色教学为主有所不同的是，本规划教材将更多关注美术院校背景下的基础、技术和理论的普适性教学。作为美术院校的规划教材，不仅应该把学科最基本、最重要的科学事实、概念、原理、方法、价值观等反映到教材中，还应该反映美术学院的办学定位、培养目标和教学、生源特点。美术院校教学与社会现实关系密切，特别强调对生活现实的体验和直觉感知，因此，规划教材需要从生活现实中获得灵感和鲜活的素材，需要与实际保持紧密而又生动具体的关系。规划教材内容除了反映基本的专业教学需求外，期待根据美院情况，增加与社会现实紧密相关的应用知识，减少枯燥冗余的知识堆砌。

使用

艺术的思维方式重视感性或所谓"逆向思维"，强调审美情感的自然流露和想象力的充分发挥，对于建筑教育而言，这种思维方式有助于学生摆脱过分的工程技术理性的约束，在设计上呈现更大的灵活性和更加丰富的想象，以至于在创作中可以更加充分地体现复杂的人文需要，并且在维护实用价值的同时最大程度地扩展美学追求；辩证地运用教材进行教学，要强调概念理解和实际应用，把握知识的积累与创新思维能力培养的互动关系，生动有趣、联系实际的教材对于学生在既有知识经验基础上顺利而准确地理解和掌握课程内容将发挥重要作用。

教材的使命永远是手段，而不是目的。使用教材不是为照本宣科提供方便，更不是为了堆砌浩瀚无边的零散、琐碎的知识，使用教材的目的应该始终是让学生理解和掌握最基本的科学概念，建立专业的观念意识。

教材的使用与其说是为了追求优质的教学效果，不如说是为了保证基本的教学质量。广义而言，任何具有价值的现实存在都可以被视为教材，但是，真正的教材永远只会存在于教师心智之中。

吕品晶　张惠珍
2008 年 10 月

前　言

　　建筑学专业英语，是中国高校建筑院系在高年级开设的专业选修课程，其教学目标是使学生能够运用英语这一工具，通过阅读英语文献获取国外与本专业有关的科技信息。专业英语是建筑学专业学生必备的基本修养。

　　本教材有以下几个特点：

　　1. 由点及面：统计资料显示，在每一个专业的科技文献中，本专业最常用的术语只有几百个，而且它们在文献中重复出现的频率很高。本书将以建筑学专业英语常见词语为突破口，罗列常见相关词汇、短语等近千条，帮助学生消除建筑学专业英语阅读中的拦路虎——生词，使那些已通过大学一、二级英语学习的学生，很快树立对建筑学专业英语学习的兴趣。我们相信，克服了阅读专业英语的恐惧感之后，学生们就能有信心读懂英文的建筑学专业文献。

　　2. 由浅入深：在第2章中，我们选取了当代著名建筑师的代表作，并作中英对照。由于学生大多已了解这些建筑的特点，因而学生会较容易读懂这些建筑的英文表达。此外，还安排了环境艺术设计、室内设计及中外名画与雕塑等相关内容。

　　3. 理论与实践：在第3章中，我们选取了当代部分建筑师的理论文章，这部分的文章涉及建筑师的设计哲学，故较难理解。

　　4. 实用性：在第5章中，我们选取了第七届 OISTAT 国际建筑设计竞赛要求，并作中英对照。考虑到国内建筑系学生越来越多地参加国际建筑设计竞赛的现状，这部分内容将帮助学生阅读此类信息，掌握一定的模式性语言。在第6章中，我们选取了美国建筑专业的施工图图纸，中英对照。随着世界各地的建筑名家来中国实践，大量英文图纸也出现在中国建筑领域，此章节将帮助学生了解英文的建筑图表达。

　　笔者承担建筑学专业英语教学工作多年，一直苦于没有一本简明适用的教学参考书，今尽绵薄之力，感到十分欣慰。本教材不仅适用于在校学生，对于有志提高专业英语阅读能力的建筑行业广大工程技术人员，也是适用的自学教材。

本书由武云霞主编，何晓昕校审。参加编写工作的还有夏明、陈雳、林磊、尤立、肖素红、宋育华、杨丽、颜美华。其中，武云霞：3.4、3.5；夏明：第1章、2.1.3、2.1.4、2.2.5；陈雳：2.1.1、2.1.2、2.2.2、3.3、4.1；林磊：2.2.1、4.2、4.3；武云霞、宋育华：第5章；尤立、刘嵩松：第6章；肖素红、赵世勇：2.4；杨丽、何晓昕：2.2.4，2.3；颜美华、李婕：2.2.3。

刘嵩松、李婕、赵世勇参与整理、文字录入工作。

《专业英语 阅读与提高》是我们编写对口专业阅读教材的一次尝试，由于编者、译者水平及经验有限，教材中难免存在不妥之处，敬请广大读者批评指正，以待今后修正完善。

本书编写工作得到上海大学教材建设专项经费资助。

目　录

总序
前言

001　第1章　专业词语

- 001　1.1　房间名称
- 003　1.2　建筑类型
- 005　1.3　常见建筑表现图用词
- 006　1.4　建筑构件
- 007　1.5　建筑材料
- 008　1.6　建筑中常见几何形
- 009　1.7　建筑美学与评论用语
- 011　1.8　建筑结构
- 012　1.9　建筑历史中常见词语
- 014　1.10　其他
- 016　1.11　重要建筑组织及派别
- 017　1.12　外国著名建筑师
- 019　1.13　外国著名建筑
- 022　1.14　建筑文献中常见国家及地区
- 023　1.15　常见植物名称

025　第2章　设计实例选译

- 025　2.1　建筑设计
- 025　2.1.1　毕尔巴鄂的古根海姆博物馆
- 027　2.1.2　帝国饭店
- 029　2.1.3　萨伏伊别墅
- 033　2.1.4　范斯沃斯住宅
- 039　2.2　环境艺术设计
- 039　2.2.1　华盛顿西雅图奥林匹克雕塑公园
- 042　2.2.2　北京奥林匹克公园
- 045　2.2.3　澳大利亚昆士兰市布里斯班河规划
- 046　2.2.4　格拉斯小镇

048	2.2.5	改建项目——贝加莫市 Nembro 新市政图书馆
050	**2.3**	**室内设计**
050	2.3.1	某度假村室内设计
051	2.3.2	某起居室室内设计
052	2.3.3	某走廊室内设计
053	2.3.4	某起居室室内设计
054	**2.4**	**中外名画与雕塑**

059　第 3 章　设计理念选译

059	**3.1**	**可持续发展的关键问题**
059	**3.2**	**城市发展的选择**
061	**3.3**	**格罗皮乌斯和包豪斯**
064	**3.4**	**[日]黑川纪章：意义的生成**
065	3.4.1	从认识论到本体论
070	3.4.2	旨意＝主题(Text)；意义的生成
075	3.4.3	信息社会的建筑
079	**3.5**	**[日]伊东丰雄：现代之外的主体意象：是否存在无"临界"的居住建筑**
079	3.5.1	当代社会的分歧
081	3.5.2	对临界的误解
082	3.5.3	一群隐遁的美学家
083	3.5.4	一座最纯粹的现代主义住宅，或奥戈曼悲剧
086	3.5.5	现代之外的主体意象

089　第 4 章　专业英语课外阅读

089	**4.1**	**佛光寺**
091	**4.2**	**滨水区设计标准**
099	**4.3**	**街道设计标准和规则**

122　第 5 章　第七届 OISTAT 国际剧场建筑竞赛

130　第 6 章　国外建筑设计图选译

第1章 专业词语[1]

1.1 房间名称

词	词性	释义
access [ˈækses]	n.	接近，进入，通路
activity room		活动室，儿童游戏室
administrative office		行政办公室
apartment [əˈpɑːtmənt]	n	公寓，套间
architect [ˈɑːkitekt]	n.	建筑师，设计师
architectural [ˌɑːkiˈtektʃərəl]	a.	建筑学的，建筑上的
architecture [ˈɑːkitektʃə]	n.	建筑学
atrium [ˈɑːtriəm]	n.	中庭；门廊
atelier [ˈætəliei]	n.	画室，工作室
auditorium [ˌɔːdiˈtɔːriəm]	n.	观众席，讲堂，礼堂
baseball court		棒球场
basement [ˈbeismənt]	n.	地下室，底层
bathroom [ˈbɑːθruːm]	n.	浴室，盥洗室
bedroom [ˈbedrum]	n.	卧室
billiard room		桌球室
booking office		售票处，订票处
breakfront [ˈbreikfrʌnt]	n.	正面入口
call box		电话间
classroom [ˈklɑːsrum]	n.	教室，课堂
cloak [kləuk]	n.	覆盖(物)
cloakroom [ˈkləukruːm]	n.	衣帽间
closet [ˈklɔzit]	n.	密室，小房间，壁橱
courtyard [ˈkɔːtjɑːd]	n.	庭院，院子
dayroom [ˈdeirum]	n.	(学校等的)休息室，(营房等的)娱乐室
dining room		餐室
entrance [ˈentrəns]	n.	进入，入口，进口
fitness room		健身房
flat [flæt]	n	套间，居室
foyer [ˈfɔiei]	n.	门厅，休息室
function room		宴会厅
garage [ˈgærɑːdʒ]	n.	汽车库

---

[1] 本章所列专业词语的中文翻译以建筑中的用法为主。

续表

gate [geit]	n.	大门，城门
gate post	n.	门柱
gateway ['geitwei]	n.	门口，入口
guardian's room		管理员室
hangar ['hæŋə]	n.	飞机库
	vt.	把(飞机)放入机库
ice-cream parlor ['pɑːlə(r)]		冷饮店
information office		问讯处
karaoke room		卡拉OK厅
kitchen ['kitʃin]	n.	厨房
laboratory [lə'bɔːrətəri]	n.	实验室
landing ['lændiŋ]	n.	楼梯平台，斜路平台，梯台
larder ['lɑːdə]	n.	贮藏间，食品柜
lavatory ['lævətəri]	n.	盥洗室，厕所
lecture room		演讲厅
living room		起居室
lobby ['lɔbi]	n.	门厅，门廊
locker room		衣帽间，更衣室
loft [lɔft]	n.	阁楼，顶楼，(仓库、工厂、教室)楼层
lounge [laundʒ]	n.	休息室
male/female changing room		男/女更衣室
multipurpose room		多功能厅
night duty room		值班室
night-keeper's room		值班室
playground ['pleigraund]	n.	操场
porch [pɔːtʃ]	n.	(上有顶棚的)门廊，走廊，游廊
portal ['pɔːtəl]	n.	门，正门
porter's room		传达室
portico ['pɔːtikəu]	n.	(有圆柱的)门廊
quash court		壁球场
reading room		阅览室
reception room		接待室，会客室
refectory [ri'fektəri]	n.	(修道院，学院等处的)食堂，餐厅
repository [ri'pɔzitəri]	n.	贮藏室
roof garden		屋顶花园
sauna ['sɔːnə]	n.	桑拿浴室
shower room		淋浴室
sitting lounge		休息间
square [skwɛə]	n.	广场，正方形
stock room		贮藏室
storage ['stɔːridʒ]	n.	贮藏库，仓库

续表

studio [stjuːdiəu]	n.	(画家、雕刻师、摄影者、艺术家等)工作室
sun deck		日光晒台
swimming pool		游泳池
table tennis room		乒乓球室
telephone box		电话间
tennis court		网球场
toilet ['tɔilit]	n.	盥洗室,浴室,厕所
vestibule ['vestibjuːl]	n.	门厅,前厅
warehouse ['wɛəhaus]	n.	仓库
W. C. (Water Closet)		厕所

1.2 建 筑 类 型

academy [əˈkædəmi]	n.	高等专科院校,研究院,学会
airfield [ˈɛəfiːld]	n.	飞机场
airport [ˈɛəpɔːt]	n.	机场,航空站
aquarium [əˈkwɛəriəm]	n.	水族馆
Arena [əˈriːnə]	n.	竞技场,舞台
barber's shop		理发馆
bookstore [ˈbukstɔː(r)]	n.	书店
cafe [kæfei;(美)kəfei]	n.	咖啡馆,餐馆,酒吧
cafeteria [kæfiˈtiəriə]	n.	自助食堂
campus [ˈkæmpəs]	n.	校园,学校场地
castle [ˈkaːsl]	n.	城堡(多指中实际贵族的要塞)
chateau [ˈʃaːtəu]	n.	城堡(尤指法国的)乡间邸宅,别墅
cinema [ˈsinimə]	n.	电影院,电影
circus [ˈsəːkəs]	n.	杂技场,马戏团
club [klʌb]	n.	俱乐部,夜总会
community center		居住区中心,公共会堂
complex [ˈkɔmpleks]	n.	综合体,建筑群
creche [kreiʃ]	n.	托儿所
department store		百货商店
detached [diˈtætʃt] house		点式住宅,独立式住宅
dormitory [ˈdɔːmitri]	n.	宿舍
dwelling [ˈdweliŋ]	n.	住所,寓所
dwelling house		住宅
greenhouse [ˈgriːnhaus]	n.	温室,暖房,花房
grocery [ˈgrəusəri]	n.	食品杂货店
gymnasium [dʒimˈneisiəm]	n.	体育馆
headquarters [ˈhedˈkwɔːtəz]	n.	总部,总店
high-rise	a.	有多层楼房并装有电梯的

续表

		n.	摩天的高层建筑
hospital ['hɔspitl]		n.	医院
hostel ['hɔstəl]		n.	在校外的学生宿舍，旅店，招待所
hotel [həu'tel]		n.	旅社
ice hockey rink			冰球场
ice rink			溜冰场
inn [in]		n.	小旅馆，客栈
institute [institju:t]		n.	学校，研究所，专科学校
kindergarten [kindəga:tn]		n.	幼儿园
laundry ['lɔ:ndri]		n.	洗衣店，洗衣房
library ['laibrəri]		n.	图书馆
local dwelling			民居
lodging ['lɔdʒiŋ]		n.	寄宿，住所
lodging facilities			住宿设施
mansion ['mænʃən]		n.	官邸，宅第
market ['ma:kit]		n.	市场
monument ['mɔnjumənt]		n.	纪念碑，纪念馆
motel [məu'tel]		n.	汽车旅馆
museum [mju(:)'ziəm]		n.	博物馆
office building			办公楼
pagoda [pə'gəudə]		n.	塔
pavilion [pə'viljən]		n.	亭子，（博览会的）馆
Plaza ['pla:zə]		n.	购物中心，广场
post office			邮局
prison ['prizn]		n.	监狱
pub [pʌb]		n.	（英国）小酒馆，小旅馆
railway station			火车站
recreation centre			康乐中心
residence ['rezidəns]		n.	住宅，公馆，居住
restaurant ['restərɔnt]		n.	餐馆，饭店
retail ['ri:teil]		n.	零售，零卖
semi-detached house			半独立屋(两套房子连在一起共用一个屋顶，英国常见)
stadium ['steidiəm]		n.	体育场，体育馆
station ['steiʃən]		n.	车站
shopping mall [mɔ:l]			商业街
silo ['sailəu]		n.	地窖，筒仓
skyscraper ['skaiskreipə(r)]		n.	摩天大楼
stock exchange			证券交易所
theatre ['θiətə]		n.	剧场，戏院
the Great Exhibition			博览会
terrace house			一排房屋中的一座，毗邻式住宅
tower ['tauə]		n.	塔，塔楼
twin-pagoda			双塔

1.3　常见建筑表现图用词

a great plan/master plan		总平面图
a perspective plan		透视图
a rough plan/draft plan		设计草图
a set square		三角板
a working plan/construction plan/drawing		施工图
axonometric [ˌæksəˈnɔmitri] drawing		轴侧图
bird's-eye view		鸟瞰图
compass [ˈkʌmpəs]	n.	指北针
cross sections		剖面图
delineation [diˌliniˈeiʃən]	n.	示意图
design specification		设计任务书
design of plan		平面设计
detail drawing		详图
diagram [ˈdaiəgræm]	n.	图，图式
dimension [diˈmenʃən]	n.	尺寸，尺度
draft [drɑːft]	n.	草图
drawing board		图板
elevation [ˌeliˈveiʃən]	n.	立面图，高度，标高，海拔
flow diagram		流线图
graphic [ˈgræfik]	a.	图的，图解的，绘画的
	n.	图画，图表
graphics [ˈgræfiks]	n.	制图法
ground floor/first floor		一层平面
illustrate [ˈiləstreit]	n.	说明，图解，插图
perspective [pəˈspektiv]	n.	透视
plan [plæn]	n.	平面图，设计图
preliminary design		初步设计
profile [ˈprəufail]	n.	侧面，外形，外观，形象
	vt.	描……的轮廓，绘……的侧面图
regional planning		区域规划
scale [skeil]	n.	比例，比例尺，刻度，规模
scheme design		方案设计
second floor		二层平面
section [ˈsekʃən]	n.	剖面
sketch [sketʃ]	n.	草图，速写，素描
third floor		三层平面
T square		丁字尺

1.4 建筑构件

air-vent	n.	通风口
aisle [ail]	n.	(教堂、戏院的)通道,甬道,走廊
arcade [ɑːˈkeid]	n.	连拱廊,有拱顶的街道
attic [ˈætik]	n.	小阁楼
balcony [ˈbælkəni]	n.	阳台
blinds [blaindz]	n.	百叶窗
canopy [ˈkænəpi]	n.	挑棚,雨篷
carpet [ˈkɑːpit]	n.	地毯
ceiling [ˈsiːliŋ]	n.	顶棚,吊顶
clerestory [ˈkliəstəri]	n.	楼座,长廊,天窗,高侧窗
coffer [ˈkɔfə]	n.	藻井
	vt.	把……装入箱子
corridor [ˈkɔridɔː]	n.	走廊
crown [kraun]	n.	顶部,拱顶
	vt.	为……加顶
cupboard [ˈkʌbəd]	n.	碗碟橱,食橱,小柜
curtain [ˈkəːtn]	n.	帘子
dado [ˈdeidəu]	n.	护壁板,墙裙
dormer [ˈdɔːmə] window		老虎窗
draught [drɑːft]	n.	通风
elevator [ˈeliveitə]	n.	电梯
escalator [ˈeskəleitə]	n.	自动扶梯
facility [fəˈsiliti]	n.	容易,简易,设备,工具
fire escape		太平梯,安全出口
fire hydrant [ˈhaidrənt]		消火栓
fireplace [ˈfaiəpleis]	n.	壁炉
fireproof [ˈfaiəpruːf]	n.	防火,耐火
fire wall		防火墙
flight [flait]	n.	楼梯
floor [flɔː]	n.	地面,地板,楼面、楼层、楼盖
fresco [ˈfreskəu]	n.	壁画
full high window		落地窗
furniture [ˈfəːnitʃə]	n.	家具
gable [ˈgeibl]	n.	山墙,三角墙
gable and hip roof		歇山
gallery [ˈgæləri]	n.	长廊,游廊,门廊
grille [gril]	n.	格子窗
handrail [ˈhændˈreil]	n.	扶手,栏杆
hip roof		庑殿
lamp [læmp]	n.	灯

续表

layer [leiə]	n.	层
loggia ['lɔdʒiə]	n.	凉廊
mo(u)lding ['mouldiŋ]	n.	(凹凸)线脚
natural ventilation [venti'leiʃən]		自然通风
parapet ['pærəpit]	n.	女儿墙
partition wall		隔墙
penthouse ['penthaus]	n.	(靠在大楼等边上搭的)披屋，阁楼
plug [plʌg]	n.	塞子，栓，消火栓
pyramidal [pi'ræmidl] roof		攒尖
skylight ['skailait]	n.	天窗，天上的光
staircase ['steəkeis]	n.	楼梯间，楼梯
story ['stɔːri]	n.	(层)楼
straight stair		直跑楼梯
terrace ['terəs]	n.	倾斜的平地，露台，平台，阳台
ventilation [,venti'leiʃən]	n.	通风
walkway ['wɔːkwei]	n.	走道
wardrobe ['wɔːdrəub]	n.	藏衣室，衣橱
wing [wiŋ]	n.	侧厅，翼

1.5 建 筑 材 料

aluminium [ælju'minjəm]	n.	铝
asbestos [æz'bestəs]	n.	石棉
asphalt ['æsfælt]	n.	沥青
asphalt felt		油毛毡
blue curtain wall		蓝色玻璃幕墙
brick [brik]	n.	砖
bronze [brɔnz]	n.	青铜
cast-iron ['kaːst'aiən]	n.	生铁，铸铁
celloglass ['seləglaːs]	n.	赛珞玻璃
cement [si'ment]	n.	水泥
ceramic [si'ræmik]	a.	陶器的，陶瓷的
china ['tʃainə]	n.	瓷器
clay [klei]	n.	黏土，泥土
concrete ['kɔnkriːt]	n.	混凝土
fabric ['fæbrik]	n.	织物，布
flag stone		(铺路用的)石板，板石
ferroconcrete [,ferəu'kɔnkriːt]		钢筋混凝土
ferro-cement	n.	钢丝网水泥
free stone		毛(乱，易切，软性)石

续表

frosted glass		磨砂玻璃
glass [glaːs]	n.	玻璃
glazed [gleizd]	a.	上釉的
glazing ['gleiziŋ]	n.	(总称)玻璃窗；抛光
granite ['grænit]	n.	花岗石
granolithic [ˌgrænəu'liθik]	a.	人造石铺面的
gypsum ['dʒipsəm]	n.	石膏，灰泥板
limestone [laimstəun]	n.	石灰石
marble ['maːbl]	n.	大理石，云石
membrane [membrein]	n.	薄膜
metal ['metl]	n.	金属
paint [peint]	n.	油漆，涂料，颜料
painted ['peintid]	a.	着色的，上了漆的
panel board		镶板，心子板
pebble ['pebl]	n.	卵石，细砾
plaster ['plaːstə]	n.	灰泥
plastic ['plaːstik]	n.	塑料
reinforced concrete		钢筋混凝土
steel tube		钢管
stainless steel		不锈钢
tile [tail]	n.	瓦片，瓷砖
whitewash ['(h)waitwɔʃ]	n.	粉饰，白色涂料

1.6 建筑中常见几何形

conoid ['kəunɔid]	n.	圆锥形，圆锥体
conoidal ['kəunɔidəl]	a.	圆锥形的
cupola ['kjuːpələ]	n.	圆顶
cylindrical [si'lindrik(ə)l]	a.	圆筒形的
ellipse [i'lips]	n.	椭圆
elliptic [i'liptik]	a.	椭圆形的
geometric [dʒiə'metrik]	a.	几何学的，几何图形的
hyperbolic [haipə'bɔlik]	a.	双曲线的
irregular [i'regjulə]	a.	不规则的，无规律的
octagonal [ɔk'tægənl]	a.	八角形的
ogee ['əudʒiː]	n. & a.	S形曲线(的)
paraboloid [pə'ræbəlɔid]	n.	抛物面
pyramid ['pirəmid]	n.	金字塔，角锥(体)，棱锥(体)
shell [ʃel]	n.	壳，壳体
single-curved shell		单曲壳

续表

skew-grid		斜格子
square-grid		方格子
triangle ['traiæŋgl]	n.	三角形，三角板
two-curved shell		双曲壳

1.7　建筑美学与评论用语

abandonment [ə'bændənmənt]	n.	放弃，抛弃，遗弃
aesthetic [i:s'θetik]	a.	美学的
aesthetics [i:s'θetiks]	n.	美学
ambiguity [ˌæmbi'gju(:)iti]	n.	不明确性，含混性
amendment [ə'mendmənt]	n.	改正，修正，改善
amenity [ə'mi:niti]	n.	(环境、气候的)舒服，(性情)愉快
alternative [ɔ:l'tə:nətiv]	a.	选择的，两者挑一的
	n.	抉择
artist ['a:tist]	n.	艺术家；美术家
artistic [a:'tistik]	a.	艺术的；美术的
assessment [ə'sesmənt]	n.	估价，评价
asymmetry [æ'simitri]	n.	不对称
appraisal [ə'preizəl]	vt.	估价，评价，鉴定
appreciate [ə'pri:ʃieit]	vt.	欣赏，鉴赏，鉴别
appreciation [əˌpri:ʃi'eiʃən]	n.	欣赏，鉴赏
character ['kæriktə]	n.	特性，性质，特征，品质
climate ['klaimit]	n.	气候；思潮
cluster type		多簇式
comfortable ['kʌmfətəbl]	a.	舒适的
conservative [kən'sə:vətiv]	a.	保守的，守旧的
contemporary [kən'tempərəri]	a.	当代的
coincidence [kəu'insidəns]	n.	符合，一致，巧合
coincident [kəu'insidənt]	a.	同时发生的，巧合的，一致的
composition [ˌkɔmpə'ziʃən]	n.	构成，构图
conventional [kən'venʃnl]	a.	常规的，传统的
corrugate ['kɔrugeit]	a.	波纹的
criterion [krai'tiəriən]	n.	标准，尺度
current ['kʌrənt]	a.	通用的，流行的，现行的
delicate ['delikit]	a.	细软的，娇嫩的，奢侈的
dominate ['dɔmineit]	vt.	支配，统治
duality [dju:'æliti]	n.	两重性，二元性
elaborate [i'læbərit]	a.	精心制作的
	vt.	精心制作

续表

elaboration [iˌlæbəˈreiʃən]	n.	精心制作，精致
enormous [iˈnɔːməs]	a.	巨大的，庞大的
estimate [ˈestimeit]	vt.	估计，估量，预算
	vi.	估计，估价
	n.	估计，预算
flexibility [ˌfleksəˈbiliti]	n.	柔韧性
golden section		黄金分割
habitual [həˈbitjuəl]	a.	习惯性的
harmony [ˈhɑːməni]	n.	调和，协调，和谐
horizon [həˈraizn]	n.	地平，地平线
horizontal [ˌhɔriˈzɔntl]	a.	地平的，水平的
	n.	水平线，水平面
identify [aiˈdentifai]	vt.	认出，识别，鉴定
identity [aiˈdentiti]	n.	同一(性)，一致，特性
module [ˈmɔdjuːl]	n.	模数
module system		模数系统
monotony [məˈnɔtəni]	n.	单调，无变化，千篇一律
monumental [ˌmɔnjuˈmentl]	a.	纪念的
mood [muːd]	n.	心情，心境，情结，基调，情调
motif [məuˈtiːf]	n.	主题，动机
motive [ˈməutiv]	n.	动机，主旨，目的
outstanding [autˈstændiŋ]	a.	杰出的，显著的
parameter [pəˈræmitə]	n.	参数
popular opinion		流行观点
preservation [ˌprezəˈveiʃən]	n.	保存，保持，保护
proportion [prəˈpɔːʃən]	n.	比例，均衡，部分
psychological [ˌsaikəˈlɔdʒikəl]	a.	心理上的，心理学的
psychology [saiˈkɔlədʒi]	n.	心理学，心理
rhythm [ˈriðəm]	n.	韵律，格律，匀称
rhythmic [ˈriðmik]	a.	有韵律的
sensibility [ˌsensiˈbiliti]	n.	感觉，情感
standard [ˈstændəd]	n.	标准，规范
statistics [stəˈtistiks]	n.	统计，统计数字，统计资料
symbiosis [ˌsimbaiˈəusis]	n.	共生
symbiotic [ˌsimbaiˈɔtik]	a.	共生的
symbol [ˈsimbəl]	n.	象征，符号
symbolic [simˈbɔlik]	a.	象征的，象征性的，符号的
symbolize [ˈsimbəlaiz]	vt.	作为……的象征
symmetrical [siˈmetrikəl]	a.	对称的，匀称的
symmetry [ˈsimitri]	n.	对称
technical climate		技术思潮
texture [ˈtekstʃə]	n.	结构，质地，纹理

续表

unification [ˌjuːnifiˈkeiʃən]	n.	统一，联合，一致
vertical [ˈvəːtikəl]	a.	垂直的，直立的
	n.	垂直面，竖向

1.8 建 筑 结 构

bay [bei]	n.	架间，开间、节间，柱距、桁距
beam [biːm]	n.	梁
bracket [ˈbrækit]	n.	托架，托座，斗栱
Bundled Tube System		束筒体系
cantilever [ˈkæntiliːvə]	n.	悬臂
column [ˈkɔləm]	n.	柱，圆柱
Column Diagonal Truss Tube		对角桁架柱筒体系
column grid		柱网
configuration [kənˌfigjuˈreiʃən]	n.	形状，构造，外形
corbel [ˈkɔːbəl]	vt.	支撑，用梁托
cross runner		次要构件
civil engineering		土木工程
economic span		经济跨度
exposed and suspension system		外露悬吊体系
framed structure		框架结构
Framed Tube		框架筒体系
framework [ˈfreimwəːk]	n.	构架，骨架结构
framing component		框架构件
field-poured gypsum roof decking		现浇石膏屋面板
girder [ˈgəːdə]	n.	（大）梁
main runner		主要构件
megastructure [ˌmegəˈstrʌktʃə]	n.	巨型结构
mushroom post		带柱帽的柱子
precast [priˈkɑːst]	vt. & a.	预制（的）
precast concrete slab		预制混凝土板
prefabricated [priːˈfæbrikeitid]	a.	预制
pretension [priːˈtenʃən]	n.	预张
runner [ˈrʌnə]	n.	构件
scaffold [ˈskæfəld]	n.	脚手架，骨架
shear [ʃiə]	n.	剪，剪力墙
skeleton [ˈskelitn]	n.	骨架
Shear Truss Frame Interaction		剪力桁架与框架体系
Shear Truss Frame Interaction with Rigid Belt		有刚性桁带的剪力桁架框架相互作用体系
Shear Wall		抗剪墙体系

续表

Shear Wall Frame Interaction		抗剪墙框架互相作用体系
span [spæn]	n.	跨度，墩距，全长
	vt.	横跨，跨越
support [sə'pɔːt]	vt. & n.	支撑，支柱
Tube in Tube System		套筒体系
truss [trʌs]	n.	桁架，构架
vault [vɔːlt]	n.	拱顶

1.9 建筑历史中常见词语

abbey [æbi]	n.	修道院
agora ['ægərə]	n.	(古希腊)广场
alignment [ə'lainmənt]	n.	列石
altar ['ɔːltə]	n.	祭坛，圣坛
arch [aːtʃ]	n.	拱，拱门
architrave ['aːkitreiv]	n.	柱缘，线脚
baroque [bə'rəuk]	n.	巴洛克风格
base [beis]	n.	柱础，基础
basilica [bə'zilikə]	n.	巴西利卡
Buddhism [budizəm]	n.	佛教
Buddhist [budist]	n.	佛教徒
	a.	佛教的
buttress [bʌtris]	n.	扶壁
capital ['kæpitl]	n.	柱头
castle ['kaːsl]	n.	城堡
cathedral [kə'θiːdrəl]	n.	大教堂
church [tʃəːtʃ]	n.	教堂
column ['kɔləm]	n.	柱，柱身
Composite Order		组合柱式
context ['kɔntekst]	n.	上下关系，背景，文脉
Corinthian Order		科林斯柱式
Counter-fort ['kauntəfɔːt]	n.	扶垛，护墙
craft [kraːft]	n.	工艺，手艺
craftsmanship [kraːftsmənʃip]	n.	(工匠的)技术，技艺
crest [krest]	n.	顶饰，脊饰
crest tile		屋脊瓦
cross vault		十字拱
dolmen ['dɔlmen]	n.	石台
dome [dəum]	n.	圆屋顶，穹隆
Domic(al) [dəumik]	a.	穹隆式的
Doric Order		多立克柱式
dynasty ['dinəsti]	n.	朝，朝代

fly-buttress		飞扶壁
Giant Order		巨柱式
gothic [ˈgɔθik]	a.	哥特人的，哥特式的
Ionic Order		爱奥尼克柱式
Ionic Scroll		爱奥尼克涡卷
lancet [ˈlɑːnsit]	n.	尖拱，尖状饰
Latin Cross		拉丁十字
mansard roof		复折屋顶，孟莎式屋顶
Mastaba [ˈmæstəbə]	n.	玛斯塔巴
medieval [mediˈiːvəl]	a.	中世纪的
Mediterranean [ˌmedɪtəˈreinjən]	n.	地中海
Megaron [ˈmegərɔn]	n.	美加仑
monastery [ˈmɔnəstəri]	n.	修道院，庙宇，寺院
monolith [ˈmɔnəuliθ]	n.	整石柱
mosque [mɔsk]	n.	伊斯兰教寺院，清真寺
nave [neiv]	n.	中厅
niche [nitʃ]	n.	壁龛
obelisk [ˈɔbilisk]	n.	方尖碑
order [ˈɔːdə]	n.	柱式，秩序
Palladian Motif		帕拉第奥母题
pendentive [penˈdentiv]	n.	帆拱
piazza [piˈætsə]	n.	广场，市场
prehistoric [ˈpriːhisˈtɔrik]	a.	史前的
primitive [ˈprimitiv]	a.	原始的，早期的
pylon [ˈpailən]	n.	牌楼门
religious [riˈlidʒəs]	a.	宗教的，宗教上的
religion [riˈlidʒən]	n.	宗教，信仰
renaissance [rəˈneisəns]	n.	文艺复兴
rococo [rɔˈkəukəu]	n.	洛可可
romanesque [ˌrəuməˈnesk]	a.	罗马风的
secular [ˈsekjulə]	a.	非宗教的，世俗的
stalactite [ˈstæləktait]	n.	钟乳拱，蜂窝拱
Stonehenge [ˈstəunhendʒ]	n.	石环
stupa [ˈstuːpə]	n.	印度塔，窣堵坡
temple [ˈtempl]	n.	庙宇，寺院，神殿
Thermae [ˈθəːmiː]	n.	浴场
Tuscan Order		塔司干柱式
vernacular [vəˈnækjulə]	a.	乡土，地方
Ziggurat [ˈzigəræt]		观象台

1.10 其 他

英文	词性	中文
air conditioner		空调
an active volcano		活火山
archaeology [ˌɑːkiˈɔlədʒi]	n.	考古学
a pedestrian crossing		人行横道
assist [əˈsist]	vt.	帮助,援助
assistance [əˈsistəns]	n.	援助,帮助
assistant [əˈsistənt]	a.	辅助的
	n.	辅助物,助手
authenticity [ˌɔːθenˈtisiti]	n.	确定性、原真性
block [blɔk]	n.	街区,大楼
boulevard [ˈbuːlivɑːd]	n.	大街,主干道
budget [ˈbʌdʒit]	n.	预算
	vi.	编预算
capital expenditure		基建费用
carve [kɑːv]	n.	雕刻品
cascade [kæsˈkeid]	n.	瀑布;格栅
challenge [ˈtʃælindʒ]	n.	挑战
client [ˈklaiənt]	n.	委托人,顾主,业主
commercial [kəˈməːʃəl]	a.	商业的
commission [kəˈmiʃən]	n.	委任,委托
component [kəmˈpəunənt]	n.	组成部分,成分
	a.	组成的,合成的
conceive [kənˈsiːv]	vt.	构想,设想
conference [ˈkɔnfərəns]	n.	讨论,会谈
conservation [ˌkɔnsə(ː)ˈveiʃən]	n.	(环境)保护
convention [kənˈvenʃən]	n.	会议,大会,集会
conventioneer [kənˌvenʃəˈniə]	n.	到会的人
Cultural Heritage		文化遗产
decade [ˈdekeid]	n.	十,十年
decoration [ˌdekəˈreiʃən]	n.	装饰,装潢
demeanor [diˈmiːnə]	n.	行为,举止,品行
devise [diˈvaiz]	vt.	设计,计划
district [ˈdistrikt]	n.	区,区域,地区
downtown [daunˈtaun]	n.	城市商业区
earthquake [ˈəːθkweik]	n.	地震
entertainment [ˌentəˈteinmənt]	n.	招待,招待会
exterior [eksˈtiəriə]	a.	外部的,室外
footbridge [ˈfutbridʒ]	n.	人行天桥
forest [ˈfɔrist]	n.	森林

续表

fountain ['fauntin]	n.	泉水，喷水泉
garden ['gɑ:dn]	n.	花园
Genius Loci		场所精神
habitable [hæbitəbl]	a.	可居住的
habitation [hæbiteiʃən]	n.	居住
highway ['haiwei]	n.	高速公路
inhabitant [in'hæbitənt]	n.	居民，住户，常住居民
interior [in'tiəriə]	a.	内部的，室内
landscape [lændskeip]	n.	风景，景色
layout ['lei,aut]	n.	布局，陈设，安排，设计
leasable ['li:səbl]	a.	可出租的
master-piece	n.	杰作
merchandise ['mə:tʃəndaiz]	n.	商品，货物
metropolis [mi'trɔpəlis]	n.	大城市，大都会
morphological [,mɔ:fə'lɔdʒikəl]	a.	形态学的
morphology [mɔ:'fɔlədʒi]	n.	形态学
neighborhood ['neibəhud]	n.	邻接，附近，街坊
ornament ['ɔ:nəmənt]	n.	装饰物，装饰品，装饰
park [pɑ:k]	n.	公园；停车场
pedestrian [pi'destriən]	a.	徒步的
peripteral [pə'riptərəl]	a.	围柱式的
pond [pɔnd]	n.	水池，池塘
preservation [,prezə(:)'veiʃən]	n.	保护，维护
Pritzker Architecture Prize		普利兹克奖
recreation [,rekri'eiʃən]	n.	消遣，娱乐
register/List ['redʒistə]/[list]	n.	注册/表，名单，编目
rehabilitation ['ri:(h)əbili'teiʃən]	n.	复兴，复原
resident ['rezidənt]	a.	居住的
sculpture ['skʌlptʃə]	n.	雕刻，雕塑
statue ['stætju:]	n.	雕像，塑像
suburb ['sʌbə:b]	n.	郊区，郊外
sustainability	n.	可持续性
tornado [tɔ:'neidəu]	n.	龙卷风，旋风
typological [,taipə'lɔdʒikəl]	a.	类型学的
vehicular [vi'hikjulə]	a.	车辆的
volcanic [vɔl'kænik]	a.	火山(性)的
		活火山
volcano [vɔl'keinəu]	n.	火山
urban ['ə:bən]	a.	城市的，都市的
waterfall ['wɔ:təfɔ:l]	n.	瀑布

1.11 重要建筑组织及派别

abstractionism [æbˈstrækʃənizəm]	n.	抽象派艺术
Allusionism [əl(j)uːˈʒənizəm]	n.	引喻主义
Archigram [ˈɑːkigræm]	n.	阿基格拉姆派
Arcological City		仿生式城市
Arts and Crafts Movement		工艺美术运动
Art Nouveau		新艺术运动
Bauhaus [ˈbauhaus]		包豪斯
biology [baiˈɔlədʒi]	n.	生物学，生态学
Brutalism [ˈbruːtəlizm]	n.	粗野主义
Charter of Athens		雅典宪章
Charter of Miachu-Picchu		马丘比丘宪章
Chicago School		芝加哥学派
Classical Revival		古典复兴
Classicism [ˈklæsisizm]	n.	古典主义
CIAM(Congre's Internationaux d'Architecture Moderne)		现代建筑国际会议，简称CIAM
City Industrial		工业城市
Colonial Style		殖民时期风格
Constructivism [kənˈstrʌktivizəm]	n.	构成派
Contextualism [kənˈtekstjuəlizəm]	n.	文脉主义
Deconstruction [ˌdiːkənˈstrʌkʃən]	n.	解构派，解构主义
De Stijl		风格派
Deutscher Werkbund		德意志制造联盟
Eclecticism [eˈklektisizəm]	n.	折衷主义
Elementarism [ˌeliˈmentəri]	n.	要素派
ethnology [eθˈnɔlədʒi]	n.	人种学，民族学，人类文化学
Existentialism [egziˈstenʃəliz(ə)m]	n.	存在主义
Eexpressionism [ikˈspreʃəniz(ə)m]	n.	表现派
Floating City		海上城市
Formalism [ˈfɔːməlizəm]	n.	典雅主义
Formalism [ˈfɔːməlizəm]	n.	形式主义
Functionalism [ˈfʌŋkʃənəlist]	n.	功能主义
Futurism [ˈfjuːtʃəriz(ə)m]	n.	未来派
Garden City		花园城市
Gridiron City		方格网城市
High-Tech		高技派
ICCROM (International Centre for the Study of the Preservation and Restoration of Cultural Property, Rome)		国际文物保护与修复研究中心，简称ICCROM
ICOMOS (International Council on Monuments and Sites)		国际历史建筑与遗址理事会，简称ICOMOS
Impressionism [imˈpreʃəniz(ə)m]	n.	印象主义，印象派

International Style			国际式建筑
Late Modernism			晚期现代派
Linear City			带形城市
Metabolism [meˈtæbəlizəm]		n.	新陈代谢派
Modernism [ˈmɔːdənizəm]		n.	现代主义
Neo-Plasticism			新造型派
Ornamentation [ˌɔːnəmenˈteiʃən]		n.	装饰主义
phenomenology [fɪnɔmiˈnɔlədʒi]		n.	现象学
phenomenon [fiˈnɔminən]		n.	现象
Plug-in City			插入式城市
Post Modernism			后现代派
Purism [ˈpjuərizəm]		n.	纯粹主义
rationalism [ˈræʃənəlizəm]		n.	理性主义
romanticism [rəˈmæntisizəm]		n.	浪漫主义
Space City			空间城市
Submarine City			海底城市
The Venice Charter			威尼斯宪章
UIA (Union International des Architects)			国际建筑师协会，简称 UIA
UNESCO (United Nations Educational, Scientific and Cultural Organization)			联合国教科文组织，简称 ONESCO
Village New Harmony			新协和村

1.12 外国著名建筑师

Adolf Loos	阿道夫·路斯
Arne Jacobsen	阿诺·雅各森
Aldo Rossi	阿尔多·罗西
Alvaro Siza	阿尔瓦罗·西扎
Alvar Aalto	阿尔瓦·阿尔托
Antonio Gaudi	安东尼奥·高迪
Arata Isozaki	矶崎新
A. & P. Smithson	史密森夫妇
Balkrishna Doshi	巴尔克什那·多什
Bernard Tschumi	贝尔纳·屈米
Ceasat Pelli	西萨·佩里
Charles Correa	查尔斯·柯里亚
Charles Jencks	查尔斯·詹克斯
Charles Moore	查尔斯·摩尔
Christian de Portzamparc	克里斯蒂昂·德·鲍赞巴克
Christopher Alexander	克里斯托弗·亚历山大
E. D. Stone	E·D·斯东

续表

Eero Saarinen		小沙里宁
Eliel Saarinen		老沙里宁
Frank Lloyd Wright(Organic architecture/Prairie House)		弗兰克·劳埃德·赖特(有机建筑/草原式住宅)
Frank O. Gehry		弗兰克·盖里
Fumihiko Maki		槇文彦
Glenn Murcutt		格伦·穆科特
Gordon Bunshaft		戈登·邦沙夫特
Gottfried Boehm		戈特弗里德·伯姆
Hans Hollein		汉斯·霍莱因
Hans Scharoun		汉斯·夏隆
Herzog & de Meuron		赫尔佐格与德梅隆
Hippodamus		希波丹姆斯
Jacques Herzog		杰奎斯·赫佐格
James Stirling		詹姆斯·斯特林
Jean Nouvel		让·努维尔
Joseph Paxton		约瑟夫·帕克斯顿
J. Utzon		J·伍重
Karl Fredrich Schinkel		卡尔·弗雷德墨克·辛克尔
Ken Yeang		杨经文
Kenzo Tange		丹下健三
Kevin Roche		凯文·林奇
Kisho Noriaki Kurokawa		黑川纪章
Kunio Maekawa		前川国男
Le Corbusier(Vers une Architecture)		勒·柯布西耶(走向新建筑)
Ieoh Ming Pei		贝聿铭
L. B. Alberti		L·B·阿尔伯蒂
Luis Barragan		路易斯·巴拉甘
Louis Henry Sullivan (Form follows function)		路易斯·亨利·沙利文 形式追随功能
Louis Kahn		路易·康
Mario Botta		马克奥·博塔
M. Breuer		M·布劳耶
Michael Graves		迈克尔·格雷夫斯
Mies Vander Rohe (Less is more. /Total Space)		密斯·凡·德·罗 少就是多/全面空间
Minoru Yamnsaki		雅马萨奇
Norman Foster		诺曼·福斯特
Oscar Niemeyer		奥斯卡·尼迈耶
Paul Roudolph		保罗·鲁道夫
Paulo Mendes da Rocha		保罗·门德斯·达·罗查
Peter Behrens		彼得·贝仑斯
Peter Eisenman		彼得·艾森曼

续表

Pierre de Meuron		皮埃尔·德·默隆
Philip Johnson		菲利普·约翰逊
P. L. Nervi		P·L·奈尔维
Rafael Moneo		拉斐尔·莫尼欧
Rem Koolhaas		雷姆·库哈斯
Renzo Piano		伦佐·皮亚诺
Richard Meier		理查德·迈耶
Richard Rogers		理查德·罗杰斯
Robert Venturi		罗伯特·文丘里
Robert A. M. Stern		罗伯特·斯特恩
Santiago Calatrava		圣地亚哥·卡拉特拉瓦
SOM(Skidmore, Owings & Merrill)		史欧姆建筑事务所，简称SOM
Sverre Fehn		斯维尔·费恩
TAC(The Architects Lolaborative)		协和建筑事务所
Tadao Ando		安藤忠雄
Thom Mayn		汤姆·梅恩
Marcus Vitruvius Pollio (De Architectura Libri decem)		维特鲁威（《建筑十书》）
Walter Gropius		沃尔特·格罗皮乌斯
Zaha Hadid		扎哈·哈迪德

1.13　外国著名建筑

Acropolis, Athens	雅典卫城
AEG Tubine Factory	德国通用电气公司透平机车间
Asume House, Osaka	住吉的长屋
Art and Architecture Department Building, Yale University	耶鲁大学艺术与建筑系大楼
AT&T Headquarters Building	电报电话公司总部大楼
Baker House Dormitory, M. I. T	贝克大楼
Barcelona Pavilion	巴塞罗那博览会德国馆
Bianchi House at Riva San Vitale, Ticino	圣维塔莱河畔比安希住宅
Brandenburger Tor, Berlin	柏林勃兰登堡门
Cambridge University History Faculty Library	剑桥大学历史系图书馆
Casa Mila	米拉公寓
Centre National des Industries et Techniques	巴黎国家工业与技术中心陈列大厅
Children's Home, Amsterdam	阿姆斯特丹儿童之家
City Hall, Kurashiki	仓敷市厅舍
Colosseum, Rome	罗马大角斗场
Congress Building, Brasilia	巴西议会大厦
Crown Hall	克朗楼（皇冠厅）

续表

Crystal Palace	水晶宫
Cultural Center, Tokyo	东京文化会馆
Church of Sagrada Familia, Barcelona	神圣家族教堂
Douglas House, Harbor Springs, Michigan	道格拉斯住宅
Dulles International Airport	杜勒斯国际机场候机厅
Eiffel Tower	埃菲尔铁塔
Einstein Tower, Potsdam	波茨坦市爱因斯坦天文台
Embassy of U.S.A. New Delhi	新德里美国大使馆
Empire State Building	帝国大厦
Engineering Faculty Building, University of Leicester	莱斯特大学工程系馆
Erechtheion	伊瑞克先神庙
Extension to the Staasgalerir, Stuttgart	斯图加特美术馆扩建
Fagus work	法古斯工厂
Farnsworth House	范斯沃斯住宅
Falling Water	流水别墅
Galerie des Machines	机械馆
Gallaratese 2 Residential Complex, Milan	米兰加拉拉泰西公寓
Gandi Smarak Sangrahalaya	甘地纪念馆
General Motors Technical Center, Detroit	通用汽车技术中心
Grand Louvre, Paris	巴黎卢佛尔宫
Guggenheim Museum, Bilbao	毕尔巴鄂古根海姆博物馆
Guild House Retirement Home	老年人公寓
"Habitat" Apartment Block at Expo'67, Montreal	蒙特利尔世界博览会集合住宅
Harvard Graduate Center	哈佛大学研究生中心
Headquarters for the Hong Kong Bank	香港汇丰银行
House of Parliament	英国国会大厦
I.I.T. (Illinois Institute of Technology)	伊利诺理工大学
Imperial Hotel	帝国饭店
Isabel Roberts House	罗伯茨住宅
Jewish museum, Berlin	柏林犹太人博物馆
John Hancock Center	约翰·汉考克大厦
Josioh Quincy Community School	何塞·昆西公立学校
Johnson and Son Inc. Administration Building	约翰逊公司总部
Kagawa Prefectural Government office	香川县厅舍
Kanchanjunga Apartments, Bombay	干城章嘉公寓
Kanshi International Airport Passenger Terminal Building	关西国际机场候机楼
Kimbell Art Museum, Fort Worth	金贝尔美术馆
La Chapelle de Ronchamp	朗香教堂
Lake Shore, Chicago	芝加哥湖滨公寓
Larkin Building	拉金公司大楼
Le Centre National d'art et de Culture Georges-Pompidou	蓬皮杜国家艺术与文化中心
Lever House	利华大厦

续表

Lincoln Cultural Center	林肯文化中心
L'unite d'Habitation, Marseille	马赛公寓
Maison Carre, Bazoches-Sur-Guyonne, Paris	卡雷住宅
Marquette Building	马奎特大厦
Mcgregor Memorial Conference Center	麦格拉格纪念会议中心
Monadnock Building	蒙纳诺克大厦
Municipal Library viipuri	维堡市立图书馆
Museum of Modern Art, San Francisco	旧金山现代艺术博物馆
Nakagin Capsule Tower	中银舱体楼
National Gymnasiums for Tokyo Olympics	东京代代木国立室内综合体育馆
New National Gallery West Berlin	西柏林新国家美术馆
Notre Dame, Paris	巴黎圣母教堂
Palais de Versailles	凡尔赛宫
Pantheon	罗马万神庙
Parc de La Villete	拉维莱特公园
Parc Guell, Barcelona	古埃尔公园
Parthenon	帕提农神庙
Pavillim Suisse A la Cite University, Paris	巴黎瑞士学生宿舍
Peachtree Center Plaza Hotel	桃树中心广场旅馆
Pearl Palace	珍珠宫
Philharmonic Hall, Berlin	柏林爱乐音乐厅
Piazza and Piazzetta San Marco	圣马可广场
Piazza d'Italia, New Orleans	新奥尔良意大利广场
Pirelli Tower	皮瑞利大厦
Public Service Building, Portland	波特兰市政大楼
Railway Station, Helsinki	赫尔辛基火车站
Red House	红屋
Richard Medical Research Building	理查医学研究中心
Robie House	罗比住宅
Roof Roof House, Kuala Lumpur	"双屋顶"住宅
Seagram Building	西格拉姆大厦
Sears Tower	西尔斯大厦
Sheldon Memorial Art Gallery	谢尔屯艺术纪念馆
South Bank Art Center, London	南岸艺术中心
Spiral, Minato, Tokyo	东京螺旋大厦
St. Joseph's Fountain	圣约瑟喷泉
Steiner House, Vienna	斯坦纳住宅
Summer Palace	颐和园
Sydney Opera	悉尼歌剧院
Taj Mahal	泰姬·马哈尔
Taliesin West	西塔里埃森
The Guggenheim Museum, New York	古根海姆美术馆

续表

Tsukuba Center Building	筑波中心大厦
Teatro del Mondo for Venice Biennale	威尼斯双年展水上剧场
Technical Center for General Motors	通用汽车技术中心
The Doge's Palace	威尼斯公爵府
The East Building of the National Gallery of Art	国家美术馆东馆
The Guggenheim Museum	古根海姆博物馆
The Headquaters of United Nations, New York	联合国秘书处大厦
The United States Capitol, Washington D. C.	美国国会大厦
Thermae of Caracalla	卡瑞卡拉浴场
Tjibaou Cultural Centre, Noumea, New Caledonia	特吉巴欧文化中心
Town Hall of Säynatsalo	珊纳特赛罗镇中心主楼
Triumphal Arch	凯旋门
Tuberculosis Sanatorium at Paimio	帕米欧肺病疗养院
Tugendhat House	吐根哈特住宅
TWA Terminal	美国环球航空公司候机楼
Utrecht House	乌德勒支住宅
Vanna Venturi House	文丘里母亲住宅
Villa Savoy	萨伏伊别墅
Water Tower Place Building	水塔广场大厦
West Bridge Water Elementary School	西水桥小学
Wexner Center for the Visual Arts, Columbus, Ohio	维克斯纳视觉艺术中心
Wolfsburg Cultural Center	奥尔夫斯贝格文化中心
Woolworth Building	渥尔华斯大厦
World Trade Center	世界贸易中心大厦
Yamanashi Press and Broadcasting Center	山梨县文化馆

1.14 建筑文献中常见国家及地区

Amsterdam [ˈæmstəˈdæm]	n.	阿姆斯特丹 [荷兰首都]
Babylon [ˈbæbilən]	n.	巴比伦
Barcelona [ˌbɑːsiˈləunə]	n.	巴塞罗那 [西班牙港市]
Brasilia [brəˈziːljə]	n.	巴西利亚 [巴西首都]
Brussels [ˈbrʌslz]	n.	布鲁塞尔 [比利时首都]
Byzantine [biˈzæntain]	a. & n.	拜占庭的；拜占庭人
California [ˌkæliˈfɔːniə]	n.	加利福尼亚 [美国州名]
Copenhagen [ˌkəupnˈheigən]	n.	哥本哈根 [丹麦首都]
Danish [ˈdeniʃ]	a.	丹麦的，丹麦人的
Dutch [dʌtʃ]	a. & n.	荷兰人的；荷兰人
Edinburgh [ˈedinbərə]	n.	爱丁堡 [英国城市]
German [ˈdʒəːmən]	a. & n.	德国的；德国人

续表

Houston ['hju:stən]	n.	休斯敦［美国港市］
Indianapolis [indiə'næpəlis]	n.	印第安纳波利斯
Irish ['aiəriʃ]	a. & n.	爱尔兰的，爱尔兰人的；爱尔兰人
Nara ['na:rə]	n.	奈良［日本城市］
Oriental [,ɔ:ri'entl]	a.	东方的，远东的
Oriental architecture		东方建筑
Pennsylvania [,pensil'veinjə]	n.	宾夕法尼亚［美国州名］
Seattle [si'ætl]	n.	西雅图［美国港市］
Swedish ['swi:diʃ]	a.	瑞典的
Swiss [swis]	a.	瑞士的
Utopian [ju:'təupjən]	n.	乌托邦
Vienna [vi'enə]	n.	维也纳［奥地利首都］

1.15 常见植物名称

acacia [ə'keiʃə]	n.	洋槐
Apricot ['eiprikɔt]	n.	杏
bamboo [bæm'bu:]	n.	竹
banyan ['bænian] tree		榕树
beech [bi:tʃ]	n.	山毛榉
begonia [bi'gəunjə]	n.	秋海棠
boxtree ['bɔkstri:]	n.	黄杨
bush [buʃ]	n.	灌木，矮树，灌木丛
camellia [kə'mi:ljə]	n.	山茶
camphor ['kæmfə] tree		樟树
cherry (blossomes) ['tʃeri]	n.	樱花
Chrysanthemum [kri'sænθəməm]	n.	菊花
Cockscomb ['kɔkskəum]	n.	鸡冠花
dahlia ['deiljə]	n.	大丽花
elm [elm]	n.	榆树
fragrant ['freigrənt] olive ['ɔliv]		桂花
gingko ['giŋkəu]	n.	银杏
hemp [hemp] palm [pa:m]		棕榈
ivy ['aivi]	n.	爬山虎
Japanese ['saipris] cypress [prəs]		丝柏
laurel ['lɔrəl] tree		月桂
marvel-of-peru ['ma:vəl-əv-pə'ru:]		紫茉莉
moth [mɔθ] orchid ['ɔ:kid]	n.	蝴蝶兰
mulberry ['mʌlbəri]		桑
peony ['piəni]	n.	芍药

续表

phoenix [ˈfiːniks]	n.	梧桐
pine [pain]	n.	松树
plum [plʌm]/damson [ˈdæmzən]	n.	李
rape [reip] blossoms [ˈblɔsəm]		油菜花
rhododendron [rəudəˈdendrən] azalea [əˈzeiliə]	n.	映山红（杜鹃）
rose [rəuz]	n.	月季花
sandalwood [ˈsændlwud]	n.	檀香
spruce [spruːs]	n.	云杉
sunflower [ˈsʌnflauə]	n.	向日葵
tea(plant) [tiː]	n.	茶花
teak [tiːk]	n.	柚木
tree peony [ˈpiəni]		牡丹
tulip [ˈtjuːlip]	n.	郁金香
ume [juːm]	n.	梅
white birch [bəːtʃ]		白桦
willow [ˈwiləu]	n.	柳

第 2 章　设计实例选译

2.1　建筑设计

2.1.1　毕尔巴鄂的古根海姆博物馆[1]
The Guggenheim Museum in Bilbao

The Guggenheim Museum in Bilbao, completed in 1997, is the result of a collaboration between the Basque Country Administration, which finances and owns the project, and the Solomon R. Guggenheim Foundation, which will operate the museum and provide the core art collection. The museum represents the first step in the redevelopment of the former trade and warehouse district along the south bank of the Nervion River. Directly accessible from the business and historic districts of the city, the museum marks the center of a cultural triangle formed by the Museo de Bellas Artes, the university and the Old Town Hall. The Puente de la Salve Bridge, which connects the nineteenth-century city center with outlying areas, passes over the site at its eastern edge, transforming the museum into a gateway to the city.

毕尔巴鄂的古根海姆博物馆（图 2-1），于 1997 年落成，是巴斯克国土局（给予财政支持并拥有该项目）与所罗门·R·古根海姆基金会（管理博物馆并提供核心艺术品）合作的成果。博物馆代表着重建内尔韦恩河南岸老商贸区的第一步。从城市商业区和历史街区均可以直接到达，博物馆标志着由贝拉斯艺术博物馆、大学和老市政厅构成的文化三角地中心。保存桥越过基地东部一角，将博物馆化作城市之门，连接着 19 世纪的老城中心及其外延区域。

A public plaza located at the entrance of the museum

The Guggenheim Museum in Bilbao

● 图 2-1　古根海姆博物馆

（图片来源：http://blog.3608.com/UploadFiles/2008/4/28/ZHANGQINMIAO28093808734.jpg）

encourages pedestrian traffic between the Guggenheim and the Museo de Bellas Artes, and between the old city and the river-front. Public facilities, including a three-hundred seat auditorium, a restaurant, and retail spaces, are accessible from the main public plaza as well as from within the museum itself. This dual access enables the spaces to operate independently from the museum, allowing them to play an integral part in the urban life of Bilbao.

一个公共广场位于博物馆的入口，引导古根海姆博物馆和贝拉斯艺术博物馆之间的步行人流，也联系着老城与河岸。博物馆的公共设施，包括一个 300 座的礼堂、一家旅馆和一个零售区，它们均有通道与主公共广场及博物馆本身相连。这种双重连接使空间能够于博物馆之外独立运作，也让它们成为毕尔巴鄂城市生活中一

---

[1] 资料来源：Frank O. Gehry, Francesco dal co, Kurt W. Forster, hadley Arnold. Phaidon Press, 2003.

个不可缺少的组成部分。

The main entrance to the museum is through a large central atrium, where a system of curvilinear bridges, glass elevators, and stair towers connects the exhibition galleries concentrically on three levels. A sculptural roof form rises from the central atrium, flooding it with light through glazed openings. The scale of the central atrium, rising more than 150 feet above the river, is an invitation to monumental site-specific installations and special museum events.

博物馆的主入口穿过一个大的中心庭院，那里，由曲桥、玻璃电梯和楼梯塔所组成的一套体系，将同心分布于三个楼层的公共展厅连接起来。雕塑般的屋顶高耸于中心庭院之上，光线透过玻璃窗洒满大厅。中心庭院，以高出河面150ft❶的尺度，邀请人们来到这个不朽之地，那里有精良的设备和独特的博物馆活动。

The Guggenheim Foundation required gallery spaces to exhibit a permanent collection, a temporary Collection, and a collection of selected living artists; in response, three distinct types of exhibition space were designed. The galleries for the exhibition of the permanent collection are relatively conservative in design. This collection is housed in two sets of three consecutive square galleries stacked on the second and third levels of the museum. The temporary collection is housed in a more dramatic, elongated rectangular space that emends to the east. This space passes underneath the Puente de la Salve Bridge and terminates in a tower on its far side, integrating the bridge into the overall composition of the museum. The interior of the space is entirely tree of support columns, permitting the museum to stage large-scale art installations that would otherwise not be feasible. The exhibition of the work of selected living artists is housed in a series of eleven distinct galleries, each of unique spatial quality and generous ceiling height. Back-of-house functions, such as loading, art staging, storage, and conservation, are housed in the lower level of the museum.

古根海姆基金会要求陈列空间能够展示常设的（永久性）馆藏展品、临时性展品以及经过筛选的当代艺术家的作品；作为回应，三种显然不同的展览空间被设计出来。永久性馆藏的展示馆设计相对保守。这些展品放在两套三个连续的方形展览空间中，分别位于第二、第三层。临时藏品摆放在一个更加戏剧性的长方形空间中，以协调东侧。该空间穿行于保存桥之下，终止于该桥远端的一座塔，将桥与整个复合的博物馆连成一体。内部空间全是些如树木般的支撑柱子，这使博物馆得以存放大型的艺术装置，否则是不能存放的。经过筛选的当代艺术家的作品，存放于11个个性鲜明的序列展厅，每一展厅都具有独特的空间品质和丰富的顶棚高度。内部功能，如装载、艺术品舞台、储藏和修复室，则放在博物馆较低的楼层。

The major exterior material on the rectangular buildings of the museum is Spanish lime stone, while the more sculptural shapes of the building are clad in titanium panel. The interior walls of the galleries are a smooth-finish plaster. Large, glazed curtain walls open to views of the river and surrounding city. Mechanical systems maintain a strict temperature and humidity control. The galleries for the permanent collection are lit by direct exhibition lights with a flush—mounted power system, while the galleries for the temporary collection and for the living-artists collection are lit by a theatrical catwalk-mounted lighting system. In addition, custom-designed wall-wash fixtures create an even illumination of ten to twenty foot-candles at eye level in all the galleries. Natural light is introduced through skylights with supplemental blackout shades for daylight control.

博物馆矩形建筑物的外部材料主要是西班牙石灰石，然而更多的雕塑般的建筑物外表皮则包覆钛板。展厅内的墙体是打磨光滑的石膏。巨大的闪光幕墙朝向河

---

❶ 长度单位，ft 即英尺。1ft＝0.3048m。

流及城市周边开启。机械系统保持着严格的温度和湿度控制。馆藏展品大厅采用嵌入式电源系统的直接照明，临时展品厅和当代艺术家展品厅则采用剧院的悬空支架结构灯光系统照明。此外，按习惯设计，墙板设备均匀照明，所有展厅有107.6～215.2lx（10～20英尺烛光）（照度单位）的均匀照度。自然光由天窗引入，并附以遮光片调控日光。

The 256,000 square-foot, one-hundred-million-dollar, project is one of many redevelopment projects the Basque city is undertaking to commemorate its seven-hundredth birthday, in the year 2000. Other projects include a foot-bridge over the river by Santiago, Calatrava, new metro stations by Sir Norman Foster, a transportation hub by Michael Wilford and Partners, a new airport terminal by Calatrava, and a master plan of the city's business district by Cesar Pelli.

该工程25.6万平方英尺，斥资1亿美元，是巴斯克都市重建项目之一，为了在2000年纪念其建市700周年。其他的工程包括河上的步行桥(由圣地亚哥·卡拉特拉瓦设计)、新车站(由诺曼·福斯特爵士设计)、转运中心(由米切尔·威尔福德及伙伴事务所设计)、一座新的机场航站楼(由卡拉特拉瓦设计)以及城市商业区的总体规划(由西萨·佩里设计)。

2.1.2 帝国饭店[1]
IMPERIAL HOTEL

Wright's most extraordinary commission, the Imperial Hotel occupied the bulk of his energy for eight years, from 1915 to 1923. This unique project provided him an opportunity to intimately experience the country he had so long admired and translate his understanding of its culture into form.

赖特所接受的最不同寻常的委托是设计帝国饭店(1915～1923年)，八年间耗费了他大部分精力。这项独特的项目给他提供了一次机会，使他能够亲密接触这个令他仰慕已久的国家，并且将他对其文化的理解融入建筑设计之中(图2-2，图2-3)。

● 图2-2 帝国饭店

(图片来源：世界建筑 NO.53 台北：胡氏图书出版社，1983)

● 图2-3 帝国饭店室内

When the hotel opened in 1923, Shufuntomo magazine boasted, "The new Imperial Hotel… makes an unhesitating use of modern science and civilization… In fact this grand hotel is attested to be without peer in Japan and the world." Louis Sullivan, Wright's mentor, declared in *Architectural Record* that the Imperial Hotel stood "unique as the high water mark thus far attained by

---

[1] 资料来源：Lost Wright, Simon & Schuster Editions. Rockefeller Cente, 1996: 127.

any modern architect. Superbly beautiful as it stands——a noble prophecy."

1923年，饭店开业之际，某杂志夸耀说，"新帝国饭店……毫不犹豫地使用了现代科技文明……事实上，这座豪华的饭店被证明在日本以及全世界都是无与伦比的。"赖特的老师，路易斯·沙利文，在《建筑实录》上宣称，帝国饭店站在"独特的高水准之上，远高出任何现代建筑师的成就。它的雄伟壮丽就像它所展现的那样——是一个高贵的预言。"

The three-story masterpiece had two 500-foot-long wings with 285 guest rooms. The central core included a theater seating one thousand people, a cabaret, a banquet hall, and a formal dining room. Promenades 300 feet long connected the guest wings with the public spaces. The modern mechanical and electrical systems were hidden in the building's columns. A reflecting pool greeted entering guests, while inner garden courts provided a quiet refuge.

该杰作3层高，两个500ft长的侧翼，285间客房。中心部分包括一个可容纳千人的剧院，一个卡巴莱（带餐馆的歌舞厅），一个宴会厅，一个正规的餐厅。300ft的长廊连接着客房与公共空间。现代机械和电气系统隐蔽在建筑的柱内。一个泛着波光的水池迎候着入住的客人，内部的庭院提供了一个静谧的私密场所。

Art was integrated into the fabric of the building. The sculptural forms Wright had carved from volcanic oya stone were as much Mayan as Japanese. Murals, urns, carpets, furniture, and tableware were all designed as elements of the unified composition of textures, colors, and forms.

艺术被融入到建筑结构之中。赖特用火山大谷石雕刻的形式兼具日本风格与玛雅风格。壁画、茶壶、地毯、家具和餐具都被作为与材质、色彩、形式相统一的混合元素来设计。

On September 1, 1923, just as the opening ceremony for the hotel began, the great Kanto earthquake struck, destroying three-quarters of Tokyo, setting 134 fires, and displacing 1.5 million residents. Because of the unique floating, reinforced-concrete foundation, which Wright and the engineer Paul Mueller had designed, the hotel remained standing, but it was damaged and its decline had begun.

1923年9月1日，饭店开业典礼的当日，发生关东大地震。东京的3/4被毁，地震造成了134起火灾，150万居民流离失所。因为赖特和工程师保罗·慕勒设计的独特的筏式钢筋混凝土基础，饭店依然直立，但是，它受到损坏，并开始倾斜。

The fire bombing of Tokyo in 1945 during World War II destroyed the banquet halls and south wing and exacerbated a sag in the central core. Repairs were not taken seriously, and the oya stone was whitewashed during the American occupation of Japan. By the 1960s only the lobby and a promenade remained in original condition. Rationalizations for demolition—the concealed mechanical systems were difficult to update air conditioning and television, the wooden roofs did not meet new building codes-grew, along with the management's fears that the hotel was not the most economically productive use of the valuable center—city land. Finally the hotel was razed. The lobby was saved and rebuilt as part of the Meiji Mura Outdoor museum near Nagoya. A new Imperial Hotel has risen in its place.

在1945年第二次世界大战的轰炸中，宴会厅和南翼被毁，中心部分剧烈下沉。修复没有得到重视，大谷石在美军占领日本期间被涂成白色。到了20世纪60年代，只有大厅和步廊尚保留原样。拆除建筑的合理化原因是：隐蔽的机械系统难以更新空调和电视，木屋顶不符合新的建筑规范，再加上管理层担心该饭店所处的市中心土地昂贵，而该建筑并非最经济地利用土地。最终饭店被夷为平地，大厅被保存下来，并作为靠近名古屋的明治村室外博物馆的一部分得以重建。一座新的帝国饭店在原址上拔地而起。

2.1.3 萨伏伊别墅[1]
VILLA SAVOYE

The Villa Savoye at Poissy-sur-Seine is related to the whole range of Le Corbusier's architecture and urban planning. Built between 1929~1931, the last of Le Corbusier's so called 'Four Compositions', the Villa Savoye illustrates with extreme clarity and is perhaps the most faithful in its observation of his 'Five Points of a New Architecture' made in 1925: the columns; the roof of garden; the free plan; the long window; the free façade.

在波瓦西·休尔·塞纳(Poissy-sur-Seine)的萨伏伊别墅与勒·柯布西耶的整个建筑及城市规划理念有着密切的关系。萨伏伊别墅建于1929~1931年间，是勒·柯布西耶被称为"四种住宅组合成分"中的最后一个作品，非常清楚地(也可能是他所有作品中最忠实地)表明了勒·柯布西耶于1925年提出的"新建筑五要素"理念。这便是：底层架空；屋顶花园；自由平面；横向长窗；自由立面(图2-4，图2-5)。

Villa Savoye

● 图2-4 萨伏伊别墅

(图片来源：世界建筑.NO.13.台北：胡氏图书出版社，1983)

However, the Villa Savoye is much more than a part of Le Corbusier's rational development and clarification of an architectural doctrine. It is a masterwork of modern architecture-a poetic interpretation of life, exemplary of Le Corbusier's grand unity of purpose and indicative of the coherent continuity of the whole of his creative process.

Interior of villa Savoye

● 图2-5 萨伏伊别墅室内

然而，萨伏伊别墅绝不仅仅是柯布西耶建筑理论的理性发展与表白而已，它还是现代建筑中的杰作——对生命所做的诗的诠释，是勒·柯布西耶那伟大的人生目标的代表，也是他的创作过程中不懈追求的明证。

Le Corbusier's own sketch of the four compositions, 1. Maison La Roche 2. Maison a Garches 3. Maison a Stuttgart and 4. Villa Savoye, show where he placed this building in the hierarchy of compositions. The Villa Savoye was an integral part of his life work and was also conceptually related to the dwelling types that come before and after; the Domino Houses of 1914, the Citrohan House of 1922, the Villa Meyer of 1925 and the Marseilles apartment block, and all of the subsequent Unites'd habitation. In all of these he pursued with remarkably unsentimental logic the observation that dwellings should be a flexible container for the new species of nomad that is modern urbanized man. But beyond that, it is a poetic interpretation of life; and exemplary of the great unity of purpose of his own life, which was directed to provide a coherent body of theory to inform about, not only his own

---

[1] 资料来源：世界建筑 NO.13.台北：胡氏图书出版社，1983.

creative endeavor, but all of the spatially constructive acts of the machine age society. The seeds of this theory are, in many respects, as related to social philosophy as to aesthetics or machine production, and in fact the special purpose expressed in the freedom of the plan at the Savoye house is 'to provide a place for relaxation in the open air and a revolution in the way of living.'

勒·柯布西耶自己对这四栋作品所做的草图：①勒·罗许（La Roche）住宅；②加奇（Garches）住宅；③斯图加特住宅；④萨伏伊别墅，显示其在这些作品中的地位。萨伏伊别墅是柯布西耶一生作品中不可或缺的部分，同时在建筑理念上也与他设计这一作品前后所作的其他住宅形态有着密切的关系。比如1914年的多米诺（Domino）住宅、1922年的雪铁汉（Citrohan）住宅、1925年的迈耶别墅、马赛公寓，以及以后所有的集体住宅。在这些作品中，他以令人惊讶不带情感的逻辑，追求其对现代建筑所做的观察，那就是，住宅应该为新的流浪者——现代都市人，提供一种自由且富有弹性的居住空间。除此之外，它是对生命之诗的诠释。这更是其人生中伟大目标的最佳典范，不仅展示他创造性的努力，更为自己的机械化时代社会的空间构造活动提供了一个统一的理论体系。这一理论的根源是多方面的，与社会哲学有关，也与美学或机械生产有关。事实上，萨伏伊别墅自由平面所表现的空间，其目的是"提供一个场所，使人可以在开放的空间中放松紧张的神经，同时也是对生活方式所作的一种变革。"

A building can be considered as a set of carefully related elements and one of the methods that Le Corbusier uses in relating elements is the 'regulating line'. In *Towards a New Architecture*, he describes the regulating line as, "a satisfaction of a spiritual order which leads to the pursuit of ingenious and harmonious relations. It confers on the work the quality of rhythm. The regulating line brings in this tangible form of mathematics which gives the reassuring perception of order. The choice of a regulating line fixes the fundamental geometry of the work. It fixes therefore one of the 'fundamental characters.' The choice of the regulating line is one of the decisive moments of inspiration, it is one of the vital operations of architecture."

一栋建筑可以被看成一组经过细心经营的相关元素，勒·柯布西耶处理这些相关元素所使用的一个方法是"规则线"。在《走向新建筑》一书中，他如此描述规则线："一种精神秩序的满足，引导我们追求富有创意而和谐的关系，它赋予作品以韵律感。规则线带来了如数学般明确的形式，重新肯定了秩序感。规则线的选择决定了作品的基本几何形式，也因而决定了其'基本的特质'，选择规则线是灵感表现的决定性时刻，也是建筑设计中最为重要的一步。"

Le Corbusier has made the superstructure and all elements of the Villa Savoye related with the proper attributes of completeness by rigorous use of a Palladian grid. The regulating line, "a basis of construction", gives measure to the grid of columns and bays and establishes the relationship between the systems of structure and volume; structure and geometry; structure and enclosure; and structure and circulation. At Villa Savoye where the importance of the golden section proportion may be analyzed, there is a stretching of an otherwise square plan in the direction of the entry and the main circulation ramp, indicating some deformation about the central axis without disruption of the structural grid.

由于严密地应用了帕拉第奥网格，勒·柯布西耶赋予萨伏伊别墅的结构与所有要素以恰当而完整的品质。作为"构造的基础"的规则线决定了柱列与柱间跨度的尺度，并建立起结构系统与空间体量的关系、结构与几何的关系、结构与四周包围的空间以及结构与动线间的关系。在萨伏伊别墅，应分析黄金分割的重要性，由入口方向主要交通动线的坡道所作的延伸，使得原本方形的平面产生变化，改变了中央轴，却没有破坏原有的结构秩序。

Entry and circulation help disengage the rear and front facades from the column grid, helping to establish a dominant central axis reinforced by the narrower central bay containing the interior ramp. The columns of the building are defined by a system of walls independent of the structure. The exterior walls enclose the structure with a relatively simple symmetrical form in dialogue with the asymmetrical interior organization. The strip windows exist in an arrangement which allows a non-alignment of column and plan grids and establishes a system free of the requirements of structure and circulation but creating a tension between them.

入口与流线的处理使前后立面得以从柱列中解放出来，并建立了具有支配性的中央轴线，该中央轴线因一组室内斜坡所在的较窄一些的中央柱距得以强调。建筑中的柱子由与结构分离的墙板系统界定。包围结构的外墙为一个相当简单、对称的形式，与内部的非对称组织相呼应。带状的横向长窗独立排列，与柱子、平面不发生关系，因而不受结构与流线的限制，但又在其间形成了一种张力。

The building has a long history. It was occupied and badly desecrated by the Germans during the Second World War, and afterward deteriorated simply by neglect until advancing development threatened it with complete destruction. At that time, in1959, concern on the part of the international architectural community, combined with the efforts of France's subtle and effective Minister of Culture, Mr. Andre Malraux, succeeded in obtaining the reservation of the house as a national monument and restored it to its present condition.

Of the Poissy site, 30km from Paris, Le Corbusier wrote: "It is a magnificent property shaped by a large pasture and orchard forming a dome-like rise encircled by a belt of full grown trees."

这栋建筑历史久远，在第二次世界大战中它被德军占领且严重受损，之后又因疏于整理而受到更多损坏。到了1959年，新的开发几乎导致其彻底的损毁。也就是在此时，国际建筑界的关注，加上当时法国敏锐且能干的文化部部长安德烈·马尔罗（Andre Malraux）先生的多方努力，该建筑才作为国家纪念碑而得以保留，并予以修复还原成它目前的状况。

波瓦西（Poissy）的这个基地，距离巴黎30km，对此，勒·柯布西耶曾写道："那是一个很大的产业，由一大片牧场及果园所构成，一圈高大茂密的树林围成一个穹顶般的小丘。"

Entry to the property is through a gate at one end of a high stone wall which parallels the street. Located at this entry is a small gate-keeper's lodge which is consistent in design with the main house, a white stucco enclosed volume on second level raised on columns, and whose plan organization could well serve as a unit dwelling in a multi-family housing block. The Villa Savoye is visible through the trees from the lodge. The worn old country road was kept in order to disturb the forest and the meadow as little as possible, and one travels this road by car, through the open field, directly to the entry door of the house. The main portion of the house is raised on columns which are set on the grass plane, and the car enters the house under the columns, turn around the service compartments to arrive on the central axis of the building at the vestibule door and then to continue into the enclosed carport, or to proceed on the return route. According to Le Corbusier this was the basic given as the house was designed to have a "front". The semi-circular wall on the ground level which guides and expresses the flow of traffic around the carport was determined dimensionally by the minimum turning radius of a car.

进入这片地界，需要穿过与街道平行的、位于高大石墙一端的入口通道。该入口处有一栋小门房，门房的设计与主体建筑一致，一座由白灰浆粉刷所包裹的体量，置于由柱子撑起的二层之上。它的平面组织正好构成了一个多家庭集合住宅的居住单元。从门房可透过树林看到萨伏伊别墅。古老而破损的村路被保留下来，以免破坏森林及草原的景致，人们可搭车经由此路，穿过空旷的原野，直达别墅的大门。建筑的主要部分由柱子撑起，柱子则立于草地之上，车子在柱下进入屋内，绕过服务空间抵达建筑物中轴的前厅大门，然后继续驶入一个封闭的车库，或转停到返程的路线上。根据勒·柯布西耶的说法，房子的设计要求有一个"正面"，因此这就是基本的所谓正面了。地面一层的半圆形墙引导并表现出车子的流线，其尺度由车子的最小转弯半径决定。

The recessed enclosed space on the ground level which was originally painted rust and dark blue embodies the entrance, the garage, service compartments and the servant's quarters of the building. In addition, it contains the gallery space and gently sloping ramp which leads one almost imperceptibly to the living level above.

一层退缩在柱子里的空间最初被饰以铁褐色及深蓝色，以显示此处为入口、车库、服务性空间及佣人区。此外，这里还有柱廊以及坡度平缓的斜坡，引导人们几乎难以觉察地来到上面的居住层。

The second level with the open garden terrace, as a extension of the main rooms of the house is lifted upon columns in such a way as to permit distant views of the horizon. It contains all the major living spaces; living-dining areas, kitchen, master bedrooms and bathrooms. The living area, which opens on the south to the garden through large floor-to-ceiling sliding glass doors, is positioned so as to take advantage of a view to the north as well as allowing the sun to penetrate into this space through the garden. The original scheme and the built scheme of Villa Savoye essentially differ in accommodation and consequent spatial displacement. In the original scheme, the living-dining area occupied the entire width of the building; whereas in the built plans the kitchen has been placed in the north-west corner of that space. Clearly the plan became more influenced by the clients' spatial requirements during the development and the built plan is less 'pure' in its order than the original scheme.

带有开敞式屋顶花园平台（从主要房间延伸出来）的第二层被置于支柱之上。如此，可以看到更远的景色。这一层包括了所有重要的生活空间：起居室兼餐厅、厨房、主卧室和浴室。起居室南面的花园可以经由落地玻璃推拉门进入，其位置的选择除了可以使太阳光由花园射进来以外，还可以向北远眺。萨伏伊别墅包括原先的设计和后来实施的方案在内涵所表达出的空间构成有本质上的差异。在原来的设计中，起居室兼餐厅占据了建筑物的整个宽度，而建成后，厨房则被放在该部分的西北角。显然，平面更多地受到业主对空间要求的影响，所以最后实施的平面在秩序上就比原先的设计来得较不"纯粹"。

For Le Corbusier the plan is the generator, the expression of the master idea. Although there is at the Villa Savoye an external symmetry to the building, and although it is basically a centralized plan with a tendency towards two preferential sides, (entry and rear), which is expressed by the shallow cantilevers beyond the 4bay x 4bay square grid, the internal organization is free of this grid and all of the walls and, the movement system is independent of it. Within Le Corbusier's self-imposed square "the spiraling qualities of asymmetry, rotation and peripheral dispersal" are expressed by the ramp, which is placed on axis of the entry doors on the ground level, and ascends to the second level where it then becomes an exterior promenade from the garden terrace to the roof solarium. For Le Corbusier the promenade is extremely important here uniting one level with another. He writes, "in this house it is a matter of a true architectural promenade, offering aspects which are constantly varied, unexpected and sometimes amazing. It is interesting to get so much variety when you have, for example, from a structural standpoint, permitted only a system of pots and beams of absolute rigor."

对勒·柯布西耶来说，平面是设计形成的源头，是总构想的表达。尽管萨伏伊别墅有一个对称的外观，尽管它基本上是一个集中的平面，并带有偏好两边（入口及背面）的趋势（我们可以从每边四个柱子的正方形平面的柱位上方的些微出挑看到），但是，内部的组织则完全自由，丝毫不受柱子的限制，所有的墙面及动线系统均脱离平面而独立存在。在柯布西耶式的方形空间内，他的"非对称、旋转及扩张式的螺旋状空间特质"通过斜坡表达出来,此斜坡设置在底层玄关入口的中央轴上,但在登上二楼之后,斜坡就成为从二楼的花园平台到屋顶日光浴室之间的室外散步场所。对勒·柯布西耶来说,这个散步场所非常重要,它连接了一层与另一层。他写道:"在这栋建筑物中,它是一个真正的建筑散步场所,步移景迁,出其不意,有时甚至令人惊讶。举例来说,当你从结构的角度去审视,若只能允许绝对严谨的柱梁系统,如此多样的变化就显得十分有趣了。"

Although other architects had experimented with one of more of his Five Points, Le Corbusier was the inventor of these principles and he was the first to identify them and to develop an integrated theory of architecture which clarifies and defines their use. With regard to the Villa Savoye Le Corbusier has made his intention extremely clear, "The inhabitants come here because this rustic landscape goes well with country life," and specifically with regard to the suspended garden located on the living level lifted above the ground and supported on pilots, "if you stand in the grass, you don't see very far. Besides grass is damp and unhealthy etc. to live in. So the true garden of the house shouldn't be on the ground but 3 and a half meters above it. This will be the suspended garden whose soil is dry and healthy and from where you can see the countryside so much better than if you had stayed on the ground."

虽然,其他的建筑师在他之前已实验过一个或更多的(他提出的)"新建筑五要素",勒·柯布西耶仍是这些原则的发明家,同时也是第一位对这些要素加以确认并发展出一整套建筑理论体系,明确并界定如何运用这些要素的建筑师。至于萨伏伊别墅,勒·柯布西耶极为清晰地阐明了他的创作意图:"这里的居住者,是因该地块的田园风景与乡村生活相配而来的"。关于由底层列柱所支撑的起居层上的空中花园,他强调说:"如果你站在草地上,根本无法远眺,况且潮湿的草地有害健康,也不宜居住。因此,房子的真正花园不该在地面上,而应该在其上的3.5m处;这便是土壤干爽且有益于健康的空中花园,这里,你会看到比在底层更好的乡村景致。"

The upper level solarium, modified from the original so that it no longer contains a bedroom suite, is open to the sky and complete with those elements which again allow the landscape to enter into life in segments and provide a semi-protected exterior environment with ample sun and verdure. The coherent continuity of Le Corbusier's creative process is exemplified by the roof garden at Villa Savoye which is related to the whole range of his architecture and urban planning as he claimed that, "the radiance of the sun and the open sky were the birthright of everyman."

最上层的日光浴场,修改了当初的设计,不再带有卧室套房,而是敞向空中。由此,完成了那些新建筑的构成元素,再次允许景观嵌入生活,并提供了一个有充足阳光与草地的半室外环境。勒·柯布西耶创作的连贯性在萨伏伊别墅的屋顶花园中得以体现,这一手法与他所有的建筑及城市规划理念密切相关。正如他宣称的:"璀璨的阳光及开阔的天空是每个人与生俱来的权利。"

2.1.4 范斯沃斯住宅❶
The Farnsworth House

THE SITE: The Farnsworth House is situated on the right bank of the Fox River, south of Plano, approximately 75 km west of Chicago. The size of the surrounding land originally acquired by Dr. Edith Farnsworth was 3.8ha. The mostly flat meadow is broken by groups of trees, including in the immediate vicinity of the house two enormous sugar maples. Carefully placed among them, the house is oriented with its long axis in an east-west direction.

基地:范斯沃斯住宅坐落于芝加哥以西约75km的布兰诺布(Plano)南郊,在福克斯(Fox)河的岸边。该地

---

❶ 资料来源:世界建筑 NO. 27. 台北:胡氏图书出版社,1983.

块最初由伊迪丝·范斯沃斯博士购置,约 3.8hm²❶。一片平坦的草地上,间以一簇簇茂密的树木,建筑近旁还有两棵巨大的糖枫树。该建筑的长轴沿东西向布置,建筑巧妙地坐落于茂密的树林中(图 2-6,图 2-7)。

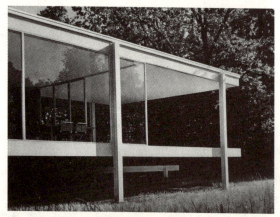

Farnsworth House

● 图 2-6 范斯沃斯住宅

(图片来源:世界建筑 NO.27. 台北:胡氏图书出版社,1983)

Entrance of Farnsworth House

● 图 2-7 范斯沃斯住宅入口

THE STRUCTURE: The house is a steel skeleton of I-beam supports welded to floor and roof frames. The supports rest on massive, individual concrete footings. The frames provide perimeter channels which hold secondary I-beams spanning the short direction. The spaces between these beams are filled in with precast concrete slabs, which produce the thin roofs and floor planes. In the latter, the precast slabs were used as forms for an additional top layer of poured-in-place concrete which, in the exposed deck area, is shaped to slope toward center openings to allow drainage. The floor is, however, deep enough to accommodate the waste pipes from the two bathrooms, at either end of the core element, and the kitchen, in between.

结构:这幢房子是一座以 I 形钢柱直接焊接于地板和屋顶钢架上的钢骨架结构,这些支柱则安放在块状、各自独立的混凝土基础上。楼板和屋顶的周边由槽形钢制成,用来承托跨过建筑短边的 I 形钢梁。在这些钢梁之间,安装了预制的混凝土板,形成薄薄的屋顶及地板。当建造楼板时,这些预制混凝土板便成了现场浇灌混凝土的模板。露台处,为了排水,现场浇筑的混凝土,朝着中央口部分略为倾斜。建筑的地板被抬高以便容纳来自房子核心两端浴厕及中间厨房的排水管道。

All pipes and other utility lines are compressed into one stack which connects the elevated house with the ground. An elongated roof element above the core contains exhausts for the kitchen, the bath and boiler rooms, and for the fireplace in the sitting area. Heating is provided through hot water in a coil system embedded in the floor. It is supplemented by a hot-air system which allows the temperature to be raised instantly from the average of 10℃ maintained by the hot-water system during the winter. There is no air conditioning, but low window openings in the bedroom area provided cross ventilation with the entrance door at the opposite end of the house. In the porch section the floor and roof frames are equipped with grooves for the installation of screens. Tracks along the edge of the ceiling permit curtains to be drawn in front of the glass walls on all sides of the house.

建筑所有的管道及配线,均集中于连接地面与抬高的楼板之间的方筒之内。在核心位置伸出屋顶的部分,用来排出厨房、浴厕、热水炉及起居室壁炉的废气。建筑的供暖系统主要是嵌入地板中、盘绕的热水管装置,但另有一个辅助的暖风系统,当冬季严寒时,可以迅速地将热水供暖系统所维持的平均 10℃ 的室温予以提高。

---

❶ 面积单位,hm² 即公顷。1hm² = 10⁴m²。

在这个建筑里,并未装置空调设备,但在卧室部分设有低窗,可与房子对角的入口处产生空气对流。在门廊部分,地板与屋顶框架间设有沟槽,以便安装纱窗。天花板的边缘均设有窗帘盒,在房子的每一边都可以拉上窗帘,以遮蔽玻璃墙。

In spite of its modest size, the Farnsworth House presented a considerable challenge for the contractor because of the unprecedented tolerances and rigorous standards Mies demanded in the execution. In order to guarantee utmost precision in the erection of the steel frame, levels of extra length had to be custom made. The welding of the columns to the roof and floor frames was limited to the top and bottom sections of the fasciae and plug-welding from the rear of the fasciae through to the I-beams was done to minimize unsightly marks. In addition the entire steel frame was sand-blasted to ensure an immaculate surface.

这幢建筑的规模并不算大,但由于密斯对于施工上要求史无前例的精确度以及严格的标准,对建造者来说,范斯沃斯住宅是一个巨大的考验。为了确保钢框架安装的高度精确性,超长的水平构件是特制的,钢柱与屋顶及地板框架的焊接也限制在柱顶板的上下缘之间。而点焊则自柱顶板的背面与I形钢梁联结,将不雅观的焊痕减至最少。此外,为了使所有的支架表面光洁无瑕,钢材均经过喷砂磨光处理。

THE DIMENSIONS: The house is laid out on a horizontal grid expressed in the pattern of the travertine floor slabs, each of which measures 0.61m by 0.76m. The length of the entire house is 23.5m, the width 8.5m; the length of the attached deck is 16.8m, the width 6.7m. The floor level of the house is 1.5m above ground, of the deck 0.61 m; and the interior height of the house is 2.9m. The four supports on both long sides are spaced 6.7m apart, the floor and roof extending 1.7m on either end beyond the last column. The latter dimension represents the interval between the secondary beams which number 4 per bay for a total of 13 in the floor and roof frames, and of 9 in the deck frame. The fasciae of both frames are 0.38m wide. The house is enclosed with 6 mm-thick panes of plate glass, and the length of the panes between the columns is 3.2m. The 2.1m-wide entrance is off-center by 0.3m toward the south side, adding wall space to the dining corner and leading more directly into the sitting area. The core element, finished in primavera wood, is 7.5m long and 3.7m wide. It leaves a 3.7m-wide space on the south side and a 1.2m-wide space on the north side that serves as the kitchen gallery; in the long axis, it leaves a 5.4m space for the dining corner and a 3.7m space for the sleeping area. A second cabinet element only 1.8m high by 3.7m long and 0.66m deep, contains drawers and a built-in record player, and functions as a backdrop for the bed. Preliminary drawings show another low partition screening a bed in the present dining corner, originally intended for guests.

尺度:该建筑平面由0.61m×0.76m的石灰华板所构成。建筑总长23.5m、宽8.5m,平台长16.8m、宽6.7m。房子的地板高出地面1.5m、平台则高出地面0.61m。室内的高度为2.9m,长边两侧的四个支柱相距6.7m,屋顶及地板两端,各自支柱边缘挑出1.7m,这个尺寸,也就是梁与梁的间距。在每一跨度间有4支小梁,地板及屋顶的小梁总共有13支。而平台则有9支小梁,框架宽0.38m。整幢房子四周镶嵌6mm厚的平板玻璃,支柱与支柱之间的玻璃长度是3.2m。2.1m宽的入口向南侧偏离中心0.3m,入口与餐厅之间设隔屏,使入口更直接地导向起居室。建筑的核心部分,以木皮饰面,长7.5m、宽3.7m。在这个核心部分的南侧留有3.7m宽的空间,北侧留有1.2m宽作为壁橱。在长轴方向,有5.4m的空间作为进餐的位置、3.7m的空间作为卧室。另有一个1.8m高、3.7m长、0.66m深设有抽屉及嵌入唱机的橱柜,其功能犹如床的靠背,从原始草图上可以看出,在餐厅角落处,隔屏划分出一个床空间,可供客人使用。

When put up for sale by Edith Farnsworth it was fortunate that the house was bought by an admirer of Mies. Although Peter Palumbo's home is London, he not only undertook an extensive restoration of the building and improvement of the site, but he also equipped the house for the first time with furniture designed by Mies Vander Rohe.

伊迪丝·范斯沃斯出售这幢住宅时,很幸运地,买主彼得·帕隆博(Peter Palumbo)是密斯的仰慕者。彼得的家乡虽在伦敦,但他不仅着手修缮房屋,并且还首度以密斯·凡·德·罗亲自设计的家具作为这幢房子的摆设。

Thirty years after its conception, the Farnsworth House is now generally accepted as one of the classic examples of modern architecture. It is the last house in the work of Ludwig Mies Vander Rohe, and the only one built after his immigration to the United States. It marks the transition to his late work, dominated by a preoccupation with structure, better than any of the other projects he designed in the decade after his arrival in 1938. And, it represents one of those rare occasions in the history of architecture where neither the client nor the commission itself made restrictive demands on the architect.

自范斯沃斯住宅诞生,迄今30年来,它已被大众接受并成为现代建筑的经典范例之一。它是密斯所设计的最后一幢住宅,也是密斯移居美国后完成的唯一住宅。范斯沃斯住宅标志着密斯后期工作的转折点——全神贯注于结构形式,同密斯于1938年赴美后10年内的任何作品相比,范斯沃斯住宅更为杰出。而且,它也是建筑历史上一次罕见的机缘,无论业主或委托业主本身,对建筑师均给予了无限的自由。

Considering the program, one could call it a minimal house intended to function only as a secondary residence for a single person. In its bucolic setting, the extremely simple and light structure suggests a pavilion in the classic sense of the European 18th century or the Japanese tradition. It is no accident that the Farnsworth House is the only structure in which Mies Vander Rohe had all the exposed steel elements painted white. The favorite color of modern architecture contributes here to the dematerialization of the structure by denying the steel a symbolic expression of its nature.

考察这幢住宅的功能,我们可以说它是为单身业主的次要居住而设计的极简别墅,功能被置于次要位置。其田园式的环境、极端单纯轻巧的结构似乎暗含着18世纪欧洲的古典意识或日本传统所孕育的亭榭意蕴。范斯沃斯住宅是密斯所设计的钢结构建筑中,唯一将外露的钢构件漆成白色的作品。此事绝非偶然,这是现代建筑所偏爱的色彩,这里的贡献在于:否定了钢铁所象征的特质,而将结构物本身抽象化。

As with any building, the configuration of the Farnsworth House is the result, to a large extent, of the specific conditions of the site, which Edith Farnsworth had acquired before she had chosen the architect. The land, lying low along the Fox River, is regularly inundated, and the house therefore had to be raised above the average flood level. Yet this functional requirement does not suffice to explain the choice of form, which can also be interpreted as a negative version of the podium that Mies employed for a number of projects.

在很大程度上,范斯沃斯住宅的外形基于其特殊的基地条件。伊迪丝·范斯沃斯在未选定建筑师之前,即拥有了这片草地。这块土地沿着福克斯河,以低缓舒坦的姿态展开,每年总要遭受河流规律性的泛滥。因此,房子的底层不得不提高到洪水的平均水位之上。但是,这个功能上的要求并不足以解释其外形的由来,它也可以被解释为密斯在若干其他作品中所惯用的基座的否定版本。

In spite of the acrimonious controversy that later ended the relationship of Edith Farnsworth and Mies Vander Rohe, one must acknowledge that she was, as a client, one of a small number of enlightened individuals who have made history along with the great architects chosen to execute their commissions. A physician noted for her involvement in research, she had originally studied music. Whether she felt, like so many of her generation, a moral commitment to modern architecture as an expression of a progressive life style is an unanswered question. It was, however, her declared intention to build a house that would make a major contribution to modern architecture, and it had to be, therefore, the work of one of its major exponents. Having asked the Museum of Modern Art in New York for advice, she was given the names of Frank Lloyd Wright, Le Corbusier and Mies Vander Rohe. The latter was finally chosen, perhaps only for his accessibility, and accepted the commission in 1945, without, however, producing any concrete designs during the years immediately following.

尽管激烈的争执结束了伊迪丝·范斯沃斯与密斯·凡·德·罗之间的关系，我们必须承认，伊迪丝·范斯沃斯是少数开明而有远见的业主之一，这些人和建筑师们共同开拓了建筑的历史。范斯沃斯以其从事研究的医生身份为人知晓，但她原先学的是音乐。她是否也像其同时代的许多其他人一样，基于一种伦理性的感知，把现代建筑看作进步的生活方式的象征，我们尚不得而知。但是，她宣称要建造一幢可以对现代建筑有所贡献的建筑物，因此必须由能够代表现代建筑的建筑师来设计。征询纽约现代艺术博物馆的意见后，她得到的提名是：弗兰克·劳埃德·赖特、勒·柯布西耶以及密斯·凡·德·罗。而后者终于被她选中，这很可能是由于密斯的平易近人。委托合约是在 1945 年签订的，但在随后的几年内，并没有完成任何具体的设计方案。

Mies, who throughout his life exercised the art of creative inactivity, may have felt that the specific solution of the Farnsworth House had to await its time. Indeed, it stands at the beginning of a new phase in his work characterized by the pre-eminence of structure, which had increasingly occupied him since his arrival in Chicago. The new direction was apparent in the buildings he designed and built for the IIT campus during the 1940s. the symbolic, segregated presentation of the architectural elements-floor and ceiling planes, supporting columns, interposed wall elements-had been abandoned, and with it the more pronounced articulations of the "open plan". The supporting I-beams had receded into the brick walls and, although still definable as separate elements, reinforced the tendency toward the all-enveloping skin.

毕生追求静态美的密斯，可能认为设计范斯沃斯住宅必须静待时机。确实，这个设计正是密斯以卓绝的结构为特色展开其历史新页的起点。在抵达芝加哥之后的年代，他的这种风格日益彰显。这一倾向在密斯于 20 世纪 40 年代所设计的美国伊利诺工学院校舍中十分显著。这种建筑构件的象征性、各自分离的表现法——地面及天花板、支柱、隔墙——全部被摒弃了，紧跟着来的是更有力量的观念"开放性平面"。支撑的 I 形钢隐没在砖墙内，虽然仍可以界定为分离构件，它却越来越强调表皮化的倾向。

The formula for the IIT buildings had precedents in German factory construction, in general, and in Mies Vander Rohe's own work of the 1930s, where the atrium houses he projected show increasingly solid brick walls. In one sketch, however, for a House on a Hillside, a steel frame appears in the form of a cage-like truss cantilevered like the beginning of a bridge from an abutment, and supported only at one point by a by a pair of posts above the ground. This project implies not only the completed "bridge" solution of the Resor House of 1938 but also anticipates the Farnsworth House and the formulations that went beyond the IIT buildings.

伊利诺理大学校舍的建筑形式，以德国的工厂为先例，而且在密斯·凡·德·罗 20 世纪 30 年代的作品中亦曾出现过。在密斯所做的一幢山麓住宅的草图中，一个形似笼子的结构，犹如桥梁一般自桥墩挑出，并且仅由一对支柱作用于一点而将房屋架离地面。这种形式不仅暗含着 1938 年里索住宅的桥式解答，并且渗入范斯沃斯住宅的设计之中，甚至于延续到伊利诺理工大学校舍之后的一切设计中。

In their placement outside of the enclosing skin, the i-beam supports of the Farnsworth House seem a pre-figuration of the mullion element of all later curtain walls. It has been observed that even the attachment of these columns to the fasciae of the frames had a precedent in one of Mies Vander Rohe's early exhibition designs-a table-top connection used at the World Exposition in Barcelona in 1929. This, in turn, has been traced to the earlier de Stijl influence, which had indeed introduced the lateral connections to suggest a by-passing, rather than a meeting, of the vertical and horizontal elements.

在范斯沃斯住宅中,安置在表皮之外的 I 形钢支柱,似乎成为他此后无数幕墙形式的原型。我们可以观察到,甚至连支柱与结构框架的联结方式,都可以在密斯·凡·德·罗早期的展示场馆设计——1929 年用在巴塞罗那世界博览会的屋顶与柱的结合法中找到先例。这可以追溯到构成派,构成派确曾引入了侧面连接的形式,以表现水平与垂直构件有意错开而非直接连接。

The externalization of the columns in the Farnsworth House is also indicative of another aspect of his preoccupation with structure: In spite of its small scale, the house can be recognized as the first of Mies Vander Rohe's remarkable clear-span structures. Their progression leads from Crown Hall of 1952-1956 at IIT, where the external supports are joined by overhead girders, to the New National Gallery in Berlin of 1968, where an enormous, stiff roof plate rests on two peripheral columns on each of the four sides. With this building, Mies Vander Rohe returned to the separation of the constituents, elements, as well as to the principles of the "open plan" in at least the exhibition system he devised for the main hall. The wall elements suspended from the ceiling offer an almost infinite number of arrangements and, therewith, of patterns for the flow of space. Such possibilities did not exist in the Farnsworth House, where the supremacy of the horizontal planes had been revoked by the cage effect of the external supports, and where the interior dimensions restricted the ability of the core and cabinet elements to effectively modulate the space..

范斯沃斯住宅支柱"外部化"的手法,也从另一方面显示出密斯对结构的关注。尽管这幢房子的规模非常小,它可以被看作密斯(设计的)那些卓越的有明确跨度的结构物的首例。这种风格的发展,自 1952~1956 年期间,伊利诺理工大学克朗楼的外部支柱与屋顶的大构架联结,到 1968 年柏林新国家艺术馆的巨大、坚实的屋顶板放在每边一对的外围支柱之上。在这两幢建筑中,密斯重新追求构件的分离、要素的分离。同时经由大厅的展示系统,密斯再度显示了其"开放空间"的魅力。自天花板悬吊而下的展示墙,也呈现出一种空间的无限性,而这种可能性在范斯沃斯住宅是不存在的。因为外柱的形式加强了箱笼的效果而瓦解了平面的优势,并且室内的尺度,也限制了核心部分及橱柜有效变换空间的可能性。

Yet the experience of the actual situation seems to contradict this assessment. Unlike any other building by Mies, even the atrium houses of the 1930s which had carefully framed views into the landscape, the spatial composition of the Farnsworth House seems to embrace its entire surroundings. With the total dissolution of the walls into glass, individual trees, or groups of trees and shrubs assume the role of the interposed wall elements as regulators of the space continuum. Only once before, in the project for his own house in the Tyrolean Alps of 1934, did Mies integrate a building so closely into the landscape. There are, however, no field-stone walls in the Farnsworth House, which not only maintains the autonomy of the structure, but introduce, in an almost contrapuntal manner, a contrast between man-made object and natural environment. As if to emphasize the temporariness of the invasion, the house is made to hover above, rather than to touch, the ground. Such strict distinction between architecture and nature had not been attempted since the end of the 18th century when romantic landscaping began to eliminate all transitional zones around the building.

然而,现实的经验似乎与这个评估相左。迥异于密斯的任何其他建筑,甚至与 20 世纪 30 年代细心布置花木的庭院住宅相比较,范斯沃斯住宅的空间组织,其开放性似乎拥抱了整个周围环境。由于外墙完全是玻璃,那些树木、树群，以及灌木丛担当了空间构成的主要角色，使空间连成一体。过去仅有一次，密斯将建筑完全与环境融合在一起，那便是1934年在阿尔卑斯山，提洛尔人为自己所建造的住宅中。然而，范斯沃斯住宅并无任何实墙，玻璃墙面非但强调了结构本身的自主性，也同时以一种近乎对等的姿态展示了人造物与自然环境之间的对比。仿佛为强调洪水侵袭的暂时性，这个房子更像是悬浮而非立于大地之上。自18世纪末浪漫主义造园术开始淘汰所有围绕建筑物四周的过渡区以来，将建筑与自然如此断然划分的手法，再没有被尝试过。

While the site prompted the elevated frame structure, the program facilitated the reduction to essentials, and both contributed to the exceptional circumstances which enabled Mies to achieve the monumental simplicity that has become synonymous with his name. In retrospect, the Farnsworth House appears as the ultimate formulation that even Mies may not have surpassed had he accepted another commission for a house. While parts and details have been copied many time and entered into the vocabulary of contemporary architecture, the house itself has remained a singular case and-if one regards Philip Johnson's early work as a parallel development-without succession. It seems, rather, to reach back in time, evoking the primeval hut, or perhaps more concrete associations with prehistoric lake dwellings. A house that only our age could have built, it has, at the same time, the agelessness of the archetype.

基地的特质促成了这个高抬的构架，内容则促进了对建筑本质的还原，两者均造就了独特的环境，使密斯获得那已成为与"密斯"两字同义的不朽的单纯性。范斯沃斯住宅表现出一种终极的建筑形态，即使密斯本人再接受其他的住宅设计委托时，也不可能超越它。虽然它的部分形式和细部被多次模仿并已经成为当代建筑语汇，这幢建筑本身仍然独特非凡。菲利浦·约翰逊早期作品虽也呈现类似的发展，却后继乏力。这幢住宅，似乎可追溯到原始时代的小屋，更确切地说与史前时期的湖居有着一脉相承的原始性。这是一个只

有在我们这个时代才可能建造的住宅，同时也是永恒的建筑原型。

2.2　环境艺术设计

2.2.1　华盛顿西雅图奥林匹克雕塑公园❶
Olympic Sculpture Park, Seattle, Washington

Lead Designer: Weiss/Manfredi
Landscape Architect: Charles Anderson
client: Seattle Art Museum
Project Statement
Envisioned as a new urban model for sculpture parks, this project is located on Seattle's last undeveloped waterfront property-an industrial brown field site sliced by train tracks and an arterial road. The design connects three separate sites with an uninterrupted Z-shaped "green" platform, descending 40 feet from the city to the water, capitalizing on views of the skyline and Elliot Bay, and rising over existing infrastructure to reconnect the urban core to the revitalized waterfront.

主设计师：韦斯/莫弗雷迪
景观设计师：查理斯·安德森
业主：西雅图艺术博物馆
项目综述

作为城市雕塑公园的一个新的构思模式，场地位于西雅图最后一块未开发的滨水地区，是一片被铁轨和公路分割的工业棕色用地❷。设计采用一个不间断的"Z"字形"绿色"平台，将三部分连成一体。这条"绿色"平台，从市区向水域延伸40ft，利用天际线和艾略特（Elliot）海湾的天然景观，开发现有的基础资源将市中心连接到复兴的滨水地区（图2-8，图2-9）。

---

❶ 资源来源：http://www.asla.org/awards/2007/07winners/267_wmct.html

❷ "棕色土地"一词，20世纪90年代初期开始出现在美国联邦政府的官方用语中，用来指那些存在一定程度的污染，已经废弃或因污染而没有得到充分利用的土地及地上建筑物。

● 图2-8 西雅图奥林匹克雕塑公园1

(图片来源：http://www.asla.org/awards/2007/07winners/267_wmct.html)

● 图2-9 西雅图奥林匹克雕塑公园2

Most large North American coastal cities are oriented around once-active ports where streets, roadways, and rail lines were organized to move labor and materials efficiently. Over the past several decades, many ports have become obsolete and industry has moved away, leaving behind an antiquated system of urban infrastructure. Highways and rail lines that facilitated the flow of commerce have become barriers blocking public use of urban waterfronts. The site of the Olympic Sculpture Park was emblematic of this condition.

多数大型北美沿海城市都面向周围一度活跃的港口，那里的街道、道路和铁路线都曾被用来高效地运送劳动力和物资。在过去的几十年间，许多港口已经过时，产业搬迁后，留下陈旧的城市基础设施系统。曾经促进了贸易流通的公路和铁路线，现已成为阻挡公众利用城市水滨的障碍。奥林匹克雕塑公园这块基地就具有这种典型性。

Until the late 19th century, the local shoreline was characterized by the rising slope of Denny Hill. To accommodate growing industrial development, the City of Seattle radically transformed its topography by using hydrological power to level the waterfront bluff and to create new landfill.

19世纪末期，当地海岸线的特征是丹尼山的大斜坡。为了容纳不断增长的工业发展，西雅图市利用水利拉平了海滨的峭壁，建设了新的堆填区，将其地形进行了根本性的改变。

Used primarily for industrial purposes, the site declined in value in the 1960's and 1970's. More recently, it has become prime for residential speculation and would have been highly developed had it not been for the intervention of the Seattle Art Museum. Formerly owned by Union Oil of California (Unocal), the area was used as an oil transfer facility. Before construction of the park, over 120,000 tons of contaminated soil was removed. The remaining petroleum contaminated soil is capped by a new landform with over 200,000 cubic yards of clean fill, much of it excavated from the Seattle Art Museum's downtown expansion project.

主要用于工业用途的这块基地在20世纪六七十年代开始贬值。最近，如果不是因为西雅图艺术博物馆这个项目的介入，它或已主要成为住宅投机地块并进行高度的开发。这块地前身(原)为加利福尼亚石油联盟所有,作为石油运输设施。在建设公园之前,移走了超过 12 万 t 的污染土壤,再用超过 20 万 yd³❶ 的清洁土壤,以一种新的地貌形式来覆盖剩下的石油污染土壤,这些清洁土壤大部分是从西雅图艺术博物馆的市中心扩建工程挖掘而来。

Winner of an international design competition, the design for the Olympic Sculpture Park capitalizes on the forty-foot grade change from the top of the site to the water's edge. Planned as a continuous landscape that wanders from the city to the shoreline, this Z-shaped hybrid landform provides a new pedestrian infrastructure. Built with a system of mechanically stabilized earth, the enhanced landform re-establishes the original topography of the site, as it crosses the highway and train tracks and descends to meet the city. Layered over the existing site and infrastructure, the scheme creates a dynamic link making the waterfront accessible. The main pedestrian route is initiated at an 18,000-square-foot exhibition pavilion and descends as each leg of the path opens to radically different views. The first stretch crosses a highway, offering views of the Olympic Mountains; the second crosses the train tracks, offering views of the city and port; and the last descends to the water, opening views of the newly created beach. This pedestrian landform now allows free movement between the city's urban center and the restored beaches at the waterfront.

作为国际设计竞赛的获奖作品,奥林匹克雕塑园的设计充分利用了基地制高点与水边的 40ft 高差变化。把都市蜿蜒至海岸线的景观规划为一个连续的景观,Z 形的混合地形为参观者提供了一个新的步行设施。建立在土方机械平衡系统的基础上,抬高了的地形穿越高速路和铁路与都市景观相融合,重新确立了基地原有的地形。该设计在现有的基地和公共设施上进行分层设置,为海滨的可达性创造了一个动态链。主要的步行路线是(由)一个 1.8 万 ft²❷ 的展示馆(出发),向不同的视阈开辟出不同的道路。第一条道路穿越了一条高速路,提供指向奥林匹克山的视阈;第二条道路穿越铁道,提供指向都市和港口的视阈;最后一条道路引向水面,提供新造岸线的视阈。现在这一适于行人的地形可以让人们在市中心和重建的海滨沙滩之间自由穿梭。

After winning the international design competition, the designers worked with the client to select a team of local consultants. A consulting landscape architect familiar with local species worked within the tilting landforms of the Z-shaped design to create distinct micro-settings for diverse ecological environments with plantings characteristic of the Northwest. As the route descends from the pavilion to the water, it links three re-created archetypal landscapes of the northwest: a dense and temperate evergreen forest lined with ferns; a deciduous forest of Quaking Aspens with seasonally changing characteristics; and a shoreline garden including a series of new tidal terraces for salmon habitat and saltwater vegetation. Throughout the park, landforms and plantings collaborate to direct, collect, and cleanse storm water as it moves through the site before being discharged into Elliott Bay.

设计师与业主在赢得了国际性的设计竞赛之后,挑选了一群当地的顾问。一位在这个 Z 形斜坡地上工作的景观设计咨询师熟悉当地物种,试图利用西北植物的生态特征创造出有着多样生态环境的独特的微型环境。由于路线是从展示馆延伸到水面,它串联了三个重建的西北典型的景观:长有蕨类植物的浓密的温带常绿阔叶林;有季节性变化特征的白杨落叶林;以及海岸花园,包括一系列新的适于做鲑鱼栖息和海产植被生长的梯田。整个公园地形地貌的处理和种植相结合,直接排放、收集和净化流过基地表面的雨水,然后才流注到埃利奥特湾。

As a "landscape for art", the Olympic Sculpture park defines a new experience for modern and contemporary art outside the museum walls. The topographically varied park provides diverse settings for sculpture of multiple scales. Richard Serra's Wake is contained in the

---

❶ 体积单位,yd³ 即立方码。1yd³=0.764555m³。
❷ 面积单位,ft² 即平方英尺。1ft²=9.29030×10⁻²m²。

Valley, Tony Smith's Stinger and Wandering Rocks are seen within the Aspen Grove, and Mark Di Suvero's kinetic sculpture Shubert Sonata is activated by the winds along the waterfront. Deliberately open-ended, the design invites new interpretations of art and environmental engagement, reconnecting the fractured relationships of art, landscape, and urban life.

作为"艺术景观",奥林匹克雕塑公园在博物馆墙外空间,为现代艺术和当代艺术阐释了一种新的体验。该地形多变的公园为设置不同尺度的雕塑提供了多种背景。理查德·塞拉(Richard Serra)的作品"Wake"就设置于山谷之中,托尼·史密斯(Tony Smith)的作品"Stinger"和"Wandering Rocks"可以透过白杨小树林看到,马克·德·苏维洛(Mark Di Suvero)的能动的雕塑作品"舒伯特奏鸣曲"是由海滨的风能来驱动的。为了特意做成开放的场所,这个设计鼓励对艺术与环境融合做出新的诠释,重新连接艺术、景观与城市生活断裂的关系。

2.2.2 北京奥林匹克公园[1]
Olympic Green, Beijing

Olympic Green is the landscaped setting for the principal events during the 2008 Beijing Olympics. In July 2002 Sasaki Associates convinced the international competition jury with their master plan and later won 20,000 public votes during an exhibition of finalist's designs. As with any large master plan there were dissenting opinions on the practicality of the scheme. *The China Daily* of 27 July 2002 reported that Lan Tianzhu, the director of the cultural, health and sports subcommittee, doubted as to whether water resources would be adequate when he saw the proposed water system covering more than 100 hectares. "It will possibly become a stinking open basin if there is insufficient water or if it becomes stagnant after the Olympics," he warned. Shanjixiang, the director of the Planning Committee, who rejected this criticism, said the amount of water used by industry and agriculture in Beijing had decreased, while the volume assigned for environmental use was expected to rise in 2002 to 400 million cubic meters. Moreover, the Beijing water situation would benefit from the trans-regional south to north water—transfer project being completed for the 2008 Olympics and only recycled water was to be used for planting and irrigation.

奥林匹克公园是2008年北京奥运会的主要场地(图2-10,图2-11)。2002年7月,佐佐木事务所(Sasaki)以他们设计的总体规划折服了国际方案竞赛评审团。之后,在参赛设计展中获得2万公众选票而胜出。像很多大型规划一样,许多人对方案的实用性提出异议。《中国日报》在2002年7月27日报道:(北京)文化卫生体育委员会主任蓝天柱在看了方案中水系覆盖超过100hm²之后,怀疑是否有足够的水源。他警告说:"如果没有足够的水源,或奥运会后维护滞后,这里将会变成一池臭气弥漫的大水塘"。北京市规划委员会主任单霁翔反对这一观点,他说,北京的工业农业用水已经减少,而环境用水量在2002年预计增长到40亿m³。此外,北京水资源状况将受益于为2008奥运会而完成的南水北调项目,而且只将再生水用于种植和浇灌(园区)。

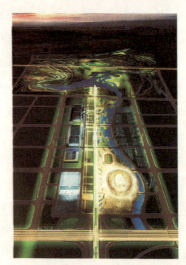

Olympic Sculpture Park, Seattle, Washington

● 图2-10 北京奥林匹克公园鸟瞰

(图片来源:Layla Dawson, China's New Dawn—An Architectural Transformation, 2005.151、153)

---

[1] 资料来源:Layla Dawson. China's New Dawn—An Architectural Transformation, 2005.150-153

奥林匹克公园最北边，一片面积为 700hm² 的自然生态森林公园将会成为各种生物安居的栖息地，其中包括湿地、草地和丘陵森林三种类别。这也会帮助提高城市中心的生物多样化。南面的文化轴线，集中了中华5000 年历史王朝之瑰宝，并融入奥林匹克轴线，轴线两边是新的体育场馆。其中包括已有的亚运会体育馆、由赫尔佐格 & 德梅隆设计的新国家体育馆，以及由 PTW 建筑设计公司、中国建筑工程总公司和奥雅纳事务所（Arup Group）联合设计的国家游泳中心。整个中轴线由南至北连接了从天安门广场、紫禁城到森林公园及其周围的格局。整个中心区域的规划框架基于原有的城市网格，覆盖着 4km 长的大道。其规模无可比拟，中心轴在整个布局以其刀斧神工脱颖而出。

From the south a pedestrian approach starts at the Olympic Gate and runs in a straight processional line northwards beside the Olympic Way with its flags of competing nations. The Olympic entry section continues this northern route with a commemorative site leading into the cluster of major stadiums. The southern tail end of Forest Lake embraces the National Stadium and then snakes northward to enclose several decorative rock islands providing habitats for wild fauna and flora. Along the axis there are squares, a fountain and possible open air Olympic Gallery. A transport node and more cultural sites are planned along the northern stretch of the axis which terminates at Forest Park Square. Here an elliptical amphitheatre can stage major civic gatherings and performing arts.

Olympic Sculpture Park, Seattle, Washington

● 图 2-11 北京奥林匹克公园平面图

At the North end of the Olympic Green, the 700—hectare, 'natural' ecological Forest Park will be home to multiple biotopes, three types 0f wetlands, meadows and upland forests, and help increase bio-diversity in the urban centre. Progressing south the Cultural Axis, which highlights the achievements of China's great historical dynasties over 5,000 years, flows into the Olympic Axis, which is flanked by the new sports venues. These include the existing Asian Games stadium, the new National Stadium, designed by Herzog & de Meuron, and the National Swimming Centre designed by PTW Architects with CSCEC and Arup Group. The complete Central Axis, linking all these sections, runs from Tiananmen Square and the Forbidden City in the south to Forest Park in the north. The framework for the layout of this entire central zone is the existing city grid which covers the four—kilometer—long tract. The scale is monumental and the Central Axis itself overpowering in its dynamic cut through the landscape.

人行路从南边奥林匹克大门开始，笔直的大路向北延伸，相伴的是布满各参赛国国旗的奥林匹克之路。奥林匹克入口部分延续向北大路，走过纪念场地，前面就是主要体育馆群。南部线的尾端是森林湖，湖水环绕着国家体育馆，并蜿蜒向北点缀着几个装饰性岩石小岛，是野生动植物的栖息之所。沿中轴线规划了几处广场，一个喷泉以及可开启为露天的奥林匹克画廊。中轴线向北设计了一个交通网站和许多文化场所，终点是森林公园广场。这个椭圆形阶梯广场可以作为群众聚会和艺术演出场地。

Incorporating the three Olympic ideals, sports, culture and environment, this planning concept aims to achieve urban balance and integration, between east and west, technology and nature, historical and modern times. Conceived as a poetic narrative Forest Park symbolizes the cradle of Chinese civilization with water flowing from its artificial lake southward into a canal which runs alongside the green borders of the central axis. The ecological aspects of the plan are considered pivotal in the later development of a sustainable urban environment, with green lungs and public sports facilities. A further educational aim is to reintroduce indigenous wild life into the city and give ordinary citizens a chance to experience 'nature'.

结合了奥运会三大主题：体育、文化和环境，该规划理念旨在平衡与融合城市的东、西方，技术与自然，历史与现代等元素。作为一个富有诗意的叙述，森林公园象征了中华文明的摇篮，人工湖的流水向南蜿蜒汇成小河，流淌在中心轴的绿色边带。规划的生态理念是可持续性城市环境后期发展的关键，表现在绿色结构和公共体育设施上。下一步的教育主题是向城市重新引入土著野生动物，让普通市民有机会体验"自然"。

For the Olympic National Stadium at the heart of the Olympic Green, designs by Herzog & de Meuron, working with the China Architecture Design Institute, the Beijing Architecture Design Institute, and AXS of Japan with Tsinghua University Architecture Design Institute, were picked from a total of forty-four entries by the international competition jury. An exhibition at the Beijing International Convention Center in March 2003 attracted 6,000 visitors, of whom 3,506 voted for the Herzog & de Meuron and China Architecture Design Institute's design.

奥林匹克国家体育馆位于奥林匹克公园中心，由赫尔佐格&德梅隆公司设计，与中国建筑设计院，北京建筑设计院和日本 AXS 事务所与清华大学建筑设计院共同努力完成。该方案由国际方案竞赛评审团从 44 家投标方案中筛选而来。北京国际会议中心在 2003 年 3 月举办的展览吸引了 6000 名观众，其中 3506 票赞成赫尔佐格 & 德梅隆公司和中国建筑设计院的设计方案。

The competition entry had a series of raked 1.5 meter-deep, steel box girders sixty—seven meters high which crisscrossed. giving the impression of woven twigs. Early in the process Herzog&·de Meuron consulted with Beijing artist Ai Weiwei, known for his Dadaist attitudes and, for Chinese sensibilities. provocative ideas on value and authenticity in Chinese culture. Ai Weiwei encouraged the architects to develop the crazy, Chaotic structure of the stadium and first sketched a tree and a bird's nest, both classical Chinese poetic images, to illustrate his concept.

该入围方案拥有一系列 1.5m 深的钢箱支架，高 67m 呈十字交叉状，表现出枝桠编织的风格。设计早期，赫尔佐格 & 德梅隆公司曾与北京艺术家、以达达艺术态度而著名的艾未未商讨过中国观众的敏感性、挑衅性的思想价值以及中华文化中的原真性。艾未未鼓励这位设计大师扩展该体育馆疯狂、混乱的结构，并第一次画出两个经典的中国诗歌意象，树和鸟巢，以此阐明他的概念。

The facade and structure were originally designed to be identical. An invisible membrane of inflated cushions. as the stadium's weatherproof skin was to fill the openings between girders. Inside the bowl stadium there should be no visible structure to hinder the 100,000 spectators sightlines. Visitors would enter through a covered foyer with restaurants and shops from which a spacious concourse would then open out with stands in three, unbroken, continuous tiers, reinforcing the impression of a simple bowl. According to the architects. "The crowd is the architecture." In bad weather a translucent membrane roof with a grid structure was intended to Slide across the sky. Placed on a gentle rise in the Olympic Green landscape the stadium was conceived as 'a collective bowl'. an image which sits well in the land of rice bowls with a recent ideology of communal sharing.

对于体育馆的正面和结构，当初的设计目的是使它们保持一致,许多隐形的膨胀垫用作体育馆预防天气的外皮,填充在支架的露天空隙处。内部碗形体育馆应没有可见的结构物遮挡10万观众的视线。观众应通过封闭大厅(带有餐厅和商店)进入开敞的体育场,然后是3层连绵不断的结构强化单一碗形的印象。按照设计师的说法,"人群即是建筑"。天气恶劣之时,网架结构的透明膜屋顶将覆盖天空。建筑在奥林匹克公园微微起伏的地带,该体育馆曾被构思为一个碗形综合体,饭碗状的表现呈现出公众分享的最新理念。

This is just one of the many architectural projects which have been affected by the criticism of the Chinese government over inappropriate spending on over—dimensioned national gestures. In August 2004 work was stopped for a financial audit of the design. The original budget was reported in *the Peoples Daily* 23/8/04 to have been reduced by deleting the retractable roof, enlarging the size of the roof top opening and so reducing the amount of latticework steel Construction. To what extent the structure's original visual impact has been diluted remain s to be seen.

这仅仅是众多建筑项目中的一个,因其庞大的尺度而引起的不恰当开支,遭到中国政府的批评而受到影响。2004年8月,建筑停工以进行设计财政审计。2004年8月23日,《人民日报》刊登了原有的预算。为了缩减开支,需要去掉可收缩屋顶,并扩大顶部开口而减少格子钢结构数量。如此,原有结构的视觉冲击力在多大程度上被削弱仍有待观察。

2.2.3 澳大利亚昆士兰市布里斯班河规划 Plan the Brisbane River in Queensland, Australia

In the very center of the city, planners at one time proposed a highway fronting the Brisbane River in Queensland, Australia. Lend Lease and its team of designers, however, had ideas and urged the city of Brisbane to consider alternative proposals. Thus in the early 1980s, Belt Collins worked with Lend Lease, and architect Harry Seidler, on a total urban concept for a portion of the waterfront. That concept has become Riverside Centre, a prestigious office tower development in the city's commercial center.

规划师们曾经建议,在澳大利亚昆士兰市市中心的布里斯班河前修建一条高速公路,然而伦德·里斯(Lend Lease)和他的设计团队对此却有其他想法,并且希望布里斯班在此两项计划中择其一进行。为此,在80年代早期,伦德·里斯与贝尔·高林(Beit Collins)以及哈里·塞德勒(Harry Seidler)合作,对整个城市的滨水部分做概念规划。这一规划现已变成现实,河畔中心已成为城市商业中心的一个著名办公发展区(图2-12,图2-13)。

Brisbane River in Queensland, Australia

● 图2-12 昆士兰市布里斯班河规划1

Brisbane River in Queenslay, Australia

● 图2-13 昆士兰市布里斯班河规划2

Anchoring the project is a 3.5-acre landscape design that includes major plaza spaces, a riverfront promenade, rooftop gardens and a major connection from the waterway activities to the hub of the commercial activities in downtown Brisbane.

In the early discussions of the landscape plan, the clients said they wanted a heroic tree as the centerpiece for the plaza. Belt Collins was able to find a 20-meter ficus tree some distance up river. At the time, no tree of that size had ever been transplanted in Australia. The huge tree simply could not be moved over land. The solution was to build a special barge, which floated the tree down river to the plaza where it was craned into place.

这一项目正式启动为一块 3.5acre❶ 地块的景观设计，其中包括主要的广场空间、滨水步道、屋顶花园及一个主要联系枢纽，联系水滨活动区和布里斯班市区的商业中心。

在早期景观规划的讨论中，业主希望由一棵高大的树木作为广场的重心（标志）。贝尔·高林在河的上游找到一棵 20m 的杉树。当时澳大利亚还没有过移植此类尺寸树木的先例，如此巨大的树当然不能简单地移动。解决这一难题的方法是为此建造了一艘特殊的船，用它载着这棵树顺着河流向下游运至其定位的广场。

Riverside Centre was the first major development to address itself to the river with a ferry landing and riverside promenade. Twenty years later, the entire riverfront is connected with a promenade, river ferries and other riverside activities from the Storey Bridge to the Brisbane Botanic Gardens, a distance of several miles.

Today Riverside Centre forms the heart of the city's financial district. It is said that the plaza has etched itself into Brisbane life, forming the well-attended Sunday Riverside Market, while during the week it provides a vibrant setting for outdoor relaxation by city workers and visitors.

河畔中心是第一个用小码头渡口和滨水散步道来与水互动的主要发展区。20 年之后，整个滨河地带从斯托里（Storey）桥至几英里远的植物园之间均由散步道联系，设有渡口及滨河活动区域。

今日，河畔中心成了城市金融区的核心，据说这一广场已经融入了布里斯班的生活，形成吸引众多人流的周日河畔集市，并为城市上班族和游人在一周的工作日中提供充满活力的户外放松休闲设施。

2.2.4 格拉斯小镇
Grasse Town

The small town named Luneng·Grasse, which is using the French town of Grasse as the theme, is located in the heart of the Beijing East Sea villa at the eastern outskirts of Beijing. Close to the Wenyu River, a number of small standalone units can form a community together, and the individual buildings could be either separated or combined each other. Such diversities make them not only confined to commercial buildings, but also a new mode of commercial real estate.

以法国格拉斯小镇为借鉴题材的鲁能·格拉斯小镇，坐落于北京京郊东海别墅社区的核心位置，与温榆河的老河紧密相邻。多个小建筑单体功能相辅相成，围合成一个建筑群落。各个建筑单体可分可合，多样化的建筑平面功能使其不仅仅局限为商业建筑。这是一种新的商业地产模式（图 2-14～图 2-16）。

The Site Plan

● 图 2-14　规划总平面

---

❶ 面积单位，即英亩。1acre=4046.8642m²。

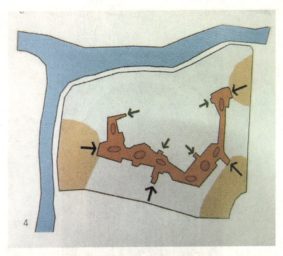

Sketch of space

● 图 2-15 空间示意图

Bird's eye view of the town

● 图 2-16 小镇鸟瞰图

The concept of the small town starts from the old cove, and the subject unfolds around the celebrations of the small Grasse Town. The series of celebration events are anticipated to be one of the important functions. The layout is from the mode of the traditional town, and due to the small scale, the major roads to the east and south will be fuller. And the changes of the node blocks inside the street complete the model of the layout. When you walk in the town, you'll see that with the changes in the street, you always have various choices for paths and destinations. It provides people with comfortable conditions to "stroll around the street" and greatly raises the free-dom of people in the town, so that the town is full of energy.

格拉斯小镇的构思沿着老河湾开始，围绕着格拉斯小镇的庆典主题展开。按照预想，系列庆典活动将作为小镇重要功能之一。小镇的建筑布局是由传统小镇的街区模式转化而来，在小镇建筑规模不大的条件下，沿东、南两侧主要道路分布的建筑布局较为丰满，在内街空间变化的建筑节点完成街区模式的布置。当人们在街道中行走的时候，随着内街的空间变化，人们的行进方向和目的总有多种选择，这为人们"逛"街提供了条件。人们在小镇中的自由度大大提高，从而使小镇充满了生气。

Although the flexible building layout has provided people a variety of choices, nodes and the main line provide a framework to determine the structure of the town. In the small town's landscape plan, the five most important node spaces are the center park along the river, the small public square at the northeast corner, the river public square at the southwest corner, the public square in the entrance of the small town and the center platform of the business street. The connection of the five nodes forms the two major axes of the small town.

尽管灵活的建筑布局形式为人群的流动提供了多样化的可能性，然而节点空间和主线的确定才为整个小镇的结构提供了骨架。在小镇的规划设计中，沿河中心花园、东北角的小广场、西南角的滨河休闲广场、小镇入口广场以及商业街中心平台是整个小镇的最重要的五个节点空间，这五个节点的联系成为小镇最重要的两条轴线。

The main axes begin from the public square in the entrance of the small town, then through the center platform of the business street to the center garden in the small town. Finally, it leads to the beautiful old cove. And the minor axes starts from the small public square at the northeast corner in the business street, connecting to the river public square at the southwest corner, crossing the center platform of the business street. In this system, the etiquette space in the entrance of the small town, people's traffic space, party space, celebration space, and commercial space are combined in an orderly manner. The complete small-town style has been formed by changes in the elevation of the ground, management of the street width, and acceptance of landscape.

其中主轴线从小镇入口广场开始，经商业街中心平台通向小镇中心花园，并最终通向美丽的老河湾；而次轴线从商业街东北角小广场开始，连接到西南角的滨河休闲广场，并和主轴线在商业街中心平台处形成交叉。在这个基本体系里，小镇入口礼仪空间、人流交通空间、休闲聚会空间、庆典空间、商业活动空间等有序地结合在一起。并通过地面标高变化、街道尺度控制、景观的收纳来丰富整体规划，最终形成了完整的小镇风貌。

2.2.5 改建项目——贝加莫市 Nembro 新市政图书馆❶
New Municipal Library of Nembro

A building erected in 1897, originally as a primary school, has seen many changes of use over the years, becoming town hall, then day nursery and finally clinic. The municipality today intends to renovate the dilapidated building in order to turn it into a library, to give the city a facility for the education and information of its citizens. The strategic position within the urban tissue, the architectural character of the original structure, closed on three sides, and the need for more space, has made it necessary to add a new wing, in the form of a new construction that is placed so as to close the only open side and form an enclosed open-air court.

该图书馆始建于 1897 年，起初此建筑是一所小学，在多年来的演变中，该建筑的功能有多次的改变。从小学校到成为市政厅，以及托儿所和后来的医院门诊部。目前该市决定将此建筑改造成为一座公共图书馆，并希望此建筑能够为市民提供一个学习知识与获取信息的场所。原有建筑，在城市结构中处于重要位置，三面围合。出于增加空间的需求，有必要在开敞的一边增加一个新体量，从而形成一个围合的内部庭院（图 2-17，图 2-18）。

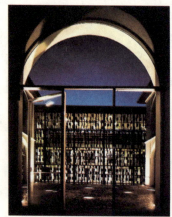

图 2-17 贝加莫市 Nembro 新市政图书馆 1

（图片来源：新建筑改造实例. 北京：中国建筑工业出版社，2008：44-47.）

图 2-18 贝加莫市 Nembro 新市政图书馆 2

The new wing communicates with the existing building through the basement, and is detached from the old structure on all sides; in spite of the connection between the two structures, this arrangement serves to underscore the architectural difference between the older, historical part and the new. The new, completely transparent body is in fact characterized by a facade in 40 cm×40 cm earthenware tiles, glazed in carmine red, held in place by a structure of coupled steel profiles; this construction method makes it possible to screen and filter the daylight.

新增加的一翼通过地下空间与现有建筑相连接，并

---

❶ 资料来源：新建筑改造实例. 北京：中国建筑工业出版社，2008：44-47. 编者摘选、修改.

与旧结构完全脱离。这样的空间组织在建筑意义上强调了新与旧的对比。新建部分的外立面由规格为 40cm×40cm 的陶土砖组成。陶土砖表面进行了深红色釉化处理，由成对的钢构件固定。这样的立面构成使得建筑成为一个完全通透的体量，外立面本身可以作为遮挡或过滤阳光的装置。

The "screen wall" that shields the new glass volume serves as a divisor between interior and exterior; the architectural distinctive trait of the facing, uniformly distributed on all sides, allows an alternation of filled and void areas according to the continuous pattern created by the rotation of every single earthenware element. In fact, while the use of earthenware evokes traditional building methods, at the same time it looks extremely contemporary thanks to the way it is used and the assembly method, as well as the distinctive textural quality of this material that, within the context of a surrounding lacking in identity, plays on a contrast that aims to stand the test of time. The architecture can be read from different angles, and its expressive language spaces from the plays with light and shade, the construction tissue, the structural unity and finally the use of materials and color, a research where durability is linked to innovation, venturing beyond the heritage and charm of the imitation. The entrance to the new library will be from Piazza Italia, where the original main entrance of the school was located; the visitor first enters an area that will serve as reception and information point, created by modifying and standardizing some existing openings so as to create a spacious and prestigious interior that reflects the public function of a library.

这层特殊的"幕墙"结构围护着内部的玻璃体量，同时成为内外空间的界限。外立面的这种特征在各个面上均得以表现，在每块陶土砖的开合转动之间，创造出一种连续的韵律。事实上，陶土材料的运用在突显传统建造技术的同时，最终的效果也极富现代感。建筑可从不同角度被阅读，其特殊的空间语言通过光影的变化、建造的质感、结构的统一以及材料与色彩的运用来表达，这里永恒与创新相连，冒险超越了继承和模仿的魅力。新图书馆的入口位于意大利广场，也就是原来学校的主要入口。参观者首先进入一个提供接待以及信息服务的区域，此区域在现状的基础上突显出宽敞与高雅的内部装饰风格，并反映出该图书馆的公用功能。

This interior leads to the portico area that, appropriately defined by glazing, provides access to the various rooms of the library proper, identifying a continuous itinerary with a display of new publications that the users may consult before entering the reading room. The basement features a spacious hall with computers for consulting, and communicates with the new volume that continues all the way to the reading room. The ground floor and first floor of the old building house the main study rooms for children, consulting rooms, a newspaper library and a multifunctional hall, while the new wing houses books in a single structure that serves both as book container and reading room. Characterized by the more than 9 meters tall bookcase structure, the new volume becomes the treasure chest with books available for consultation; access to its three levels is guaranteed by two projecting mezzanines with reading stations arranged along a book rest overlooking the façade.

由前台区域进入门廊，玻璃窗恰当地限定了空间，读者可以从此处到达与之相连的图书馆内不同功能的房间。该区域还呈现出一种连续性的展示效果，读者可以在咨询后进入各阅览室。位于地下的宽敞大厅与新的体量相连，这里备有电脑以便读者进行查阅，新的体量内有多条通道可通往阅览室。原有建筑的一层和二层主要作为儿童阅览室、信息查询室、报刊阅览室以及多功能大厅，新的翼状建筑的统一结构主要用于图书存放以及阅览室。以超过9m的书柜结构为特点，这个新的体量成为书的宝库；经由两个结构上突出的夹层楼面可以通达新建筑的三个楼层，在夹层楼面里，沿着读书休闲区的阅读站可以俯瞰外立面。

2.3 室内设计

2.3.1 某度假村室内设计
An Interior Design for a Holiday Village

In this summer vacation home, the Romantic design combines several distinct elements to a harmonious way. There are rattan seats woven from vines, a sofa of modern simplicity, and a coffee table in solid wood. These pieces, of different eras and different styles, come together to give a feeling of comfort. Coupled with deep curves, the scene is like a dream.

这是一个夏日度假村,整个作品运用浪漫主义的手法,将几个毫不相干的元素结合得恰到好处。其中有现代简约主义风格的沙发、藤条编织的坐椅,还有实木茶几。他们完全不属于一个时代,完全不属于一个风格,却让人们感觉非常舒服。加上极度夸张的曲线,让整个场景犹如梦幻一般(图 2-19)。

An Interior Design for a Holiday Village

● 图 2-19 室内设计

While these elements aren't directly connected, they reveal the very style and colors of simplicity. The carpet is like sharp lines, clean and frank, with simple colors to complement the elegant setting. Huge French Windows brighten and open up the space, diffusing the romantic feeling; the quiet atmosphere is interrupted by the modernist office lights, whose dynamic curves activate the calmness of static lines. The entire space is at times tight, at times relaxed.

从整体上看这些元素虽然没有直接联系,但是他们却表现出一种简约主义风格的色彩。彩色地毯就像几条犀利的直线,干脆整洁,配上古朴的颜色又使整个环境多了几分清闲与雅致;巨大的落地窗让整个空间开敞明亮,让浪漫的情怀再次抒发;具有现代风格的厅灯,其弯曲的灯杆不仅从形式上打破了安静的气氛,而且在设计方法上运用动静结合的手法用曲线的动打破直线的静,从而使整个空间显得有松有紧。

Bamboo, grown indoors, not only breathes life into its environment but adds to the classical atmosphere of the gardens of southern China. While the bamboo's grace elevates the romantic atmosphere, the simple color scheme becomes vivid, while the bamboo's grace elevates the romantic atmosphere.

室内种植绿竹,不仅为整个环境增添了生气,还注入了我国南方古典园林中的情趣,打破了室内环境简单的色调,在浪漫之中又多了几分高雅。

The starting point of the interior design is the concept of building space.

And spatial effects are the aspirations of the architectural art, while the windows and doors play a subordinate part. The subordinate part is the material basis of place and plays a decisive role. The program perfectly unites various elements to achieve a balance in how viewers feel the space.

室内设计的出发点和着眼点是建筑空间的内涵。

把空间效果作为建筑艺术追求的目标,而界面、门窗是构成空间的必要从属部分。从属部分是构成空间的物质基础,并对内涵空间使用的观感起决定性作用。这个方案完美地利用各种元素,让空间达到了一种平衡,一种美的平衡。

The great architect W. Platner says that "Compared to designing buildings, interior design is much more difficult." In the interior, "you have to deal with more colleagues, and analyze psychological factors to figure out how to make them feel comfortable or excited." The designers of this plan are not only breaking ground in the overall aesthetic, but also demonstrate the ability to unite disparate elements.

建筑大师 W·普拉特纳(W. Platner)认为室内设计"比设计包容这些内部空间的建筑物要困难得多",这是因为在室内"你必须更多地同人打交道,研究人们的心理因素,以及如何能使他们感到舒适、兴奋"。这个方案的设计师不仅从整体美感上有所突破,还表现了自己在控制各种不同元素达到某种统一的能力。

2.3.2 某起居室室内设计
An Interior Design of a Living Room

The decorative features of this work are full of Chinese tea culture. The use of the straight line makes us feel the beauty of steel and a atmosphere of quiet. Matched with Chinese vein decoration cloth, the whole environment has an effect of combining soft and hard, to form a picture which is warm and soothing. The shapes of furniture stretch, generous and attentive, coupled with the huge picture window, the entire space looks like very bright and open. Whether you're having a cup of tea or watching the scenery, the feelings are very soothing.

这幅作品融入中国茶文化的装饰特色,大胆地运用直线。既具有阳刚之美,又带有沉静之气。配上中国纹理图案的装饰布,让整个环境有了软、硬结合的效果,显得温馨又舒展,柔美而大方。家具的造型舒展、大方、稳重,加上巨大的落地窗让整个空间敞亮开阔,无论是品茶还是赏景都会使人感觉心情非常舒展(图 2-20)。

An Interior Design of a Living Room

● 图 2-20　起居室设计

To design furniture, on the one hand, designers use scientific means to carry out specialized, 3-dimensional and quantitative research on Chinese tradition furniture. Then they reveal the ideas of design and the scientific spirit, and extract the "traditional Chinese-style factor" and distill the shape and decorative elements of the traditional by the method of symbols. They try to find the impact point of traditional Chinese furniture design, by identifying the scientific and technological level, and other limited conditions of the time. On the basis of this factor, they inject modern ideas and expand the design idea, to finally provide a clear theoretical basis and operational method for modern Chinese furniture.

从家具的设计上看,一方面设计师用现代的科学手段,对中国的传统家具进行专业化、立体化和定量化的深层次研究,从而充分揭示出其中所含的设计思想和科学精神,提炼出所谓的"中国式传统因子",用符号学的方法抽提出传统中的造型和装饰的元素;并找出由于当时科技水平及其他限制条件对中国传统家具设计的影响点,在此基础上注入现代因子,拓展设计思想,为中国现代风格家具的开创提供比较明确的、可遵循的理论依据和操作途径。

A mature style of furniture must have uniqueness, stability, and consistency. Uniqueness is easy to identify from the specific characteristics. Consistency applies to the entire series of furniture and to the individual shapes of furniture, elevation, local, decoration and so on which must implement the details of this feature. Stability is to maintain basic characteristics in a fairly long period and create a representative group of works.

But to get particularity, stability and consistency of the acquisition depends on the major factors that impact them, including social, historical, ideological, cultural, practical, technological, and environmental. Without such basic harmony, and there will be no consistency of style and stability. Here designers break the shackles of the original style and play to their rich imagination, while respecting the applicability of design and the principle of functional form of obedience to create their own points of interest.

一个成熟的家具风格,必定具有独特性、稳定性和一贯性。独特性,就是具有容易辨认的明确的特点;一贯性,就是从整个家具系列到个体家具的造型、立面、局部、细节装饰等都贯彻这个特点,构思完整而统一;稳定性,就是在一个相当长的时期内,基本特点不变,并且产生一批代表作品。

而独特性、稳定性和一贯性的获得,必定有赖于它们和影响它们的主要因素,包括社会的、历史的、思想的、文化的、功能的、技术的、环境的等基本处于和谐的状态。没有这种基本的和谐状态,风格就不会有一贯性和稳定性。在这里设计师打破原有风格的束缚,发挥自己丰富的想象力,尊重设计的适用性,尊重形式服从功能的原则,创造着自己的兴趣点。

From the view of the use of design elements, whether the line order is vertical or level, it can show a refined and quiet sense, like the effect of blinds. Therefore, here comes with the partitions which embody the styles of traditional Chinese screen-grid.

从设计元素运用的角度上看,无论是垂直的还是水平的细密直线的排列,都可以表现出一种精致和静谧,如百叶窗产生的那种效果。如图 2-20 所示,结合中国古代屏风的元素设计的隔断就表现出了这种意境。

2.3.3 某走廊室内设计
An Interior Design of a Corridor

This is a design of a corridor. There is a sharp contrast between the facades of the two sides. The wood partition is a bit prudent and strict on the left wall, while the curve of the corridor makes the whole inside don't feel weakness. Incidentally, the two complement and react to each other, so the space becomes lively and interesting.

这是一个走廊的设计(图 2-21)。

An Interior Design of a Corridor

● 图 2-21 走廊设计

两边的立面一实一虚,形成鲜明的对比。左边的墙面运用庄重的方格木质隔墙,有几分稳重、严谨之感,而走廊的曲线走势让整个立面显得不致呆板无力,两者恰巧互相补充、互相作用,让空间生动有趣。

Interior design is not only to be considered as decorative art. In fact, it's more important to create wealth of space modeling and pursue peace and a realm of freedom. These are the main intentions of interior design.

There should be a clear theme in interior design, and unity can constitute all the form and nature of beauty. Using unity for planning and design could make the idea invaluable and full of meaning, it is the design realm that every designer should pursue. In these works, designers have fully displayed their talents and their design concept has been expressed very clearly.

室内设计不能被单纯地理解为艺术装饰。其实创造丰富的空间造型,并且科学性地追求平和随意、率真自由的境界更重要。这些才是室内设计的主要意旨。

室内设计要有一个明确的统一的主题,统一可以构成一切美的形式和本质。用统一来规划设计,使构思变得既无价又有内涵,这是每个设计师都应该追求的设计境界。在这幅作品中,设计师充分展现了自己的才华,将自己的设计理念表达得非常明确。

Interior design elevates personality over popularity. Different environmental and cultural backgrounds, customs, and tastes may produce different results. Therefore, interior design is constantly innovating. Don't rigidly adhere to the old point of view; it's very important to bestow each space new images through aesthetic decoration and its function. Our modern interior design is not in a determined circle, and the best things may become obsolete in modern times when people's demand is increasingly diversified. The emergence of new style is accepted, and makes interior design colorful. The most important thing for interior design is realm, and if you have realm you could reach a high level. Steady, generous, yet elegant, it is the realm of this work.

室内设计追求流行但更讲个性,具体的环境不同,文化背景、品味追求与风俗习惯不同,就可能产生不同的效果。所以室内设计不断创新,不拘泥于旧有的观点,通过功能的调整,艺术的装饰,赋予每个空间以新的形象就非常重要了。我们现代的室内设计没有一个什么定则,在人们需求日益多样化、个性化的今天,最好的东西也会过时。新的风格不断出现并被人们所接受,才使得室内设计多姿多彩。室内设计以境界为最上,有境界就能达到一定高度。沉稳、大方,又不失高贵,这就是图2-21所达到的境界。

2.3.4 某起居室室内设计
An Interior Design of a Living Room

The large-scale use of circle and curve makes this program full of energy and vitality. Designers made good use of orange and pure white colors to make the entire indoor environment more live. The use of half-tinted yellow is appropriate and strikes a balance between light and dark.

The main tune is warm, and the atmosphere of home is emphasized. A yellow-white color will be placed behind the white not only to emphasize the white walls, but also to increase the stability of the entire space.

这个方案大量使用圆和曲线,使整个空间充满了活力和生机;橘黄色与纯白色的搭配,让整个室内环境更加生动。中间色调米黄色运用得也比较恰当,不亮不暗恰到好处。

以暖色调为主,烘托出家的气氛。米黄色略重于白色,将其置于白色的后面不仅烘托了白色的墙面,还增加了整个空间的稳定性(图2-22)。

● 图2-22 起居室室内设计

From the use of modeling elements, we can see the regular circular array in the middle square, giving a sense of the security of family. The ceiling lights in oval shape have broken the silence, and give instantaneous motion to the entire space.

The curve, close to nature, evokes a sense of comfort and is the most suitable for use on cold hard objects such as iron and steel security doors, hardwood furniture, Matte decorative glass, decorative masonry and so on. For smaller rooms, whether it is a straight line or curve, "slimness" should be the basic principle. Thin extension gives people a feeling of expanding space, as demonstrated by the curtain, which is full of small pieces of flowers, running beautifully from the roof down to the floor.

从造型元素的运用上看,规矩的圆形阵列置于方形中间,让整个方案看上去有种家的安全感。椭圆形的吊顶灯造型打破了沉寂,让整个空间瞬时动了起来。

曲线,有一种亲近自然的舒适感,最适合用于硬冷的物体之上，如钢铁防盗门、硬木家具、磨砂装饰玻璃、墙饰与砖石地面装饰等。对于较小的房间，无论是直线还是曲线，都应以"细长"为基本原则。细线的延伸给人一种空间扩大的感觉，比如从房顶一直垂挂到地面的窗帘，采用小碎花加纵向直线的图案就十分清丽。

poetic vision making the effect for beyond the image of reality.

作品《岩间圣母》中的人物置于幽暗的洞穴之中，潮湿的氛围巧妙地烘托着人物。整个画面营造了一个遥远、梦幻般的场景，如诗般的画面远胜过现实的人物效果。

2.4 中外名画与雕塑

Leonardo Da Vinci. *The Virgin of the Rocks*. C. 1485. Panel, 75×43 1/2″. The Louvre, Paris

● 图2-23 列奥纳多·达·芬奇《岩间圣母》1485年/镶嵌板画75in×43 1/2in/巴黎卢浮宫馆藏

Picture：from *New History of World Art 12*，SHOGAKU-KAN，Printed in Japan，12-1994，P30.

图片来源：《新编世界艺术史12》，Shogakukau，日本写真印刷株式会社，1994（12）：30.

The figures of The *Virgin of the Rocks* emerge from the semidarkness of the grotto, enveloped in a moisture-laden atmosphere that delicately veils their forms. The whole picture creates a remote, dreamlike scene, with the

Michelangelo. *The Rebellious Slave*. 1513-1516. Marble, heigh 84″. The Louvre, Paris

● 图2-24 米开朗基罗《反抗的奴隶》1513～1516年/大理石雕刻，高84in/巴黎卢浮宫馆藏

Picture：from *New History of World Art 12*，SHOGAKU-KAN，Printed in Japan，12-1994，P169.

图片来源：《新编世界艺术史12》，Shogakukan，日本写真印刷株式会社，1994（12）：169.

The Rebellious Slave is a part of the vast sculpture program for the bomb of Julius II, which was regarded as Michelangelo's greatest achievement had he carried it out as originally planned. In this master piece, the figure of The Rebellious Slave is struggling get free from restraining, perhaps its allegorical meaning mattered less to him than the expressed content, so the evocative of the Neo-Platonic image of the body seems to show that the body is the earthly prison of the soul.

雕像《反抗的奴隶》来自意大利教皇尤里乌斯二世陵墓的大型雕塑群,该雕塑群为米开朗基罗原创的最伟大的作品。作品中的人物正在挣脱束缚,也许对米开朗基罗来说,所表达的内容要高于作品本身的寓意,这种新柏拉图式的躯干形象仿佛暗示身体是灵魂的尘世牢笼。

缺乏三维空间的真实感。

马奈毕生奉献于"纯绘画"中,每一个笔触和色块并不只代表它们本身,而是表达画家的最初的现实世界。

Edouard Manet. *A Bar at the Folies -Bergeres*. 1881-1882. $37^{1/2} \times 51''$. The Courtauld Collection. London

● 图 2-25　爱德华·马奈《佛利贝尔杰酒店》1881～1882 年/$37^{1/2}$ in×51in/伦敦康特奥德艺术博物馆博物馆藏

Picture：from *New History of World Art 22*，SHOGAKUKAN，Printed in Japan，8-1993，P45-46.

图片来源：《世界美术大全第 22 卷》,SHOGAKUKAN,日本写真印刷株式会社,1993(8),45-46.

A Bar at the Folies-Bergères shows a single calm figure, which is firmly set in the rectangle canvas, but the background matched not so well. A huge shimmering mirror image mow reflects the whole interior of the nightclub, but without the sufficient sense of three-dimensional reality. Manet devoted all his life to "pure painting", what the brush strokes and color patches are not what they stand for, but are the artist's primary reality.

作品《佛利贝尔杰酒店》展示了一个平静的人物形象,稳定地置于矩形油画布上,但是背景却不是那么相称。一面巨大的闪光镜反射出整个夜总会的场面,但却

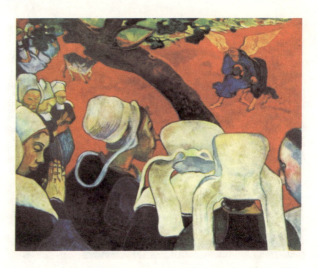

Paul Gaugain *The Vision After the Sermon*. 1888. $28^{3/4} \times 36^{1/2}''$. National Gallery of Scotland, Edinburgh

● 图 2-26　保罗·高更《布道后的幻觉》1888 年/$28^{3/4}$ in×$36^{1/2}$ in/爱丁堡,苏格兰国家美术馆藏

Picture：from *A Comprehensive Collection for Appreciation of World Art-Classics of Foreign Paintings*（Ⅱ），general editor：Zouwen, People's Fine Arts Publishing House, 5-2000, P57.

图片来源：《世界艺术全鉴——外国绘画经典（下）》邹文主编,人民美术出版社出版,2000(5)：57.

In order to escape the infin luence of Industrial society Gaugain once lived in a island in Pacific Ocean by himself. He formed a unique'art style of original mysterious meaning as well as symbolic meaning（出处同图片）. In his picture The Vision After the Sermon he tried to depict the simple faith of the western France country people with this style. The perspective and human figures in traditional painting have given way to the flat simplified picture, the dark brilliant colors and the outline of the objects.

为了逃避工业社会的影响,高更曾经一个人住在太平洋的岛屿上,在此期间他形成了自己独特的"既有原始神秘意味,又有象征意义的"艺术风格（出处同图

片）。在他的作品《布道后的幻觉》中，他试图以这种独特的风格来描绘法国西部乡下人的淳朴的信仰，平面简洁的画面、浓重华丽的色彩和物体轮廓的勾画已经超出了传统绘画对透视和人物的要求。

在对康定斯基的代表作品内涵的探索中，我们无意中会发现他的目的是用一种纯精神上的意义改变形式和色彩，用他的话说，就是通过消除所有物质世界的具体形态来获得这种效果。

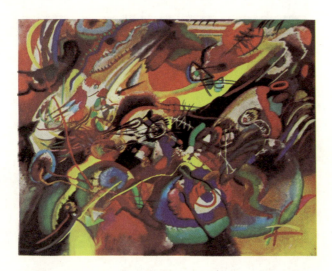

Wassily Kandinsky. *Sketch I for 'Composition Ⅶ'*. 1913. $30^{3/4} \times 39^{3/8}''$. Collection Felix Klee. Bern

● 图 2-27　瓦西里·康定斯基《构图——7号的初稿》1913年／$30^{3/4}$ in×$39^{3/8}$ in／伯恩克利私人博物馆藏

　　Picture：from *Kandinsky*, Michel Conil Lacoste, Crown Publishers, Inc. -New York.

　　图片来源：米歇尔·C. 拉科斯特著.《康定斯基》，纽约皇冠出版社.

Vincent Willem Van Gogh. *Wheat Field and Cypress Tree*，1889，National Gallery，London

● 图 2-28　文森特·威廉·梵高《麦田和柏树》，1889年，伦敦国力画廊收藏

　　Picture：from *Vincent van Gogh - Genius and Disaster*，A. M. Hammacher，Printed and bound in Japan，P134-135

　　图片来源：A. M. 哈姆马彻.《文森特·梵高——天才与灾难》. 日本印刷装订. 第134～135页.

　　As abstract as their forms of Kandinsky's work, one of the most striking is Sketch I for 'Composition Ⅶ'. Perhaps we should avoid the term 'abstract', because it is often taken to mean that the artist has analyzed and simplified the shape of visible reality. What traces of representation his work contains are quite involuntary find his aim was to change form and color with a purely spiritual meaning (as he put it) by eliminating all resemblance to the physical world.

　　在康定斯基的抽象作品中，《构图——7号的初稿》最为引人注目。也许我们应该避免使用"抽象"这一词汇，因为抽象常常意味着艺术家对可见实物的轮廓进行分析和简化。

　　Wheat Field and Cypress Tree both earth and sky show an over powering turbulence-the corn filed resembles a stormy sea, the spring trees flame bursting out from the underground, and the hills and clouds heave with the same undulant motion.

　　The dynamism contained in every brush stroke is of each one not merely a deposit of color, but an incisive graphic gesture.

　　在作品《玉米地和柏树》中，天空和大地都展示出了极度的不安，玉米地像暴风雨中的大海，春季的树木像从大地中迸发出的火焰，山丘和云朵同样也展现出起伏的动态。每一笔中所蕴含的活力不是色彩的堆积，而是清晰准确的绘画语言。

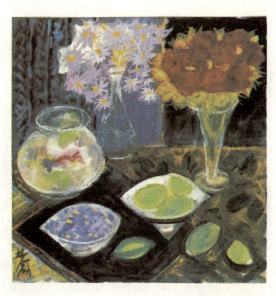

Lin Fengmian. *Still Life Painting*. 1987. Personal collection

● 图 2-29 林风眠《静物画》1987 年/私人收藏

图片来源：网络：http://images.google.cn/imglanding

Lin Feng mian, a famous creative Chinese painting master, oil painting master and who was also a famous educator in the 20th century, with profound influences to the development of the modern painting in China. He was influence by paintings of academism, impressionism and fauvism when he studied in Dijon and Paris of France in the early years, to put in his distinct savvy he finally formed his unique art character. In his picture Still Life Painting, he used square composition as usual, the red and yellow flowers echoed the tender green lemon but compared with the purple petals. He masterly mixed the Oriental and Western art together and made a common artistic language.

林风眠，一位富于创新精神的 20 世纪著名中国画大师、油画大师和美术教育家，他对中国近代绘画的发展产生了深远的影响。他早年曾赴法国在迪戎和巴黎深造，在此期间，他曾先后受到学院派、印象派和野兽派的影响，加上自己对绘画的独特悟性终于形成了独具一格的艺术特征。在其作品《静物画》中，他采用了一贯的正方形构图，红黄色的花卉既与嫩绿色的柠檬呼应又与紫色的花瓣形成色彩上的对比。他巧妙地将中西方艺术结合在一起，创造了一种共通的艺术语言。

Ren Bonian. *A Lady*. Colored on paper. Collected by Nanjing Museum

● 图 2-30 任伯年《仕女图》/纸本设色/南京博物馆藏

Picture: from *The Art of Chinese Painting*, Lin Ci, China International Press, 8-2006

图片来源：林茨.《中国绘画艺术》. 五洲传播出版社，2006.8.

Ren Bonian was not a very traditional scholar by any standard, he was especially an excellent portrait and flower-and bird painter. His A Lady, as Lin Ci wrote in his book *The Art of Chinese Painting*, 'painted with light and graceful ink strokes style, went beyond most imperial court painter in terns of accuracy, meticulousness, and radiance and clarity'. His portrait paintings take an important position in the art world. Ren Bonian is also a versatile painter, he is good at flowers and birds painting, birds and beasts painting and pottery. His painting show not only the vivid national features but also the strong emotions, which is closely connecting the epoch.

从任何标准来说，任伯年不是一位很传统的学院派画家，而是一位杰出的人物画家和花鸟画家。林茨在他编著的《中国绘画艺术》中这样描述《仕女图》，"优雅的淡墨格调，在准确、细致、光彩和清新上超越了大多数宫廷画家"。他的人物画在美术史上占有重要的地位。任伯年还是一位多才多艺的画家，在花鸟、禽兽和陶塑上均有建树。其作品不但有鲜明的民族特征，还富有强烈的情感，与时代紧密相连。

Ren Bonian. *A Lady*. Clolored on paper. Scroll painting. 117.5cm×31.5cm

● 图2-31 任伯年《仕女图》117.5cm×31.5cm/纸本设色 立轴/南京博物馆藏

ZAO Wou-ki. *Abstract Painting*. 24.5cm×24.5cm

● 图2-32 赵无极《抽象画》24.5cm×24.5cm

图片来源：网络：http://image.baidu.com

ZAO Wou-ki made his reputation from the 1950s art world in Paris, who still enjoyed the great honor and respect of international arts community now.

The abstract language of ZAO Wou-ki's Abstract Painting, came from the feeling of nature. His work is full of abstract forms but full of vigor and vitality, which makes people imagine that they see a vast nature from his paintings. He built a bridge between East-West cultures by integrated oriental aesthetics minds into western expressions, and created new image and excellent style of art. He deserves to be one of the greatest contemporary artists.

赵无极于20世纪50年代在巴黎画坛崭露头角，至今享有国际艺术界的荣誉和尊敬。

赵无极把对自然的感受上升为抽象语言，他的作品是一个完全抽象的形式世界，但是却充满生机与活力，使人浮想联翩，从画中我们可以看到变化的广袤自然。赵无极在西方表现形式中融入了东方美学思想，造就出意象新颖、风格卓异的艺术，他在东西方文化间架起沟通的桥梁，不愧为当代最伟大的艺术家之一。

第 3 章　设计理念选译

3.1　可持续发展的关键问题[1]

Key issues of sustainable development

There is no doubt that sustainable building is now a very dominant theme covering every aspect of building industry. We even go so far as to say that everyone agrees that sustainable building is a good thing. There are many relevant labels which relate to sustainable building from Low energy, Zero energy, Energy efficient, Energy conscious and Environmentally friendly to Green and Ecological. In fact there are so many labels that even the professionals are confused. So what exactly is sustainable building? It is necessary to make clear its definition and implication before we work towards it.

毋庸置疑,目前可持续建筑是建筑领域的一个主要议题,它涵盖了建筑领域的所有方面,我们甚至可以说每个人都认同可持续建筑。对于可持续建筑,有许多相关的名称。从早期的"低能耗建筑"和"零能耗建筑"到"能效建筑"、"能源友好建筑"和"环境友好建筑",以及到最新的"绿色建筑"和"生态建筑",如此多的名称使公众甚至专业人员都混乱了。那么,究竟什么是可持续建筑?在我们朝着这个目标努力之前,必须弄清楚它的具体内涵。

In 1987, the World Commission on Environment and Development defined sustainable development as Development which meets the needs of the present without compromising the ability of future generations to meet their own needs.

A current Green or Sustainable building integrates energy issues health, and comfort concerns with some ecological considerations. Chinese Ministry of Construction defines a green building as: 'a building that provides a healthy, comfortable and safe space for people's living, working and recreation based on high resource (energy, land, water, materials etc.) efficiency and minimum limit environmental impacts in its life cycle (material production, planning, design, construction, operation, maintenance, demolition and recycling). A Green building is a current sustainable building.'

1987年,世界环境发展组织提出:"可持续发展是指既满足当代人的需要,又不以影响下一代人需要为代价。"

目前的"可持续建筑"("绿色建筑")综合考虑了能源、健康、舒适问题以及一些生态因素。中国建设部将"绿色建筑"定义为:绿色建筑是指为人们提供健康、舒适、安全的居住、工作和休闲的空间,同时在建筑整个生命周期中(物料生产、建筑规划、设计、施工、运营维护及拆除、回用过程)基于高效率地利用资源(能源、土地、水资源、材料)、最低限度地影响环境的建筑物。绿色建筑是当代的可持续建筑。

3.2　城市发展的选择[2]

The city of choice

As part of this pragmatic approach, it can be recognised that while compactness has inherent advantages, this alone does not necessarily ensure sustainability. And

---

[1] 资料来源:姚润明,昆·斯蒂摩司,李百战著. 可持续城市与建筑设计. 北京:中国建筑工业出版社,2006. P6, P160.

[2] 资料来源:姚润明,昆·斯蒂摩司,李百战著. 可持续城市与建筑设计. 北京:中国建筑工业出版社,2006, P15, P166,译文略有改动。

while much of suburbia exhibits unsustainable car dependency, this is not always the case, there being numerous examples of successful low density developments within walking distance of effective public transport. Both high and low density development can thus achieve sustainability, although not necessarily by the same means. Different people have different aspirations and thus a variety of sustainable environments need to be provided. In this context it is interesting to note that after many years of decline, the population of some major western cities-such as London-is once again increasing and a popular interest in central urban living appears to have been revived.

作为这种实用主义方法的一部分，虽然紧凑型城市有其固有的优点，但是只有这些是不能保证可持续发展策略的。而造成对小汽车依赖的不可持续发展的郊区扩张也并不是绝对的，也有许多在步行范围内有效连接公共交通工具的方式，来实现城市的低密度扩展的成功范例。高密度和低密度都可以实现可持续发展，虽然它们没有必要以同样的方式去实现。不同的人有不同的看法，所以需要提供不同的可持续发展环境。就此而言，有趣的发现是，许多西方城市，例如伦敦经过几十年的人口递减后，人口又在递增，又重现了喜好都市生活的迹象。

The provision of choice can be seen as a key factor. Being close to effective public transport does not always ensure its use, but in many areas it is not even an option. In other words, car dependency is the result of lack of choice. In order to provide this choice and reduce car dependency, it would therefore be logical to discourage development in areas that are inaccessible to public transport. Urban development would then tend to concentrate in corridors along major public transport routes, leaving areas between them relatively undeveloped; in other words, linear urban development. One key advantage of linear development over nucleated development is that everyone can simultaneously be close both to the transport routes and to the countryside, thereby combining accessibility with contact with nature.

提供选择机会是一个重要的因素。靠近有效的公共交通设施，并不能确保它使用，但在很多地区还没有公共交通设施这种选择。换句话说，没有公共交通设施的选择就造成了对小汽车的依赖。为了提供这种公共交通设施的选择，以减少对小汽车的依赖性，因此，对无公共交通设施的地区应限制其发展。城市的发展就会沿着公共交通主干线，长廊式的集中发展，它们之间的一些地区会相对不发达。换言之，这是一种线性的城市发展。线性发展与集中发展相比较，其主要优点是，所有的人可以同时集中，也可以同时走向郊区，交通与自然融合在一起。

In practice what has often occurred historically is a mixture of both nuclear and linear development. The inaccessible green space in between has now, thanks to the car, become accessible. As a result, the car has unhelpfully shifted the balance from linear to concentric development, encroaching on the countryside unless it has been protected. Nevertheless, the combination of concentrations of developments along linear routes with some level of development can create a variety of settlement patterns, providing choice within a common and potentially sustainable physical framework.

在实践中，历史上经常出现线性式和集中式的混合发展。原来达不到的绿地空间，由于汽车的使用，变得可以到达。结果，小汽车无助地将重心从线性发展转移到集中发展，这样乡村土地就会被蚕食，除非它们受到保护。不管怎么说，在线性发展的基础上，结合某种程度的集中发展，可以创造出各种不同模式的居住小区，为普遍的和潜在的可持续发展提供了多种实际框架。

The principle of concentrating development along public transport corridors is so appealing to common sense that it is often adopted in planning practice. The structure plans for Copenhagen, Paris and the East London Thames Gateway project can be cited as examples. Despite this, linear urban development has received little attention as a guiding principle. There is a need to correct this, particularly because compared with the concept of constraining nuclear cities within Green belt, linear development goes more with the grain of the market. If this satisfies Breheny's criteria above and, if systematically applied, it could significantly reduce car dependency and increase efficiency and take-up of public transport. It would also provide a clear and easily comprehensible rationale for protecting the countryside.

沿交通主干线集中发展的观点非常具有吸引力，近年来在大量实际情况中得到采用。例如哥本哈根、巴黎和东伦敦泰晤士通道的设计中采用的结构规划都可作为成功范例。尽管如此，线性城市发展作为指导原则却很少提到。这是需要得到纠正的，特别是与强制绿色带中城市集中发展的观念相比较，线性发展更能考虑到实际情况。如果这些能满足 Breheny 前面提到的要求，如果能系统地实施，它可以减少对小汽车的依赖，提高公共交通的效率和使用率，也可以对周边乡村土地提供明确的、综合的具有说服力的保护措施。

3.3　格罗皮乌斯和包豪斯[1]

Gropius and the Bauhaus

Among those architects who, like Kreis, passed through an expressionist phase, none has become better known than Walter Gropius (1883~1969). Like Behrens, with whom he worked from 1907, to 1910, he did not begin as an expressionist. Trained at the Technical High School at Berlin-Charlottenburg, he was the son of an architect, Walther Gropius, and great-nephew of a more famous architect, Martin Gropius, from whom he inherited a veneration for the Prussian classicism of Schinkel. His early industrial buildings, the Fagus shoe-last factory at Alfeld-an-der-Leine, near Hildesheim (1911~1912), and the model factory and office building at the Werkbund exhibition of 1914 at Cologne, were designed with his partner, the theosophist architect Adolf Meyer (1881~1929). They are carefully controlled essays or themes inspired by Behrens and Frank Lloyd Wright. Their flat roofs, glass curtain-walling and glazed corner staircases, both rectangular and semi-circular, were to be widely influential on the post-war international modern style as transparent images of movement.

Bauhaus

● 图 3-1　包豪斯校舍

（图片来源：网络 upload.wikimedia.org）

在像克赖斯(Kreis)那样经历过表现主义阶段的建筑师当中，没有谁变得比沃尔·格罗皮乌斯(Walter Gropius, 1883~1969年)更家喻户晓。1907~1910年，格罗皮乌斯与贝伦斯共事过，而且与贝伦斯一样，开始他并不是一名表现主义者。他在柏林夏洛腾堡的工学院学习过，是建筑师瓦尔特·格罗皮乌斯的儿子；是名望更大的建筑师马丁·格罗皮乌斯的侄孙。从他们那里，格罗皮乌斯继承了对辛克尔普鲁士古典主义的崇拜。他早期的工业建筑位于希尔德斯海姆附近 Alfeld-an-der-Leine 的法古斯(Fagus)鞋楦厂(1911~1912年)，以及1914年在科隆德意志制造联盟展览会展出的示范工厂和办公楼，都是与他的合作伙伴通灵建筑师阿道夫·梅耶(Adolf Meyer, 1881~1929年)合作设计的。它们的设计主题受到贝伦斯和弗兰克·劳埃德·赖特的启发，在设计中被小心地把握着。它们的平屋顶、玻璃幕墙和闪亮的角落楼梯，有的长方形，有的半圆形，成为新建筑运动的透明图像，广泛影响着战后的国际式现代风格。

---

[1] 资料来源：David Watkin. A History of Western Architecture. Thames and Hudson, 1986 P517-520.

In the midst of the turbulent political and intellectual life of Germany following the disastrous end of the First World War and the fall of the German empire in 1918, Gropius became inspired by the radical visionary Utopianism of Taut, he joined left-wing artistic groups such as the Arbeitsrat fuer kunst (working council for art), Novembergruppe, and die glaeserne Kette (the Glass Chain), a network for the exchange of letters organized by taut. The Arbeitsrat was interested in the recreation of the medieval building-lodges, and Gropius was soon busy designing Tautian Wohnberger (mountains for living). The climax came with Gropius's proclamation of 1919, in which he published his proposal to turn the academy of fine art and the school of arts and crafts at Weimar, of which he had been appointed director that year, into a Bauhaus (house of building). The Bauhaus manifesto was illustrated with an Expressionist woodcut by Lyonel Feininger of the Cathedral of the future, depicted as the cathedral of socialism. Gropius wrote of the new structures of the future... which will one day rise toward heaven from the hands of a million workers like the crystal symbol of a new faith. Structures of this kind, the modern equivalent to the medieval cathedral, were also envisaged by Taut in his *The City Cromn* as crystal temples dedicated to the socialist brotherhood of man. Taut is also partly responsible for the note of guild socialism in the Bauhaus manifesto, which saw the new house of building as a craft workshop like the old cathedral. Thus, though the manifesto included as one of the aims of the Bauhaus the 'corporate planning of comprehensive Utopian designs-communal and cultic buildings-with long-range goals', the emphasis for the first years of the school's existence was not on architectural education but on craftsmanship and painting. The first staff appointments were painters and sculptors, including Gerhard Marcks and Lyonel Feininger in 1919 and Johannes Itten, Kandinsky and Klee in 1922. It was not until 1927 that an architect, the Marxist Hannes Meyer, was appointed head of the newly established department of building.

随着1918年第一次世界大战灾难性的结局和德意志帝国的失败，德国的政治和精神生活处于动荡之中，格罗皮乌斯受到陶特激进的幻想乌托邦主义的鼓舞，加入了左翼艺术团体，如艺术劳动协会、十一月小组、玻璃链组织，这是陶特为交流文字创作而建立的一个网络组织。艺术劳动协会的兴趣在于重建中世纪的居住建筑，格罗皮乌斯不久就忙于设计陶特堡住宅。1919年格罗皮乌斯的宣言是他活动的顶峰，他建议将魏玛工艺学校和美术学院改建为包豪斯建筑学校，当年他被任命为校长。莱昂内尔·费宁格(Lyonel Feininger)的表现主义版画"未来大教堂"对包豪斯宣言作了图解阐明，包豪斯被描绘成社会主义大教堂。格罗皮乌斯如此描述这种未来的新结构：某一天，它会从百万工人的手中升向天堂，像水晶般象征着一个新的信仰。陶特在其《城市皇冠》中设想过这种现代版本的中世纪教堂结构，并将之作为水晶殿堂献给社会主义手足兄弟。陶特也是形成包豪斯宣言中行会社会主义特点的部分原因，将校舍看作旧教堂一样的手工工场。因此，虽然宣言中所包含的包豪斯目标之一是"从长期目标，共同规划全面乌托邦式的公共建筑和膜拜式建筑"，但为了维持生存，学校头几年的重点并不在建筑教育而在于手工艺和绘画。第一批聘任的员工是画家和雕塑家，包括1919年的格哈德·马克斯(Gerhard Marcks)和莱昂内尔·费宁格，1922年的约翰尼斯·伊滕(Johannes Itten)、康定斯基(Kandinsky)和克莱(Klee)。直至1927年才将一名建筑师、马克思主义者汉内斯·梅耶(Hannes Meyer)，任命为刚成立的建筑系主任。

The most influential figure in the Bauhaus teaching program up to 1922 was Itten, who was responsible for the compulsory *Vorkurs* (preliminary course). In accordance with the naive faith of the Bauhaus that modern man must destroy the past before building the perfect earthly society, Itten's *vorkurs* rejected all the traditional goals and techniques common to Western European Culture. Instead, he provided a series of exercises intended to promote the self-discovery of the student by removing his existing intellectual and emotional impediments.

直到1922年,在包豪斯教学计划中最具影响的是伊滕(Itten),他负责必修课程。根据包豪斯的朴素信念,现代人在建立完善的世俗社会之前,必须摧毁过去,伊滕的必修课摈弃了与西欧文化相同的所有传统目标和技术。相反,他提供一系列的练习,旨在通过消除学生们现有的智力和情感障碍,促进他们的自我发现能力。

The first opportunity for the realization of the Bauhaus ideal of uniting the arts and crafts under architecture came with the commission of a house for Adolf Sommerfeld, a sawmill owner and building contractor. The Sommerfeld House at Berlin-Dahlem was designed by Gropius and Meyer as an Expressionist variant on the theme of the peasant log-house with the angular and crystalline forms fashion-able in Expressionist circles. Some of its jazzy ornamental detail, especially the notched beam ends, is similar in mood to Wright's in the Imperial Hotel, Tokyo.

实现包豪斯的理想,将艺术和手工艺统一于建筑,第一次将之实现的机会降临了,学院接到为锯木场场主和建筑承包人阿道夫·佐默菲尔德(Adolf Sommerfeld)修建宅邸的委托。位于柏林达勒姆(Berlin-Dahlem)的佐默菲尔德住宅(1920~1921年)由格罗皮乌斯和梅耶设计,它是模仿农民的圆木房屋的表现主义的变体,在表现主义建筑圈中以时尚的尖角和水晶流线外形著称。它的一些奔放的装饰细部,特别是刻有凹口的横梁末端,与赖特设计的东京帝国饭店相似。

The arrival in Weimar in 1921 of the abstract painter Theo Van Doesburg (1883~1931) brought Gropius into contact with the Calvinistic simplicity and rectangularity of the Dutch movement *De stijl* (the style). This had been founded in Amsterdam in 1917 by the painter Piet Mondrian, the architect Jacobus Johannes, Pieter Oud, and Van Doesburg, who is supposed to have claimed that 'the square is to us as the cross was to the early Christians'. The Expressionist emphasis on the crafts had doubtless been encouraged by the loss of faith in technology which had been brought about in some quarters by the mechanized mass slaughter of the First World War. However, the return of confidence in technology, coupled with the geometrical aesthetic of *De Stijl*, enabled Gropius to move to a position in 1923 of abandoning Itten's Witches' kitchen and of appointing the anti-Expressionist Hungarian artist Laszlo Moholy-Nagy (1895~1946) to run the *Vorkurs*. In contrast to Itten, Moholy-Nagy chose to dress in a kind of boiler-suit so that he looked like an industrial worker. In support of this new image, Gropius delivered an important lecture in 1923 with the 'Art and Technology-a New Unity'. Architecturally this meant a return to the factory aesthetic which he had pioneered in his Fahus Factory of 1911.

抽象派画家特奥·范·杜斯堡(Theo Van Doesbury,1883~1931年)于1921年来到魏玛,这使得格罗皮乌斯同荷兰风格派运动的加尔文式的简洁和长方形有了接触。风格派团体1917年成立于阿姆斯特丹,由画家皮特·蒙德利安(Piet Mondrian)、建筑师雅各布斯·约翰内斯(Jacobus Johannes)、彼得·奥德(Piet Oud)和范·杜斯堡(Van Doesburg)所创立。范·杜斯堡曾声称"正方形对于我们就像十字架对于早期的基督徒一样"。表现主义者对手工艺的重视无疑受到技术信心丧失的促进,而这种信心的丧失则在很大程度上来自于第一次世界大战中机械化的大规模屠杀。但是对技术信心的恢复,加上几何美学风格,使得格罗皮乌斯于1923年转到放弃伊滕的"巫婆的厨房"的立场,并且还任命一位反表现主义的匈牙利艺术家拉斯络·莫霍伊-纳吉(Laszlo Moholy-Nagy,1895~1946年)来主持基础课。与伊滕相反,莫霍伊·纳吉特意穿上了一种连衫裤工作服,使他看上去就像一名工厂工人。为了支持这种新的形象,格罗皮乌斯于1923年发表了一篇重要演讲,题为《艺术和技术——一种新的统一体》。在建筑上,这意味着以1911年的法古斯工厂为先驱的工厂美学标准的回归。

This shift of stylistic emphasis was reflected in the physical removal of the Bauhaus to Dessau from Weimar. At Dessau in 1925—1926 Gropius and Meyer put up a new home for the Bauhaus of reinforced concrete and glass curtain-walling, with a plan and elevations assembled with a studied asymmetry which was doubtless inspired by Dutch abstract or Neo-plasticist painters such as Mondrian and Van Doesburg. Resembling a factory, through there was no real justification for its doing so, it exercised a chilling influence during the next half-century on the design of a range of building types such as schools, houses and flats, which were also made to look like factories. This radical minimalist architecture was the result of an attempt to reject everything Bourgeois or Impure including pitched roofs, columns, ornament, mouldings, symmetry, generosity and warmth. The result is leaking flat roofs in constant need of repair, absence of cornices, so that the white plastered walls are always streaked and stained; rusting metal windows; narrow corridors; low rooms; lack of privacy on the one hand, and of splendour on the other; gracelessly exposed mechanical services; and excessive use of glass, causing near-insoluble problems of heat loss and gain. The survival for fifty years, even in the homes of the rich, of such an aesthetic-for aesthetic it is, lacking in functional justification-is one of the longest-running showings in history of the tale of the emperor's new clothes.

这种风格重点的转移也反映在将包豪斯校址从魏玛迁移到德骚。格罗皮乌斯和梅耶于 1925～1926 年间在德骚建起了钢筋混凝土结构、玻璃幕墙的新包豪斯校舍。新校舍的平面图和立体图的组合都呈现出一种有意设计的不对称，这无疑是受到荷兰抽象派或新造型派画家，如蒙德利安、范·杜斯堡等人的影响。它像是一座工厂，虽然这样设计并没有真正的理由，但它在接下来的半个世纪中还是对一系列的建筑类型，例如学校、住宅和公寓等产生了很大的影响，这些建筑也被设计成工厂一样的形式。这种激进的极简派艺术家的建筑是为了摒弃"资产阶级"和"不纯"的一切因素，这包括斜屋顶、圆石柱、装饰、花边、对称、宽广和热情。结果是：不断需要维修的漏水的平屋顶由于没有飞檐，涂着白涂料的墙上总是留下污痕；生锈的金属窗；狭窄的走廊；低矮的房间；一方面缺少私密性，另一方面又不恢宏壮观；粗俗外露的机械设施；过度地使用玻璃材料，造成几乎无法解决的热量散失和吸收问题。这种建筑美学标准存续了 50 年，甚至存在于那些富贵之家的住宅设计中，由于它只是一种美学标准，缺乏正当功能，它只是"皇帝的新装"这个故事在历史上最长时间的一次展示。

3.4 ［日］黑川纪章：意义的生成❶
Toward the Evocation of Meaning

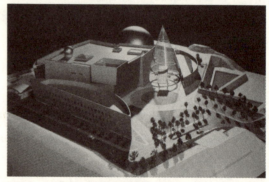

Ehime Museum of Science

● 图 3-2 爱媛县科学博物馆

（图片来源：ARCHITECTURAL DESIGN Vol64 No.1/2, January-February 1994，P29）

Hiroshima City Museum of Contemporary Art

● 图 3-3 广岛市当代艺术博物馆

（图片来源：JA No. 388 8/1989，P20）

---

❶ 资料来源：日本 SD 杂志，1989 年第 6 期，P12-22.

3.4.1 从认识论到本体论
From Epistemology to Ontology

From Greek and Roman times to the modern period, architecture has been created in a search of the answer to the question "What is architecture?" Not only architecture but the epistemological question of what being is, of what the existence of the world is, has been the central issue of Western metaphysics from the time of Aristotle, through Plato, Descartes, Hegel, and the thinkers of the modern age. The presupposition of this epistemological search has been that there is a single and true notion of existence that can be fully described based in terms of logos, or reason. The epistemology of Architecture has been that there is a sole, universal, true phenomenon "architecture," which can be comprehended logically by people of every nationality and culture. This epistemology is identical with the epistemology of the Modern Architecture of the modern age.

从希腊、罗马时期到现代，建筑创作一直在探求"建筑是什么？"这一问题。不仅建筑如此，关于存在是什么，世界的存在究竟是什么的认识论的问题，亦一直是从亚里士多德、柏拉图、笛卡儿、黑格尔，到现代思想家们的整个时代西方形而上学的中心问题。这种认识论研究的前提是认为存在一种完全可以根据理性的术语加以描述的简单而真实的存在物。建筑中的认识论认为存在一种完全可以根据理性的术语加以描述的简单而真实的存在物。监护者中的认识论认为存在一种唯一、普遍、正确的建筑现象，它能被不同民族，具有不同文化背景的人逻辑地理解。这种认识论和当代的现代建筑认识论完全相同。

The sole ideal image of Modern Architecture, the International Style, was conceived as a universal creation that transcended all differences of culture and applied the world over.

What system of values produced the icon of Modern Architecture, abstracted and universalized as the International Style? Clearly, the answer to this question is the values of industrial society, which are based on the pursuit of material comfort. We could just as correctly identify those values as the values of Western society. Here we have a phenomenon that I liken to the creation of Esperanto, which, though based on Western languages, was conceived as a universal language.

现代建筑的唯一理想形象——国际式，被作为能够超越文化差异的、适用于世界各地的通用创造物而为人接受。

是什么价值体系产生了像国际式那样的抽象且具有普遍性的现代建筑偶像呢？很显然，问题的答案是以追求物质享受为基础的工业社会价值观。我们可以恰当地把该价值观定义为西方社会的价值观。这里，存在一种我称之为世界语的创造的现象。世界语尽管建立在西方语言的基础之上，但是它被认为是一种全世界的语言。

But aren't we liable to enjoy a more richly creative world when Arthur Miller writes in English, Dostoevsky in Russian, and Yukio Mishima in Japanese? Then, through the media of translation and interpretation, we can be moved by our readings of the cultures of various nations and participate in mutual communication.

Yet the notion of the universal persists. The Cartesian linguist Noam Chomsky postulates a deep structure, a universal grammar, the existence beneath the surface of the various languages of the world. Some, encouraged by such theories, go so far as to suggest that within the heterogeneous cultures of the world there is a deep structure of sorts, a meta-level hierarchical structure common to all humanity, and from that a single and unified notion of existence, of the world, can be extracted.

但是阿瑟·米勒(Arthur Miller)用英语写作，多斯托夫斯基(Dostoevsky)用俄语写作，三岛之雄用(Yukio Mishima)日语写作，难道我们能不喜欢欣赏丰富多彩的世界吗？借助翻译和解释，我们就能欣赏各个民族的文化作品，并参与相互交往。

然而，普遍性的观点仍然存在。信仰笛卡儿哲学的语言学家诺姆·乔姆斯基（Noam Chomsky）假想，在世界各种语言的表层之下，存在一种深层结构，一种通用的语法。在这种理论的鼓舞下，有些人甚至猜测在世界各地的各种文化中，共有着一整套深层结构以及超层次的等级结构。从这种结构可以推出关于世界和存在的简单而统一的观念。

But this theory of existence by the metalinguists is an issue that is restricted to the context of Modernism, and it has been fiercely attacked by the forces of Postmodernism.

For example, J. M. Benoist, in *La revolution structural*, criticizes Chomsky's universal grammar: "We cannot but conclude that the concept of a universal grammar is nothing but the extreme generalization of a particular notion that is specific to Western culture. This concept can be easily challenged by the theory of the relativity of all cultures." The Cartesian definition of substance demands a reduction of reality to an unchanging unit, which is why Chomsky, with his theory of deep structure as universal grammar, calls himself a Cartesian linguist.

但是这种由形而上学语言学家提出的存在理论只是现代派的观点，已经受到后现代主义猛烈抨击。

例如，J·M·本罗依斯特（J. M. Benoist）在《结构改革》一书中曾批判乔姆斯基的通用语法论："对于通用语法论，我们只能做出这样的结论，它只不过是西方特定文化的个别观念的极端普遍化。所有文化的相对主义理论都很容易对这种观念提出异议。"笛卡儿哲学家给物质下定义时需要把现实事物归并成一个不变的单元，这就是为什么把自己的深层结构理论看作是通用语法的乔姆斯基自称为笛卡儿语言学家的原因。

The application of transcendent metastatements to the exterior of individual works, the metatheory of an image of existence that is shared the world over (architecture with a capital A) has been the target of criticism from the Postmodern movement. J. F. Lyotard, in his *La condition postmodern*, has remarked as follows: "As long as science refuses to limit itself to expressing a simple functional regularity and aims to pursue the truth, it must legitimatize its own rules of operation. In other words, a statement that legitimizes the status of science is required, and that statement goes by the name of philosophy. When that metastatement is based in a clear manner on some grand scheme—the dialectic of the mind; the study of the deciphering of meaning, the rational man, or the liberation of the proletariat and the creation of wealth—in order to legitimatize itself, we call the science based on those schemes, those stories, "modern". At the risk of greatly oversimplifying the matter, Postmodernism is, first and foremost, a suspicion of these metaschema." (English version based on the Japanese translation by Yasuo Kobayashi, *Posuto-modan no joken*. Edition de La Rose des Vents a Tokyo.)

把异乎寻常的变相描述强加于个别作品的外部，把现有形象的变相理论（A字大写的建筑）强加于世界各地，这已经成为后现代主义批判的目标。J·F·利奥塔得（J. F. Lyotard）在《后现代主义的条件》一书中表明："只要科学拒绝把自己限制在表达简单功能的规律性范围内。而致力于追求真理，它就必然需要使自己的操作规则正统化。也就是说需要一个使科学地位合法化的声明，而这一声明又藉哲学的名义发挥作用。一旦该声明为使自己正统化而建立在某些崇高的主题之上——如精神的辩证性、意义的解释学、有理性的人、劳动主体的解放以及财富的创造——我们就把建立在此类主题和描述基础上的科学称为'现代'。正是基于对极端简单化的事物的危机感，后现代派才成为这种超主题的最早怀疑者。"

If we can say that Modern Architecture created a universal icon based on Western culture, we can see that this was very much a metastatement (architecture with a capital A). In chapter 3 of their *Kafka: Pour une litterature mineure*, Gilles Deleuze and Felix Guattari describe minor literature as not only literature composed in minor languages but the literature created by minor peoples in a language that is widely used around the world. In the context of the overwhelming dominance of Western culture and the Modern Architecture of the West, the architecture created by architects who belong to the minority cultures of the world (in which Japan must be included), employing the languages of modern technology, materials, and structural models, can be described as minor architecture.

如果我们说现代建筑在西方文化的基础上创造了一个通用的偶像,那么就会看到这是一种极端的变相描述。在《卡夫卡:纯而小的文学》一书的第三章中,吉尔·德勒兹(Gilles Deleuze)和菲力克斯·瓜达里(Felix Guattari)把小文学描述成不仅是由小语种构成的文学,而且是由小民族用世界通用的语言创造的文学。在占绝对优势的西方文化和西方的建筑体系中,属于小文化的建筑师(日本必包括在内)创造的建筑,采用了现代技术语言、材料和结构形式。这种建筑可称之为小建筑。

Culture and tradition are not limited to the tangible. Styles of life, customs, aesthetic sensibilities, and ideas are intangible, invisible aspects of culture and traditions. Japanese culture, in particular, transmits its traditions with greater stress on its mental and spiritual aspects, its aesthetic sensibilities and ideas, than on physical objects and forms.

While Modern Architecture in Japan is extremely contemporary in its forms, it also manages to enclose the cultural tradition within itself. In the same fashion, the city of Tokyo seems at first to be a modern metropolis of no nationality; but actually Tokyo contains within itself extremely Japanese characteristics and elements.

文化和传统并不局限于有形的范围内,生活方式、习俗、审美意识和观念是文化传统的无形的、看不见的方面。尤其是日本文化,其传统的绵延中所带有的思想、精神及美学方面的影响要比客观物体和形式方面的建筑强得多。

日本的现代建筑在形式上能跟上时代,同时也试图体现其文化传统。同样,东京城乍看上去似乎是毫无民族性的现代大都会,然而事实上东京城包含着很强的日本特征与要素。

It was the cultural anthropologist Claude Levi-Strauss who first articulated the theory of the relativity of culture, stressing the importance of minor culture and the symbiosis of different cultures. By regarding Western culture from the perspective of "barbarian" cultures he relativized Western culture and offered his theory of structuralism.

I call the system of values based on the symbiosis of different cultures the philosophy of symbiosis (see my book of that title, *Kyosei no Shiso*, published by Tokuma Shuppan in 1987). What I conceive of as architecture based on the philosophy of symbiosis is created by being deeply rooted in one's own history and culture and at the same time making positive efforts to incorporate elements from heterogeneous cultures into the work.

文化人类学者列维·施特劳斯(Levi-Strauss)首先明确提出文化相关性理论,强调小文化和不同文化共生的重要性。在观察"野性的"文化基础上,列维·施特劳斯对西方文化重新思考,认识到西方文化的相对性,并提出了他的结构主义理论。

我把基于异质文化的共生之上的价值体系称为共生的思想(参见我的题为《共生的思想》一书)。我所构想的基于共生思想的建筑是深深植根于自身的历史和文化,同时试图揉合来自不同文化的要素为一体的建筑。

Since no single, universal ideal architectural icon exists, architects must first of all express their own culture. And at the same time, they must collide with other cultures, engage in dialogue with them, and, through symbiosis, create a new architecture. This new architecture must be both local and global. Whether it be a nation, an organization, or a culture, decline sets in once heterogeneous elements are rejected and a path of centripetal development is taken. It is always necessary to incorporate heterogeneous, outside elements and keep shifting the structure of the core.

由于不存在单一的、理想的建筑偶像,建筑师必须首先表达自己民族的文化，同时与其他文化比较，努力与之取得联系，通过共生手法创造全新的建筑。这种全新的建筑必须既具有地方性又具有全球性。无论是一个民族，一个组织还是一种文化，一旦拒绝异质的要素且向心发展，那么它就会开始衰落。揉入异质的、外来的要素，保持中心结构的转换状态是必要的。

The presupposition of epistemology is that it is possible to completely articulate a single, ideal concept of architecture through the medium of logos. This logos-centric view is both the tradition of Western metaphysics and one of the pillars of Modernism. The history of Modernism in the West is one of the control and suppression of nature by logos. The city is created by controlling nature, and with the unfolding of modernization, cities that had grown and evolved naturally had to be efficiently reconstituted following a geometric plan.

认识论的前提是认为借助理性可以全面表达一种唯一的、理想的建筑意象。这种理想中心主义既是西方形而上学的传统，又是现代主义的基石之一。西方的现代主义历史是靠理性控制和征服自然的历史，他们靠控制自然而创造了城市，并且随着现代主义运动的发展，那些已经形成、自然发展的城市不得不按照几何规则功利性地重建。

Architecture was also created as a means of controlling space and demonstrating the rational capacities of human beings. Reason was conceived as the means of controlling and subjugating nature, which was exterior to human existence. And the definition of modern man is one in which his interior nature-his wildness, his sensitivity-are controlled and subjugated by his reason.

The great treasure house of nature and those great sources of variety and richness, human wildness, human sensitivity, were rejected by reason, which sought a universal truth, a single, ideal conception of existence. At best, they were subject to control and subjugation.

建筑也是被作为控制空间和展示人类理性能力的手段而创造的。由于建筑被作为控制和征服自然的手段，故而建筑对人类存在来讲是外在的。现代人的解释是：它的内在本性——它的野性、它的敏感性——是由其理性控制并征服的。

大自然的伟大宝库以及作为多样性和丰富性、人类灵性的巨大源泉，都与追求一种普遍真理，追求唯一的，理想概念存在的理性排斥，至少也要面临控制和压抑。

This has become an important issue at certain times in the process of modernization because the social ideal of Modernism is industrial society, a mass society produced by industrialization. For industry, which aimed at mass production, it wouldn't do for the masses to possess wildness and sensitivity and exist in a rich variety, industrial society sought a humanity with a single, universal face.

由于现代主义的社会观念是工业化社会，一种由工业化带来的大批量生产社会，所以在现代主义运动发展过程中的特定时期，上述问题已经成为重要论题。因为工业的目标是大批量生产，它就不可能为大众有效地表达野性、敏感性以及存在的丰富性、多样性。工业化社会追求的是带着单一的、通用的面具的人类。

Universality, commonality, homogeneity, speed, and efficiency came to be more highly valued than individuality and the differences among cultures and histories. In an age of reason, science, technology, and economics take precedence over culture, art, literature, and thought.

To challenge Modernism and Modern Architecture is to challenge Western rationalism. Contemporary Postmodern architecture has not sufficiently achieved the essential conquest over Western dominance and rationalism. Levi-Strauss's structuralism, which relativized Western culture, is being further developed by poststructuralists. The deconstruction of hierarchical model of the tree and its replacement with the rhizome which has been suggested by Deleuze and Guattari and Derrida's deconstructionism are both designed to deconstruct metaphysics (philosophy based on logos) and Western dominance.

在工业化时代,普遍性、公共性、均质性、速度和效率的价值越来越高于文化和历史的个性与差异。在理性时代,科学、技术、经济的地位优先于文化、艺术、文学和思想性。

对现代主义和现代建筑的挑战就是对西方理性主义的挑战。当代的后现代建筑事实上尚未从本质上完全达到征服西方中心主义与理性主义的程度。与西方文化相关联的列维·施特劳斯的结构主义被后结构主义者作了进一步发展。树形秩序模型的被解构,并由德勒兹和瓜达里提出的根状基(rhizome)理论所取代,以及德里达的解构主义,这些都被用来消除形而上学(建立在理性主义基础上的哲学)和西方中心论。

The essential transformation that is taking place in the Post-modern age can be described as a change from epistemology to ontology. In his *Sein und Zeit*, Martin Heidegger writes, "The epistemological question has been whether we can properly describe being. In contrast, ontology asks what the nature of existence is." Existence here refers to things existing as matter: this desk, room, work of architecture, nature. Existence means the being of existing things.

后现代主义时代发生的本质变化可以描述成从认识论到本体论的转变。海德格尔在《存在和时间》一书中写道:"认识论的问题一直是我们是否能正确地描述存在的问题,与此相对应,本体论寻求的是存在的本质是什么的问题。"这里的存在是指作为物质存在的事物:桌子、房间、建筑作品、自然界。存在意味着现存事物的存在。

While the question "what is architecture?" is an epistemological one, seeking the right order of architectural being (its single, universal, ideal image), ontology asks the question "What is the meaning of architecture?" In this connection, ontology is linked to semantics.

Ontology and semantics do not seek a single, true order (notion of architecture) in the form of the universally applicable International Style, but pursue instead the evocation of meaning in architecture.

"建筑是什么?"这一问题是认识论的问题,即:寻求建筑存在的正确规律(唯一的、通用的、理想的形象)。而本体论的问题是"建筑的意义是什么?"在这一点上,本体论与语义学相关。

本体论和语义学并不寻求唯一的、正确的规则(建筑意象),如通用的国际式,而是追求建筑中意义的产生。

They do not conceive of the existence of a single, true, ideal image of architecture that exists as a truth transcending time, transcending history, transcending the differences among all the different cultures of our world. Rather, it is the differences that arise in the unfolding of time and history that produce meaning. From the epistemological standpoint of Modernism, which asked "what is architecture?" the truth was given a priori, and the problem was how to attain that truth through the power of reason.

他们并不设想存在一种唯一的、正确的、理想的建筑形象能像真理一样,超越时间、超越历史、超越世界所有不同文化,而是认为正是在时间与历史发展过程中展示的差异性产生了意义。对于寻求"建筑是什么"的现代主义认识论的观点来说,真理是先期给定的先验之物,问题是如何借助理性的力量获取之。

It is easy to see that Postmodern Architecture will evolve as the architecture of minor cultures, of heterogeneous cultures, the architecture of deconstruction that seeks to reintroduce noise, an architecture that sets itself off-center. In this sense, Postmodern Architecture is often a architecture of melange, with tendencies toward hybridization. But this hybridization is fundamentally different from the hybrid style that simply mixes together historical architectural styles of the past.

很容易看出,后现代建筑力图复活一种小而不纯的文化的建筑,再次引进杂质的解构的建筑,一种使自己脱离中心发展的建筑。在这个意义上,后现代建筑常常是混合式建筑,有混杂的趋向。但是这里的混杂同过去简单拼凑历史上的建筑样式的杂揉风格有本质不同。

Since there is no single ideal architecture, no correct

order, architecture does not express a single system of values. It is a conglomeration of many different systems of values, or an order that embraces many heterogeneous elements.

由于他们认为不存在唯一理想的建筑形式，不存在绝对正确的规则，因此建筑就不应表达单一的价值体系，而应是多种不同价值体系的一个集合体，或者是包含多种异质要素的一种秩序。

As the ontological question "what is the meaning of architecture?" suggests, architecture will be the stage for the evocation of a variety of meanings. The collision of different cultures, the introduction of different cultures as noise, creates a new culture. This is the discovery and evocation of meaning by means of our sensitivity to differences. In architecture, the conscious manipulation of different elements from different cultures is a means to evoke meaning through difference and disjunction, and in this it is fundamentally different from a simple hybridization.

本体论的问题"建筑的意义是什么？"使人们联想到，建筑将是种种意义产生的舞台，不同文化间的冲突，作为杂音的异质文化的引入，创造一种新文化。这就是经由我们对差异的敏感性而得到意义的发现和产生。

在建筑中，有意识地操作浮现于不同文化中的异质元素，是一种借助差异和分离而产生意义的方法，在这一点上，它与简单的混杂有本质不同。

3.4.2 旨意＝主题(Text)；意义的生成 Will＝Text; Toward the Evocation of Meaning

I have noted how Modern Architecture, as a Modern epistemology, is deeply rooted in Western dominance and logos. If we are to move on to Postmodern Architecture, which asks ontological and semantic questions in its attempt to create an evocation of meaning, how must we transform the design methods of Modern Architecture?

我已经指出，现代建筑作为一种现代认识论是如何深深地植根于西方中心主义与理性主义之中的。后现代建筑试图在创造意义中提出本体论和语义学问题，如若我们转向后现代建筑，我们应如何改变现代建筑的设计方法呢？

The basis for the design methods of Modern Architecture up to now has been the a priori assumption of an ideal image of architecture (an order) which is single and universal. This has been known as the International Style. It was believed necessary to articulate this ideal image(order) by means of reason. The design processes of analysis, structuring, and organization were stressed, always pursued according to principles of reason and logic. The final result of the design process was expressed as a synthesis with universal application.

Heterogeneous elements were excluded from this design process, and in each element the operations of introduction, connection, clarification, denotation, and coordination were given greatest importance. Reason and logos were always called upon to control and subjugate intuition.

到目前为止，现代建筑设计方法的基础一直是预先假定一种唯一的、普遍的、理想的建筑形象，这就是众所周知的国际式。人们过去一直相信借助推理明确表达这一理想形象是必要的。人们强调分析、结构、组织的设计过程，而且总是依照理性和逻辑原则进行探讨。设计的最后结果被表达成普遍适用的综合体。

这一设计过程把异质要素排除在外，对于每一元素，关于导入、连接、明确性、指示性和协调性的运作，被赋予了至高无上的重要性。理性总是被用来控制、抑制直觉。

Dualism and binomial opposition are inherent in Western metaphysics and logos; the dualisms of reason and sensitivity, body and spirit, necessity and freedom, and binomial opposition of science and art have dominated Western thought since Aristotle and on up through Descartes and modern metaphysics. In the history of architecture as well, the binomial opposition of reason and sensitivity has always manifested itself in a pendulum phenomenon. The industrial revolution was followed by William Morris's Arts and Crafts Movement, which was followed by Art Nouveau and the Jugendstil movements. They in turn were followed by the rationalism of Peter Behrens and Tony Garnier. After the Expressionist and Futurist movements, Modern Architecture emerged, waving its banner of functionalism. This dualistic process of action and reaction has had an unfortunate effect on Modernism and Modern Architecture.

在西方形而上学和理性中，二元论和二元对立是固有的。从亚里士多德开始，到笛卡儿和现代形而上学体系，理性与知觉、物质与精神、必然与自由的二元论和科学与艺术的二元对立一直统治着西方思想。建筑的历史同样，理性与直觉的二元对立显示出建筑总是处于一种摇摆不定的境地。工业革命之后是威廉姆斯·莫里斯的工艺美术运动，随后是新艺术运动和青年风格派，接着是彼得·贝伦斯和托尼·戛尼耶的理性主义。在表现主义和未来主义运动之后，出现了挥舞着功能主义旗帜的现代建筑。这一活动及其对立面的二元过程对现代主义和现代建筑曾产生了不良的影响。

In Modern Architecture, dominated by reason, the wild revolts, the revolts of sensitivity of such architects as Alvar Aalto, Frank Lloyd Wright, Hans Scharoun, Paolo Soleri, and Bruce Goff have always been regarded as exceptions; they have been declared geniuses, and have thus been excluded from the mainstream of Modern Architecture. But their strategies of a revolt of wildness and sensitivity against the rule of reason are also a product of the age of Modernism. The topic that's on people's lips all over the world today with the advent of the Postmodern age, the new strength of the advocates of sensitivity, of wildness, and the paeans to Gaudi, are not likely to play any role in the defeat of modernism.

在现代建筑中，理性主义占统治地位，像阿尔瓦·阿尔托、弗兰克·劳埃德·赖特、汉斯·夏隆、保罗·索莱里和布鲁斯·高夫等建筑大师的野性反叛和感性反叛总是被当作现代建筑的特例。他们被称为天才人物，因此他们被排除在现代建筑的主流之外。但是他们对理性规则的野性反叛和感性反叛战略亦是现代主义时代的产物。随着后现代时代的到来，今天世界各地人们口头上的话题显示出了对感性和野性的提倡和对高迪的赞美的新趋势，但是这些在对现代主义的攻击中似乎没有起到任何作用。

If we have no need for one, true image of architecture(order) which has been provided to us a priori, where should we direct our search for architecture? When there is a priori image of the world, a universal order, it is sufficient for architects to be led by it, to try to approach as near to it as possible. How to ride the flow of that order is what is most important. The architect's talent is the talent of successfully riding that current and expressing his personality in the appropriate manner within the confines of that rational order.

如果我们不需要事先提供一个唯一的且正确的建筑形象，那么我们研究建筑的方向在哪儿呢？如果存在一个关于世界的既定的形象，一种普遍的秩序，那么建筑师就可受其引导，尽可能地接近它，这样做就足够了，如何驾驭那种规则的变化是最重要的。建筑师的才能表现为成功地驾驭那种潮流，并能在理性规则的范围内以适当的方式表达自己的个性。

We are living in an age of the transformation or conversion of the paradigm of Modernism. Postmodern Architecture must begin from the expression of the will(=philosophy)toward the changes of the new age. The will, the philosophy that tells us what we should transform and how we should transform it will become the driving force that motivates the creativity of architects the world over. The ontology suggested by the question "What is the meaning of architecture?" of the Postmodern age will be established through the expressions of the wills of this wide variety of people.

然而，我们正生活在一个改变现代主义海市蜃楼的时代。后现代建筑以表达意愿（思想）为开端，目标是新时代的变革。意愿会告诉我们应该改变什么事物以及如何改变,并且这些意愿将成为激发世界各地的建筑师创造性的推动力。由后现代时期的问题"建筑的意义是什么?"而引出的本体论将会通过表达各式各样人的意愿而建立起来。

The expression of my own will is, as I said earlier, "the transformation of Western domination and logos." And my own will is linked with the expressions of the will that are taking the form of battle lines unfolding on a variety of fronts-in literature, philosophy, art, and many other areas.

I am deepening my personal expression of the will to transform the dominance of the West and of logos in the form of my own philosophy of symbiosis. The philosophy of symbiosis is the present expression of my will, which I have previously articulated as Metabolism and metamorphosis, and it enables me to search in my architecture for an evocation of meaning. The philosophy of symbiosis is not another metaphysic; I believe it is more accurate to call it the text of a movement.

如前所述,我自己的意愿就是改变西方中心主义和理性主义。在文学、哲学、艺术及其他许多领域中所展示的意愿的表达都与我的意愿的表达有关。

我以我的共生思想来改变西方中心主义和理性主义,并深化个人意愿的表达。即共生的思想是我目前的意愿的表达方式,而过去是新陈代谢和变形理论。它使我在建筑设计中能探讨意义的产生过程。共生的思想并不是另一种形而上学,我相信把它称之为主题运动更准确些。

The text(philosophy) of the expression of the architect's will is, first and foremost, rooted in that person's history, his culture. The architects of the Modern age sought an internationalism, a universalism that transcended their own personalities and regional characteristics. Postmodern architects, on the other hand, must set out from the expression of their own will, deriving from their own history and culture, A keen sensitivity to differences in history, in time, in culture, will enable them to evoke the meaning of architecture.

建筑师意愿表达的主题首先来源于个人的历史和文化。现代主义建筑师寻求超越他们自己个性和地方特征的国际主义,而后现代建筑师必须以表达自己的历史与文化的愿望为出发点。对历史、时代和文化中的差异保持敏感性,将使他们得以表现建筑的意义。

Whereas the ultimate goal of Modern Architecture was to achieve synthesis, the ultimate goal of goal of Postmodern Architecture will manifest itself as evocation. As far as the methodology of design is concerned, symbolization will replace analysis, deconstruction replace structuring, relation replace organization, quotation replace introduction, intermediation replace synthesis, transformation replace adaptation, sophistication replace clarification, and connotation replace denotation. These design methods will have a conclusive and important role in the evocation of meaning.

现代建筑的最终目标是达到综合,相反,后现代建筑的最终目标将是自我表现。至于设计方法,即符号将代替分析,解构将代替结构,关联将代替组织,引用将代替介绍,调解将代替综合,变革将代替适应,复杂将代替明确,内涵将代替指称。这些设计方法将在意义的产生过程中起决定性的作用。

We cannot necessarily declare that these design methods will be carried out more under the direction of intuition than on reason and logos. Rather, we can expect the simultaneous operation of reason and intuition. The processes of symbolization, deconstruction, relation, quotation, intermediation, transformation, sophistication, and connotation, however, depend greatly on a keen sensitivity to differences among times, among cultures, and among elements.

In order words, it is a sharp sensitivity which detects differences, which creates differences. That sharp sensibility is attained through liberating leaps in the unrelenting contest of reason and intuition, thought and action.

这里我们不必断言，直觉之下的设计方法会比理性与理性之上的设计方法有效得多，我们宁可希望理性和直觉同时起作用。然而，象征、解构、关联、引用、调解、变革、复杂和内涵，在很大程度上取决于对时代的、文化的和特征的差异保持敏感性。

换句话说，正是洞察到差异的敏感性创造了差别。人们借助在理性与直觉、思想与行为的不断冲突过程中的思想自由跳跃来获得敏感性。

I have already published a book on my will as text, *the philosophy of symbiosis*, so I will omit extended discussion of its contents here, but in a word it is a text(a philosophy) for the deconstruction of metaphysics (logos) and the domination of the West. The basic components of the philosophy of symbiosis are the symbiosis of: heterogeneous cultures, human beings and technology, the interior and the exterior, the part and the whole, history and the future, reason and intuition, religion and science, human beings (their architecture) and nature. It is the expression of my will as it challenges Modernism and Modern Architecture and aims to transform their paradigm.

关于我的意愿，我已出版一本书《共生的思想》，所以在这里，我不再展开来讨论它的内容。简而言之，它的主题是解构西方中心主义和形而上学。共生思想的基本组成部分是：异质文化的共生、人类与技术的共生、内与外的共生、部分与整体的共生、历史与未来的共生、理性与直觉的共生、宗教与科学的共生、人类及其建筑与自然环境的共生。向现代主义和现代建筑挑战并致力于推倒它们的幻象，这就是我的意愿。

This philosophy of symbiosis takes as its pretext the Indian Buddhist philosophy of Consciousness Only and Japanese Mahayana Buddhism. In other words, this expression of my will is rooted in Japanese culture and is also my own personal identity. I do not regard tradition as being restricted to the transmission of tangible forms; tradition includes such intangibles as styles of life, customs, thoughts, aesthetic sensibilities, and sensitivities.

In the transmission of Japanese culture in particular these intangibles are stressed. It is possible for us to transmit Japanese culture by injecting it into the contemporary architectural expression employing the latest high-technology materials. It is also possible to represent forms of an extremely traditional nature within the Japanese aesthetic sensibility, among them the absence of a center, open-endedness, asymmetry, the expression of detail, and disjunction (deconstruction).

这种共生思想以印度佛教的唯意识论和日本佛教为基础。也就是说，我的意愿表达根植于日本文化，又根植于我的个性特征。我并不认为传统只能表达成明确的形式，传统还包括一些不确定的东西，如生活方式、习惯、思想、审美意识和敏感性。

在表达日本文化时，尤其需要强调这些不确定的东西。我们有可能把日本文化的表达融进采用最先进高科技材料的当代建筑的表达方式之中。在日本的审美意识范围内表达古老的传统特性也是有可能的，如：中心空置、开放体系、非对称性、细部表达和分离（解构）。

These elements of the Japanese aesthetic manifest themselves as a sense of balance (an aesthetic), not in the form of a system but when they are disposed as separate elements. We might also say that their special character is that they possess form as atmosphere, mood, feeling. The special character of Japanese culture can be described with the philosophy of symbiosis, which is both a text for the special nature of Japanese culture and a text for the transformation of the modern paradigm.

在日本，这些美学要素不管是以体系的形式或是以分离放置的形式总表现为一种均衡感（审美意识）。我们也可以说日本文化的特点在于它把形式配制成一种氛围，一种语气或一种感觉。日本文化的独特性可以描述为具有共生的思想，共生的思想既是日本文化独特性的来源，又是对现代主义幻象加以改变的主题。

Mood, feeling, atmosphere can be described as a symbolic order without an established structure. It is through a variety of dynamic, intersecting relationships and juxtapositions-the relationship between one sign and other symbolic elements with which it stands the way the content of the sign changes when it is quoted; the existence of a medium, an intermediating space introduced between different elements; the connotations of the sign; the relations of parts to the whole-that mood, feeling, and atmosphere are created.

The meaning produced by the individual elements that are placed here and there, and the meaning produced by their relationships and disjunctions, evoke in architecture a multivalent, ambiguous meaning. When this meaning creates a feeling, an atmosphere, architecture contains the possibility of approaching poetic creation.

语气、感觉、氛围可以描述成一种不必建立结构的符号体系。通过要素间各种动态的交叉与并置——一种符号及与其共生的象征元素间的相互关系、所引用的符号的变化方式、异质元素插入的中介空间的存在、符号的内涵、部分与整体关系等——语气、感觉、氛围得以产生。

在建筑中，由放置在不同位置的单体元素产生的意义，以及由它们的相互关联和分离产生的意义会唤起一种多义的、含糊的意味。当这种意味产生一种感觉、一种气氛时，建筑就具有了一种接近诗意创造的可能性。

To regard architecture no more than actual space, a stacking of bricks on top of each other, is to accept the models of pyramid and the tree. There is an alternative: to consider all the elements of architecture as words (signs), between which new meanings, atmospheres can be created. Since all elements of the work of architecture-the pillars, ceilings, walls, stairways, windows, skylights, rooms enclosed by walls, entranceways, open spaces, furniture, lighting, door handles, the treatment of the wall-exist as quotations, as transformations, as sophistications, as connotations, as symbolizations, as intermediations, the solid, substantial architecture, the stack of bricks is already deconstructed.

Another way of describing the discovery of meaning in the intermediary space (vacant space) between elements is to say that we are evoking meaning by setting elements in relation to each other. Pillars and walls, which have only had meaning as structural elements in architecture up to now, can be deconstructed from the hierarchy of structure and given independent symbolic existence.

如果把建筑看作不过是实用的空间，一堆一块摞一块的砖头，也就等于接受了四面体和树形模式的概念。这里我们面临着选择，其一，把所有的建筑元素都看作是相互间能够产生新的意义和气氛的语汇或符号。由于所有建筑元素——柱、天花、墙壁、楼梯、窗、天窗、围合的房间、入口、开敞区域、家具、照明设施、门把手、装修——都是作为引语、变形、修辞、含蓄、象征、媒介而存在，因此这种固体的、物质的建筑、砖的砌体就被解体了。其二，在元素的中间空间（空隙中）产生意义的另一方法是，借助元素间的相互关系的配置以唤起意义。以往，柱和墙在建筑中只具有结构元素的意义，但它们还能够从秩序结构体系中解构出来，并可作为独立的符号存在。

The four bamboo poles that are set up at the Shinto-style ground-breaking ceremony which is observed before commencing construction have a fictional connotation. The element of their physical nature as bamboo poles disappears and they connote the symbolic atmosphere of the place for the the descent of the gods. In his work *Le systeme des objects* (Editions Gallimard, 1968) the French sociologist Baudrillard wrote of space enclosed by the elements called things: "Space, too has a fictional connotation. All forms are relativized as they pass through space. A spacious room has a natural effect. It breathes. When there is a lack of space, the atmosphere is destroyed because our breath is robbed by the things crowded into it. Perhaps we should read a reflection of the moral principles of separation and division in this distribution of space. If that is so, it is a reversal of the traditional connotation of space as a full, existing substance." The space he refers to above is the vacant space between objects, what is referred to in Japanese as ma, or "in-between space." It is natural in the sense that it is what is outside of existents, wild and breathing. Unlike a pile a bricks, it does not have the connotation of solidity, of actuality, but of emptiness, of nothingness.

日本在施工前的地震祭仪式上，一般布置四根竹竿，这里的竹竿有一种虚构的指示作用，竹竿的物理性能已不复存在，它们标示着一种为神的降临而设置的象征性气氛的场所。法国社会学家鲍德里拉（Baudrillard）在他的著作《物体的系统》（伽里玛出版社，1968 年）中曾谈到由被称为事物的元素构成的空间："空间也有一种虚拟的指示作用，空间中的所有形式都是相对的，宽敞的房间有自然的效果，气韵通畅。当空间狭小时，这种氛围就被破坏，因为其中堆积的物品使我们感到喘不过气来。也许，在空间的这种配置中我们应了解间隔和分离的心理反应，如果是这样的话，它就不同于以往作为完整的存在客体的空间指示作用了。"上面所涉及的空间是物体间的空隙，在日本成为"间"或中介空间。由于它在存在物的外部，原始而有活力，所以它在感觉上是自然的，与一堆砖不同，它不再有实体的、实用的指示作用，只有空旷、虚无。

Atmosphere is evoked along the threads of relation that link thing to thing. Baudrillard's theory of architecture brilliantly reverses the epistemology of Modern Architecture, transforming it into to an ontology.

If the pyramid and the tree are models of Modernist hierarchy, the models of Post-modern order are the semi-lattice structure, the rhizome. The model of the rhizome was conceived by Deleuze and Guattari, and it is developed in their book *Anti-Oedipus*. The rhizome represents the principle of union and deference, a multiplicity in which relations are possible at any number of points. It is completely different from the tree, which is a model of a unilateral, frozen hierarchy.

将事物连接在一起的相关性唤起气氛，鲍德里拉的建筑理论有力地推翻了现代建筑的认识论，并把它转换为本体论。

如果四面体结构和树形模式是现代主义秩序概念的原型，那么后现代主义的模型就是半网格系统和根状基体系。德留兹和瓜塔里设计了根状基模型，并在其著作《反对奥狄浦斯》中做了进一步的发展。根状基理论表述了统一与差异的原理，以及在任何数量的点之间都有可能建立多样性的原理，它完全不同于树形结构。树形结构是一种片面的、呆板的秩序概念。

The concept of the semi-lattice resembles that of the rhizome's multiplicity. It, too, is an open-ended order in which different points are continually evoking meaning in their relations. Julia Kristeva descries the meaning of this type of ontological relationship as a polylogue. The polylogue is the condition in which "many different logics, many different selves, exist in different places and at different times." It is "an active, parallel order of things that arise in the process of the evocation of meaning."

In any case, the evocation of meaning is not realized through some established hierarchy, it is an active state evoked in the process of relation.

半网格体系的概念类似于根状基的多样性概念，它也是一种开放体系，在这种体系中，不同点之间的相互关系不断地产生意义，朱丽亚·克里斯特娃（Julia Kristeva）把这种源自本体论的意义描述成多重对话（polylogue）。多重对话是指不同逻辑观念和不同的本性存在于不同时代和不同地点的状态，它是在意义产生过程中出现的灵活的、平衡的状态。

总之，意义的产生并不是通过一些既定的制度而实现的，它是在建立联系的过程中产生的一种积极的情形。

3.4.3 信息社会的建筑
Architecture for Information Society

While Modern Architecture has been the architecture of industrial society, Post-modern architecture will be the architecture of information society. Industrialized society promised the masses a life based on material wealth. The mass production of goods in factories was based on the assumption that Western cultural values and ways of life transcended all cultural differences and were universally applicable the world over. The universal, ideal image of architecture in the shape of the International Style also assumed the development and expansion of industrial society, and logos and Western dominance have been supported by industrial society as well.

如果说现代建筑是工业社会的建筑,那么后现代建筑将是信息化社会的建筑。在工业化社会中,人们有希望得到建立在物质财富基础上的生活。当时人们假定西方文化价值和生活方式超越了所有文化的差异,并且在世界各地普遍适用,工厂里商品的批量生产即建立在这种假设之上。以国际式为代表的通用的、理想的建筑形象同样假定工业社会将继续发展扩大,并假定理性主义和西方中心主义亦会得到工业社会的支持。

The collapse of Modernism, the repudiation of Modern Architecture is actually taking place because of the transformation of the paradigm of industrial society. In the most advanced nations, the shift from industrial production to the production of information is occurring with great speed. And, while industrialization has followed the stages of evolution described by the American economist Walt William Rostow, handed down from developed to developing nations, information society transcends economic and technological evolutionary stages and the walls of ideology, offering the possibility for the entire world to move forward at the same time.

随着工业社会范例的改变,实际上,现代主义正在崩溃,现代建筑正在被人们否定。在最先进的国家中,从工业产品到信息产品的转换正高速进行。虽然美国经济学家沃尔特·威廉姆·罗斯托(Walt William Rostow)把工业化之后的阶段描述成从发达民族到发展中民族的传递的演变阶段,但是,信息社会超越了经济、技术的演进阶段和意识形态的隔阂,为整个世界提供了同时前进的可能性。

Concretely speaking, the information industries are broadcasting, publishing, finance, research, education, tourism, design, fashion, trade, transportation, and the food, leisure, and service sectors. What all of these information industries have in common is that they do not depend mainly on the production or the assembly of things instead, their products are information, information-like added value, and culture itself.

具体地讲,信息社会有广播、出版物、金融、研究、教育、旅游、设计、时装、贸易、运输、饮食、娱乐和服务部分,所有这些信息化工业的共同之处是:他们并不主要依靠物的生产或装配,相反,它们的产品就是信息,类似信息的附加价值以及文化本身。

In the fashion industry, the added value of design is worth more than ten times the cost of the materials themselves. In restaurants, the skill of the chef, the quality of the service, and the décor are worth ten times the cost of the ingredients that make up the food served. Even in industrial products, there is a shift from the mass production of modern industrial society to limited production of a greater variety of goods in an effort to produce added value through variety, and the added value of design, too, is stressed far more than it has been in the past.

在时装工业中,涉及的附加价值多于原材料自身价值的10倍以上。在餐馆,厨师的技艺、服务的质量和室内的装修,其价值是饭菜成本的10倍。即使是工业产品,也比过去更强调设计的附加价值,开始从现代工业社会的批量生产转向多种产品的有限量生产,以借助多样化来产生附加价值。

While industrial society aimed for universality and homogeneity, information society will aim for multiplicity. Universal, homogenized information is of reduced value. In order to establish their own identities, people try to distinguish themselves from others. In this manner, things, people, and society will grow infinitely various. Nor is architecture an exception. The differentiation of architecture will be achieved in the evocation of new meanings, and the evocation of new meanings will bring differences and variety into architecture.

如果说工业化社会追求普遍性和一致性,那么信息社会便是追求多样性。统一的、类似的信息具有较小的价值,为了确立自己的个性,人们试图把自己与别人区别开来。以这种方式发展下去,事物、人类和社会将变得丰富多彩。建筑也不例外,建筑的区别将在新意义的产生过程中完成,同时,新意义的产生给建筑带来差异和变化。

It is mistaken to regard the state of the world of architecture in the Post-modern period as a chaotic transitional period. The appearance of a highly differentiated architecture, the eruption of the evocation of new meanings is the manifestation of the architecture of the age of information society. Differences are created by giving consideration to relations, or by Heidegger's "care" (Sorge). The evocation of meaning through difference will require a keen sensitivity; without that, it will be impossible.

把后现代时期的世界建筑界称为混乱的过渡时期是错误的。高度差异化建筑的问世、新意义大量产生的浪潮是信息社会的建筑宣言。差异的产生取决于所给定的关系的结果,或者是海德格尔所说的"烦"(sorge)。❶ 通过差异产生意义需要设计者有高度的敏感性,离开这一点将不可能产生意义。

Information society will create relationships in real time around the world through travel and communication. Different languages, different ways of life, and different cultures come directly into our homes through the communications industry and television. This allows for the creation of multivalent meaning that was unthinkable in the age of Western dominance. The changes of industrial society, the transformation of its paradigm to one of an information society is playing a large role in shifting the world from the dominance of the West and logos.

在信息化社会中,人们借助交通和通讯,在一定时间内将建立起遍及全球的关系网络。在通讯系统和电视的帮助下,不同语言、不同生活方式、不同文化直接进入各个家庭,这就有可能产生西方中心主义时期不可想象的多重意义。在将世界从西方中心主义和理性主义之中解脱出来的过程中,工业社会的演变以及将其幻象向信息社会的转变将是该过程中的重要内容。

Roland Barthes, in his *Mythologies*(Les Editions de Seuil), calls this the "age of the power of meaning." Since the age of information society is an age in which meaning will be evoked through differences, it will be an age in which we see a shift from the "syndigmatic" linear, explicit thought patterns of Modernism and denotation to "paradigmatic," nonlinear, latent thought patterns and connotation.

Barthes referred to transformations of meaning or the expansion of meaning achieved through connotation as the mythological function of connotation. Theodor Adorno, the German philosopher, also speaks of the importance of the mythological function (mimensis) in contemporary society. In his *Asthetische Theorie* (Suhrkamp Verlag Frankfurt am Main, 1970) he describes mimensis as the "reason of harmony." He predicts that the unfortunate dualism and binomial opposition of reason and intuition that has been produced in Western metaphysics and has persisted to the age of Modernism, will be harmoniously resolved through mimensis.

罗兰·巴塞斯(Roland Barthes)在其《神话集》中,称现在是"意义的力量的时代",由于信息社会是通过差异产生意义的时代,因此在这一时代中,我们将看到从现代主义的线性的联想、明晰的思想模式,向"虚构的"、非线性的、潜在的思想模式的转变,以及从外延向内涵的转变。

巴赛斯把借助内涵而获得的意义变化或意义扩展看作是内涵的虚构功能。德国哲学家泰奥多·阿多诺(Theodor Adorno)也谈到在当今社会中虚构功能的重要性,他在《美学理论》一书中把虚构功能描述成"和谐的推理"。他预言,在一直延续到现代主义时代的西方形而上

---

❶ Sorge 既有忧虑担心的含义又有操持置办的含义。并非两种分立的含义,而是一串含义的两端。西方传统在规定人的时候,过分突出了理性和认识,而海德格尔则强调关切、关心,不关心,就谈不上认识,谈不上认识得正确不正确。

学体系中所产生的不适当的推理和直觉的二元论和二元对立,将通过虚构作用加以协调解决。

Modernism and modern rationalism were given their basic nature through the objective rationalism of Galileo, Newton, and Descartes. The principle of identity, in which there is an objective, universally applicable view of the world that is the same for all people, is epitomized by the drafting technique of perspective, used in architecture and the visual arts. Perspective, which depicts the entire world from a single, visible point, is like the head of Medusa, which turns all who look on it to stone. In perspective, not only is the viewer himself eliminated from the picture, but all that is beyond his line of vision is rejected.

现代主义和现代理性主义经由伽利略、牛顿和笛卡儿的客观理性主义而被赋予了基本性质。同一性原理认为存在一种对所有人都适用的、具有客观的、普遍有效的世界观,这种原理通常体现于建筑和视觉艺术中的透视绘画技巧中。从一个视点描述这个世界的透视图,就像希腊神话中蛇发女怪的头一样,使所有看到她的人都变成了石头。在透视图中,不仅观看者从画面上消失,而且所有在视线以外的事物也都被抛弃了。

We must abandon single-point perspective and move the point of vision so that it reveals the relationships among all things. A point of view in which the world is seen from the point of things, or people are seen from the point of things is probably also necessary. The point of view of things is a point of view of the infinitely varied whole. Modern man, who has depended too much on his eyes to view the world, cannot understand why a person from a "primitive" tribe doesn't wear clothes. The "primitive" man answers: "My entire body is my face." This episode reveals how greatly modern man's view of the world is colored by his own doxa, by opinion.

我们必须放弃一点透视法,为了展现所有事物间的关系我们必须移动视点。我们也许需要从事物的视点看世界或从事物的视点看人。事物的视点是无限变化的整体。现代人过于依靠其眼睛去观察世界,就不能理解为什么"原始"部落的人不穿衣服,"原始"人的回答是:"我的整个身体都是面孔"。这一插曲告诉我们,现代人的观念被他自己的臆测和观念重重地蒙上了一层颜色。

Recently, in quantum physics the theory of measurement has revealed that even the one true measurement made through scientific process is actually nothing more than one state which has been accidentally selected, and that selection itself cause the instantaneous collapse of the quantum wave function, rendering the state it perceptible -that is, measurable-to us. In fact, all possible states exist at the same time, overlapping each other. This is called the Copenhagen interpretation.

最近,量子力学中的观测理论已经表明,即使是科学程序做出的唯一正确的观测,实际上仍不过是一次被偶然选出的情形。这种选择本身也会引起量子波动函数的瞬间变化,而我们所能观测到的情形,也就是变化后的情形。事实上,所有可能的状态同时存在,相互重叠,这就是哥本哈根学说。

The image of architecture revealed through reason alone, the whole established solely from the point of view of the visible, the single, correct measurement (being) made by science-is actually no more than a partial glimpse of a rhizome-like multiplicity.

Without a doubt, the architecture of the information society will shift from a paradigm of symmetry to one of asymmetry, from being self-enclosed to being open-ended, from the whole to the part, from structuring to deconstruction, from centrality to lack of a center. It will aim for the freedom and uniqueness of all human beings, for the symbiosis of different cultures, and for a spiritually rich pluralistic society.

建筑形象只通过推理显示,一切都只能从可见的视点建立,由科学来做的唯一正确的观测,实际上只不过是根状基的一部分,一样具有多重性。

无疑,信息社会的建筑将从对称原则转向非对称,从自我封闭转向开放,从整体到局部,从结构到解构,从向心性到无中心。多样化社会的目标将是体现人类的自由和个性,是不同文化的共生,是精神上丰富多样的社会。

3.5 [日] 伊东丰雄: 现代之外的主体意象: 是否存在无"临界"❶的居住建筑❷

A Body Image Beyond the Modern: Is There Residential Architecture Without Criticality

3.5.1 当代社会的分歧
Fissures with Contemporary Society

The first house I designed was completed 28 years ago. This was also the first time I used the medium of architecture to send out a message to the world. There is no doubt that the position of architecture in the city is fast losing its social meaning. But if, as a lone frail individual, one insists on lingering over the work of design after the unexpressible and futile collapse of logic in the world of architecture, the only way is to expose the absurdity of one's surroundings such as they are… For me, designing a home is a labor of tracing the desperately profound rift between myself as the designer and the home's future occupant. Perhaps one should use the term "bridge" rather than "trace" when speaking of this gap, but the fact is that we lack the common terms necessary to bridge it. This labor, then, can only begin in contradiction: by building insurmountable walls with an awareness of that unbridgeable gap. (from "The Act of Design is the Tracing of One's Thought Processes as they Become Distorted" Shinkenchiku, October, 1970).

我设计的第一座房子竣工于28年前。这也是我首次利用建筑这一媒质来向外界传递信息。毫无疑问,建筑在城市中所扮演的角色正在飞快地失去其社会意义。但是,作为一个弱小的、孤立的设计者,如果在建筑逻辑已无法表达且崩溃无用之后,仍然坚持设计工作的缜密思索,那么他唯一能做的就是把将其所处环境中的荒谬忠实于原貌地公之于众……对我来说,设计住宅的过程,就是一个探究存在于作为设计师的我,与房子未来居住者之间严重分歧的工作。也许,在论及此类分歧之时,用"弥合"这个字眼会比"探究"要顺耳些。事实却是,我们缺乏必要的共同术语来弥合这一分歧。因此,该工作只能以一种矛盾的方式开始,即带着对无法跨越的分歧的察觉,进一步建造不可逾越的墙垣(引自"设计行为是思索过程被扭曲时的一种探究"《新建筑》,1970.10)。

Diego Rivera and Frida Kahlo House

● 图3-4 某小住宅

(图片来源: Top Architect Works in Series——TOYO ITO. (韩)建筑世界杂志社 Toyo Ito)

A House

● 图3-5 迭戈·里维拉和弗里达·卡洛之家

---

❶ Criticality指一种到了极端的危险状态,我们认为其指建筑师对社会的"批评"走到极端时的状态。可翻成"临界值","临界性","临界状态","临界"……为了简洁,我们将它翻成"临界"。同时,觉得"临界"有专业术语的味道,所以加了个引号。

❷ 资料来源: James Keith Vincent. Top Architect Works in Series——TOYO ITO. (韩)建筑世界杂志社

As this passage suggests, I began the work of design as an expression of an unbearable frustration over the state of society and the city. This emotion was given blatant expression in aluminum-covered exterior walls that flaunted their dents and irregularities in the light of the sun, and cylinders of light thrusting upwards without meaning. At the time, this was the only and the greatest critical tool I had.

正如本文所表明的，我开始从事设计工作时，是将它作为对城市和社会状况无法忍受的挫折感的一种表达。这种情感通过由铝材覆盖的外墙得到一种炫耀式的表达：墙面在阳光下炫耀着其表面的凹痕和不规则，光柱则毫无意义地直刺天空。在那段时间里，这是我所能采用的唯一且最好的表现工具。

In the past ten years my design work has focused almost exclusively on public architecture. The feelings I have for this work are almost the same as those expressed in the message I sent by way of that small house 28 years ago. It is impossible to conceive of a common language to bridge the gap with the systems of actual cities and societies. We are left dumfounded by our awareness of the excessive depth of that gap. Not a few times, during discussions with local governments, I have been tempted to smash the models and storm out of the room. Recently, however, I have begun to worry that staring into that gap has closed me of from the world around me. Sometimes I wonder if I am not taking refuge in the comfort of "critique" as a selfish justification of my own condemnation of society. Architecture and other creative practices often take their inspiration from frustration and anger towards the world outside. They also sometimes stem from irritations and insecurities arising from an inability to express one's emotions directly. Whether they are hot or cool, these emotions are linked to the desire to express oneself. But however much they may have their origins in individual impulses, the resultant expressions ultimately leave the hands of their creators and acquire a life of their own.

Paintings and novels remain in the museum or the bookstore, but architecture makes its appearance in our surroundings. They are there for anyone to see in unmediated form. They are available for use in people's lives and for specific purposes. Architects have no choice but to face the social or public nature of their expressive work. Can anti-social, negative expressions arising form personal frustration and anger ever be socially redeemed as individual expressions in the negative or the interrogative? This has been the most difficult issue I have confronted over the last ten years designing public architecture. Is it possible to transform negative impulses into positive expressions evoking trust without sacrificing their energy? But even private residences take on an independent existence in their environment once they are completed. Their status as private property does not prevent them from having social meaning. In this sense the same problem exists in theoretical terms both for public and private architecture, but there is a difference when it comes to the actual process of designing public architecture.

过去的十年里，我的设计作品几乎完全集中在公共建筑上。我对这类作品的情感与我在28年前通过小住宅所传递的信息几乎一模一样。要构想出一种能弥合现行城市与社会体系之间分歧的共同话语是不可能的。对于这一深层分歧的认识使得我们瞠目结舌。在与当地政府部门的讨论中，我多次冲动地要把模型砸烂，并夺门而出。然而，最近我开始担心，老是盯着这一分歧已使我同周围的世界隔绝开来。当我私下里将"批评"作为自己非难社会的一种自我辩护时，有时候，我会疑惑自己是否真的能在"批评"的慰藉中得到庇护。在建筑设计和其他的创造性实践中，灵感常常来自于对外部世界的挫折感和愤怒感。有时，这些灵感也来自于因无法直抒其怀而产生的烦恼感和忧虑感。这些情感，无论它们是充满激情还是故作冷漠，都与表达其自身的欲望息息相关。然而不管这类情感源于多么强烈的个体冲动，作为结果而存在的表达却终究会脱离它们的始作俑者而获得自己的生命。绘画和小说留在博物馆或书店里，而建筑却将其自身展现于我们周围的环境中。无须任何媒介，公众即可感知它们。它们可以用于人们的生活起居以及其他特定的用途，建筑师们除了面对其作品所处的社会和公众外别无选择。源于个体挫折感和愤怒感的反社会的、否定的表达，是否能够作为个体消极或怀疑的措辞而免受社会的责难？这是我在过去的十年间设计公共建筑的过程中所碰到的最棘手的问题。能否将消极的情绪转化成能唤起人们信心的积极表达，而同时又不失其活力？然而，即便是私邸，即便其一旦竣工便呈现出一派独立于环境而存在的架势，它们作为私人财产的角色并不妨碍其社会意义的获得。从这个意义上讲，公共建筑和私人建筑在理论上都存在着同样的问题，但是，一旦卷入设计公共建筑的实际过程，就得另当别论了。

3.5.2 对临界的误解
The Misunderstanding of Criticality

By a complete coincidence I had no opportunities to design private residences for some time after I began designing public facilities. It was not until two years ago that I finally designed two homes for the first time in years. I was lucky enough to have two excellent clients and it was wonderful to rediscover how enjoyable it can be to design private homes. But more than that, I was just happy to be face to face with homes again. Both of the projects were low-budget, but the sites were unexpectedly large, which meant that we had to cut back on finishing materials. The exteriors ended up looking like a simple factory shed, but the projects were finally completed amidst tension-filled and yet friendly disagreement with the clients. For the first time in many years I felt certain that the clients and I were occupying the same space. This sense of commonality made them modest spaces but also kept them from descending into too radical an expression.

极好的业主。重新享受设计私邸的乐趣真是妙极了。更让我高兴的是，能够再次与住宅建筑面对面。这两个项目都是低预算的，基地却出乎意料的大，这就意味着我们不得不在外装修材料上缩减开支。竣工后的建筑看上去就像一个简易的工棚。这两个工程都是在同业主紧张却还算友好的争执中最终完成的，这是我多年来第一次真切感受到业主与我是平起平坐的。这种共识不仅使住宅的表情显得谦逊朴实，也避免了过于极端的表达。

It is impossible to experience this sort of commonality with public architecture. There are moments on certain projects when one feels that one has shared a space with specific individuals. But the communication as a whole is interrupted by a succession of gaps, nothing but an assemblage of irreparable fissures.

如此的共识在公共建筑中是不可能体会到的。偶尔，在某些项目中，建筑师与少数人可以达成共识。但就总体而言，这种密切和谐的交流关系会被接连不断的分歧打断，分歧不是别的，就是所有无法弥补之裂隙的集合。

I have used the term "criticality" to refer to the absence or presence of this kind of rupture. I once said in a roundtable discussion that there was no criticality in private residence design. For me, this was a natural expression of how I felt just after having completed the two residential projects mentioned above. I felt no fissures and no need directly to vent any anger or frustration. I felt at once disoriented and happy to have been able to design something outside of my customary obsession with the language of criticality. And yet I was not sure if this particular solution was mine alone, so I added the caveat that of course this world depend on how one defines criticality.

我一直用"临界"（criticality）一词来指代这种断裂的缺席或存在。我曾在一次非正式讨论中谈到，在私邸的设计中不存在"临界"这回事。这是在我完成上述两栋住宅项目后，切身体会的自然表述。我没感到有什么裂隙而直接发泄愤怒或挫折的必要。能够不受临界语言的习惯性困扰来做设计，让我在丧失方向感的同时感到愉快。然而我还不能确定这是否只是我个人特有的解答方式，故而我特地说明，这当然要取决于一个人如何定义"临界"。

I was thus quite astonished to read a response to this comment of mine which took it to mean that I had my sites set exclusively on public architecture, had no interest in looking for themes in private residence design, and even that established architects in general were no longer concerned with designing homes. I even felt sorry for myself at having been so roundly misunderstood. But I prefer not to bring the discussion down to so personal a level here. I think it would be more interesting to expand the theme of the criticality of residential architecture as it has developed out of my personal emotions onto a more general level. This has to do with the fact that in the seventies when I designed my first home I thought that a critical attitude toward society was part of the architect's ethic. This is, however, an idea that has been with us since the advent of modernity. Architects have maintained a negative attitude toward society ever since modernist architecture set out to change it. And they have worn their rejection by mainstream society like a badge of honor. But as long as architects fail to find more positive terms in which to speak to their society, that is to say as long as they refuse to give up the idea of criticality, they will continue to create an architecture of exclusion. And residential architecture offers us the most accessible escape route from this narrow path. This is why the theme of this essay is not "Is there criticality in residential architecture?" but "Is there residential architecture without criticality?"

当我看到一篇对于我这段评论的回应时，我十分吃惊，因为这篇文章以此断定我将自己完全定位于公共建筑中，而对私邸设计缺乏兴趣，该文甚至认为，已被社会认同的建筑师们，总体上已不再对住宅设计感兴趣了。被误解得如此厉害，我实在感到遗憾。但是，我不愿把这场辩论降低到如此个人的层面。我想，关于居住建筑之临界的话题已经超越我个人的情感而上升到一个更为普遍的层次之上，此时，将其拓展开来将更为有趣。这么说的依据是，我在70年代设计我的第一栋住宅时，就认定对社会持一种批评的态度是建筑师职业道德的一部分。无论如何，这是现代主义来临之后就一直伴随着我们的一种理念。自从现代主义建筑着手改变社会以来，建筑师们就对社会持有一种否定的态度。他们将主流社会对他们的拒绝当作荣誉勋章一样佩戴起来。但是只要建筑师们没有找到更为积极的建筑语言来与他们所处的社会对话，或者说，只要他们拒绝放弃这种临界的理念，他们就会继续创作出带有排斥性的建筑。居住建筑提供给我们的正是从这条窄路上逃脱的一个最有效的途径。这就是为什么该文的题目不是"居住建筑中是否存在临界？"，而是"是否存在无'临界'的居住建筑？"。

3.5.3 一群隐遁的美学家
A Flock of Reclusive Aesthetics

When I sat down to write this article I looked over the designs of young architects written up in this journal over the past two years and found that many of them shared a common symptom. They were large and cubic and striving toward transparency. Hasegawa Akira expertly captured the essence of the "transparency syndrome" affecting these designs in the passage I cite below in his essay for the April, 1998 issue of *Shinkenchiku*. The structures are of reinforced steel or wood-frame and the entrances extremely large with a peculiar insistence on transparency. The slightly built walls are flat, utterly neutral and without the slightest pretension to structural strength… Pleasantly light and somehow makeshift, these residences nonetheless contain inconspicuous citations of the avant-garde architecture of the twenties, with whose forms they are gracefully enlivened. These are all residences designed by young architects born in or around 1960. As I look at them my sense of taste goes numb and I feel a kind of aphasia coming on.

当我坐下来写作此文时，我翻阅了《新建筑》过去两年来所介绍的年轻建筑师的设计作品。我发现其中的许多作品拥有一个共同征状——大体量、立方体且尽其所能地透明。我下面所引用的长谷川润·阿基拉（Hasegawa Akira）为《新建筑》1998年四月刊所写的文章，就熟练地抓住了频频出现于这些设计作品中的"透明综合症"的本质：钢筋或木框架结构，特别强调透明的大尺度的入口，纤细的构造墙体是平直的、全然中性的且没有一丁点儿支撑的意图……虽然如此，这些住宅还是隐含了对20世纪前卫建筑难以觉察的引证，轻盈的且多少带有暂时性的建筑显得优雅而生动。这些住宅均由出生于1960年前后的年轻建筑师设计。当我看着这些作品时，我的审美意识变得迟钝并且感到一种失语症侵袭而至（图3-4）。

The prevalence of this kind of design in the pages of this journal may simply be a result of the editors' selection, but they have in fact become quite common in the real world as well. Of course my own work has a good deal of the same kind of character. And I am certainly self-aware enough to realize that as someone who has made lightness, provisionality and transparency my own themes I must also bear some responsibility for this syndrome affecting those born twenty years later than I. And yet I cannot help but sympathize with Hasegawa when he writes that these works have numbed his sense of taste and made him aphasic. Many of these homes built by young architects seem to be characterized by a kind of feeble introversion. Of course this does not go for all of them, but for the most part they begin and end in the sophistication of a light and transparent aesthetic. They are beautiful and delicate, but they avoid conflict with the outside and remain disdainfully closed to reality. In other words, the vast majority of homes designed today fail to come up with any clear critique even as they continue to insist on the criticality of modernism. Only a precious few manage to confront reality in a proactive fashion. But if we were to trace the roots of the negative criticality seen in these residences we would end up right back in the twenties. They do in fact subscribe to the language of modernism and are characterized by the strong critique of reality that was the goal of early modernist architecture. I myself, as I mentioned earlier, have also insisted that my own work should be critical. But I cannot help feeling that a negative attitude toward actual society tends to separate one from the land and cause one to turn one's back on it.

此类作品在该杂志中俯拾即是的情形也许是编辑选择的结果，但事实上，这一类的设计已经在现实生活中相当普遍了。当然，我自己的作品也带有许多如此的特征。而且毫无疑问，我很清醒地意识到，作为将轻盈、暂时性以及透明性当作自己作品主题的建筑师，我也必须为频频出现在那些晚我20年出生的建筑师的作品中的这些综合症负有一定的责任。然而当长谷川润写到，这些作品使得他的审美感觉迟钝起来并且患上失语症时，我不免与他深有同感。许多年轻建筑师所建造的房子似乎被赋予了微弱的内省性。当然，这情形并非存在于所有的作品中，不过大部分作品自始至终都采用混合了光和透明的美学原则。这类作品尽管美丽优雅，却回避了同外界的冲突，并且对现实保持着一种轻蔑的拒绝。换句话说，即便当今所设计的绝大多数住宅继续强调现代主义的临界性，它们未能找到一个清晰的批评方法。仅有少数难得的几个人，竭尽所能地在众人趋之若鹜的情形下，面对现实。但是如果我们追溯在这些住宅中所看到的否定临界性的根源，我们将回到20年代。事实上他们的确认同现代主义语言并且被赋予对现实强力批评的特色，这种对现实的强力批评正是早期现代主义建筑的目标。正如我稍早所提，我本人也坚持自己的作品应该具有批评性。不过我不由自主地感觉到，这种对现实社会的否定态度会让人与大地隔开，并导致其对土地的背离。

3.5.4 一座最纯粹的现代主义住宅，或奥戈曼悲剧
A Home of the Purest Modernism, or the Tragedy of O'Gorman

The last spring I curated an exhibition at a gallery in

Tokyo devoted to a single home built in the early 1930s: the "Diego Rivera and Frida Kahlo House" located in Mexico City and recently restored. I was lucky enough to see this house on a recent visit to Mexico, before which I knew nothing about it. I did not even know the architect's name. But from the moment I got out of the car in front of the grounds, this house made a powerful impression on me. First of all, its pure and stoic form was more than enough to overturn all of the images I had associated with Mexico. The house was designed by Juan O'Gorman for the two highly original painters known for their tumultuous lives and completed in 1932, just one year after Le Corbusier completed his Villa Savoye.

去年春天,在东京的一个画廊里,我策划了一次展览,专门关于一栋建于20世纪30年代初期的住宅:"迭戈·里维拉和弗里达·卡洛之家"。该住宅位于墨西哥城并于近期重建。最近一次对墨西哥的访问中我有幸得以参观,而此前我对其一无所知,我甚至不知设计者的姓名。但自我从庭院前的轿车中走出的那一刻起,我便被这栋住宅深深地打动了。首先,它纯净、恬淡的形式足以推翻我已有的关于墨西哥的印象。这栋住宅是贾安·奥戈曼(Juan O'Gorman)为两位因喧闹的生活而出名且极具创意的画家所设计的,竣工于1932年,正好比勒·柯布西耶完成的萨伏伊别墅晚一年。

The two painters were husband and wife but worked independently from each other, so O'Gorman designed the house with two living spaces and ateliers in separate wings. The two wings, connected only by a bridge from roof to roof, are each simple cubes that seem to float in mid-air. Painted Indian red and marine blue respectively to evoke the Mexican landscape, the two wings are surrounded by a fence of cacti and held aloft on pilotis, completely cut off from the ground. Composed solely in the language of pure modernism, this architecture was not only separate from the land, but seemed utterly autonomous even in Mexico, where a sense of place still hangs thick in the air. The work of Luis Barragan is perhaps most strongly associated with contemporary Mexican architecture, but this house by O'Gorman is entirely different in character. Barragan's homes are much more gently integrated into the Mexican landscape. Unlike O'Gorman he often used festive colors to promote harmony with the landscape. The rough textures that highlight his surfaces and the liberal use of trees in his substantial entryways only further heighten the sense of an intimate relation to the earth. The volume as a whole may be based in the language of modernism but there is always a tendency to downplay it, to dull its edges and cover it in vegetation in order to avoid as far as possible any confrontation with the environment. Barragan's architecture is an accommodation of modernism to the land, a revisionist truce with the local. As such it ensures not a new lifestyle, but a tranquil, rich, and established one.

这两位画家是一对夫妻,工作起来却是各干各的,因此奥戈曼为这栋住宅设计了两套起居空间和画室,分别位于两侧翼中。这两侧翼仅由架于屋顶之间的天桥相连,每个都是简单的立方体,看上去犹如漂浮于半空中。他们分别涂以印第安红和海蓝两种颜色,让人联想起墨西哥风情(图 3-5)。两侧翼为仙人掌篱笆所环绕,并支在立柱上,与地面完全脱开。该建筑由纯粹的现代主义语言所构成,它不仅凌空而起,而且即便是在墨西哥这个悬挑之风依旧浓厚的国度,也好像是完全独立自在的。也许,路易斯·巴拉根(Luis Barragan)的作品与当代墨西哥建筑的联系最为紧密,但这栋由奥戈曼所设计的房子则有着迥然不同的特点。巴拉根的住宅与墨西哥自然景观的融合更为柔和。不同于奥戈曼,他经常采用一些喜庆的色彩来增进同自然景观的调和。他那突显出建筑外观的粗糙肌理以及他在实体的入口处对树木不拘一格的做法反而进一步加强了建筑同大地的亲近感。他的建筑整体看来也许是以现代主义语言为基础而创作的,但是为了尽可能避免同周围环境的冲突,也常带有将其淡化、钝化以及利用植被将其隐蔽化的倾向。巴拉根的建筑是现代主义同大地的一种妥协,一种与本土的修正主义式的休战。就此而言,它确保的不是一种新的生活方式,而是一种平静的、丰富多彩的、已经成型的生活方式。

The Diego wing in particular, with its sawtooth roof and exterior spiral staircase out of concrete, was clearly inspired by the "Ozenfant House and Studio" (1923), but it goes even further than the early houses of Le Corbusier in its pursuit of functionality. The pursuit of rationality and economy evident in the columns, floors, walls, and staircases, all of which O'Gorman is said to have designed down to the structural calculations, is taken to its furthest horizon. The same is true for the precision of the horizontal and vertical surfaces and each element (from the doors to the window sashes, the dust shoot and gutters to the furniture) was thought out down to its last detail for the sake of pure functionality and economy. A comparison with "Villa a Garches" (1927) and "Villa Savoye" (1931), two works considered early masterpieces of Le Corbusier, will make clear the extent to which O'Gorman's work was invested in the search for pure functionality. Like the "Rivera and Kahlo House", these two houses have clean-cut edges based in simple geometrical volumes, but the architectural meanings embedded in them are quite different. Le Corbusier's works are concerned with functionality and with proposing new ways of living, but at the same time they are expertly infused with tendencies of both classicism and abstract painting. As Colin Rowe (in *The Mathematics of the Ideal Villa*) points out, the proportions and phrasing of the exteriors are reminiscent of Palladio's villas, while in the interior curved lines like those used in purist painting form layers (giving a sense of transparency). While Le Corbusier was making new proposals for a new city he also continued to incorporate both the order of historical architecture and the experiments of avant-garde art. When seen in this light, Le Corbusiers' "Five Principles of Modern Architecture" (1926) which were supposed to make possible a new lifestyle, come to look like little more than a tool to justify his own architecture through the logic of modernism. More than Le Corbusier, it was the 26-year-old O'Gorman who was dreaming up the new life to be made possible through the five points of pilotis, roof gardens, horizontal rectangular windows, and free vertical and horizontal surfaces. All five of these points are offered to society in the purest form in the "Rivera and Kahlo House". Could we not say that it was only in this moment of single-minded pursuit of functionality that the language of modernism was able to burst through its closed context and sublate its identity as critical language? The best proof we have of this is surely to be found in the fact that even Rivera and Kahlo, with all their fanatic championing of the blood of ancient Mexico and their support of the Communist movement, were so proud of this purely modernist space. But O'Gorman's pursuits were not sustainable. In the early 1930s he worked on many social programs including schools and communal residences, but gave up architecture by the end of the decade to take up painting. Later he threw himself into the mural painting movement, partly under the influence of Rivera. His commitment to social reform remained constant but its form changed to the opposite pole from the pure, abstract space of Western modernism. But O'Gorman's transformation did not end there. In 1953 he moved into a cave-like home he designed and filled with Indio décor. Finally, in 1982, he moved into a modernist house he had designed as a young man and took his own life. O'Gorman's all too pure and thoroughgoing pursuit of modernist space most likely forced upon him an all too clear vision of the fissure separating the language of modernism from the culture of Mexico. It was an irreparable fissure indeed.

显然,迪戈那一侧,带有锯齿形屋顶及混凝土螺旋外楼梯的侧翼的设计灵感,来自于"奥赞范特住宅与工作室"(Ozenfant House and Studio,1923年)。但在对功能的追求上,它比勒·柯布西耶早期设计的住宅走得更远了。对理性和经济的追求被奥戈曼发挥到了极致，这种追求明显地体现于柱子、楼板、墙体以及楼梯，所有这些据说都被他简化至仅从结构上考虑而设计的元素。这种极致同样也体现在平面、立面的精确度上，出于纯粹的功能和经济的考虑，每一要素（从门到窗框，从污水槽、排水沟到家具）的每一细节都经过仔细的琢磨和推敲。如果把这栋建筑同两个被公认为勒·柯布西耶早期杰作的加奇别墅（Villa a Garches，1927年）和萨伏伊别墅（1931年）作个比较，我们就会明白奥戈曼对纯功能的追求到了何种地步。同"里维拉和卡洛之家"（Rivera and Kahlo house）一样，勒·柯布西耶的这两个住宅都有着由简洁的几何形体所形成的鲜明的轮廓，但是蕴涵于其中的建筑意义却大相径庭。勒·柯布西耶的作品关注于功能并倡导新的生活方式，但与此同时，他的作品又被娴熟地注入了古典主义与抽象绘画的旨趣。正如科林·罗欧（Colin Rowe）在《理想别墅中的数学》一书中所指出的，勒·柯布西耶作品外部的比例及修饰让人联想起帕拉第奥的别墅，而其室内那些如同运用于纯绘画中的曲线，形成了层次（给人以通透感）。当勒·柯布西耶在为一座新的城市提出新构想时，他继续将前卫艺术的体验与历史性建筑的式样结合起来。就这一点来看，勒·柯布西耶那意图使一种新的生活方式成为可能的新建筑五要素（1926年），看上去不过是一种借助现代主义逻辑替其作品辩护的工具。较之更为甚者的是26岁的奥戈曼，他一直在梦想着借助支撑柱、屋顶花园、水平带形窗、自由的平面和立面这五点，来使这种新生活成为可能。所有这五点在"里维拉和卡洛之家"中以最为纯粹的形式回馈给社会。难道我们不能说正是在如此专心致志地追求功能性之时，现代主义语言才得以突破它自我封闭的语境，并且放弃了其作为批评式语言的身份？对此，我们绝对可以从这样的一个事实中得到最有力的验证：即便是里维拉和卡洛，这两位极力为古墨西哥文明而战的狂热者和共产主义运动的支持者，也都为这纯粹的现代主义空间而感到自豪。但奥戈曼的追求飘忽不定。在20世纪30年代早期，他做了许多包括学校和公共住宅在内的社会性项目，但是到30年代末，他放弃了建筑转而从事绘画。再往后，他又投身于壁画运动，这多少是受了里维拉的影响。他献身社会改良的初衷始终没有改变，只不过形式从西方现代主义纯净、抽象的空间转向了与其对立的另一个极端。然而，奥戈曼的转变并非到此为止。1953年，他搬进了自己设计的洞穴般的住宅，里面满是印第安人的饰品。最后，1982年搬到他年轻时设计的一座现代主义住宅中并在那儿自杀。很可能，对现代主义空间过于纯粹和彻底的追求，迫使他对于将现代主义语言从墨西哥文化中分离出来的这种裂隙，有着一个过于清晰、完整的洞察。的确，这是一种无法修补的裂隙。

3.5.5 现代之外的主体意象
A Body Image Beyond the Modern

The two worlds that Juan O'Gorman expressed symbolically in his life speak to two opposing images of his body, one conceptual and one visceral. The former is an unnatural body aiming for an abstract utopian world conceived on a conscious level, while the latter is a natural one which relates to the traditions of ancient Mexico. People of every age have tried to preserve in the space of their domiciles memories of the land inscribed in their bodies. This spatialization of memory happens not only with personal memories but also with those of families and whole local communities. Houses built in this way pass through generations of desperate struggles with nature until they become almost like extensions of human skin. At the same time, however, people have always striven to build another kind of domicile to house their future memories. Particularly in this century, when technology has made such startling advances, many have dreamt of that other house. Such are the attempts to transform the exhilarating sensations we experience in machine spaces like cars and airplanes into our homes. When people try to slip into skins made of steel, glass, aluminum, or plastic they experience a liberation of their bodies as if they were moving into another dimension. And they try and expand that feeling of liberation into another skin and another body. It is a liberation from the bonds of the land and from the customary life of earthbound families and communities. I referred to the body that seeks a home as a memory of the future as an unnatural one, but now it is changing into one which experiences the universe. By now it should be possible to think of it as one which is seeking a new and different kind of nature. The body in search of the machine has gone through further expansions until it has begun to seek nature as a memory of the future. This is what we call the virtual body.

奥戈曼在他一生中所象征性表达出来的两种世界，对应于他体内的两个相对立的意象，一个是概念上的，一个是直觉上的。前者为非自然体，旨在追求一个构想于意识层面上的抽象的乌托邦社会，后者则是自然体，与古墨西哥传统相关联。各个年龄段的人们，都曾努力在他们的住宅空间里，保存铭刻于内心的关于土地的记忆。这种记忆的空间化，不仅发生于个体记忆中，也发生于家庭和整个社区的记忆中。以这种方式建造的住宅，经过几代人与大自然殊死的抗争，直至它们几乎成为人类皮肤的延伸。然而，与此同时，人们始终在努力建造另一类可以收藏他们未来记忆的住所。尤其是在本世纪，当技术取得如此惊人的进步之时，许多人就梦想着有那样的住宅，就是尝试着把我们在类似汽车和飞机这样的机械空间里所体验到的令人愉悦的感觉，转化到我们的住宅之中。当人们试着滑进这些由钢铁、玻璃、铝材或塑料制成的表皮之内，他们体验到一种主体的释放，犹如进入了另一维空间。于是他们就尝试着将这种释放的感觉扩展到另一类的表皮和主体中去，这是一种从土地的束缚，从世俗家庭、社会日常生活中挣脱出来的释放。我前面称那种寻求能收藏未来记忆之住所的主体为非自然体，但现在，它正在变换成体验宇宙的主体。那么，至此，我们就应该有可能将它当作探求一种不同于以往的崭新自然界的主体。这个寻求机械的主体在它开始探寻作为未来记忆的自然之时，经过了进一步的扩展，这就是我们所说的虚拟主体(virtual body)。

O'Gorman's "Rivera and Kahlo House" was one in search of a body as consciousness bewitched by the machine age. But that attempt failed when it was rejected by another body of strong communal memories tied to the earth. Brought back to himself, O'Gorman tried to give himself back to the memories of the earth, only to fail again. He could not tolerate having two bodies at once. But these two bodies are still with us as we live our lives today and the chaos of our urban spaces can be considered the result of our striving toward them. Many architects continue in the modernist tradition and use its language to speak of their work, lingering ambivalently without ever finding a place to touch down. And yet the power of the land that was supposed to engage our fire has lost its strength to modernization and finds its body exposed in the shrunken world of the local. It may not be comparable to revolutionary Mexico at the beginning of this century, but it seems to me that the flock of young architects mentioned earlier symbolizes a Japan that has passed the peak of modernization and lost sight of its goals. Hasegawa lost his taste and his words to the sight of their ambiguity, to the sight of them caught without the confidence to be the heirs of modernism and without the power of meaning with which to speak to society. To lose social language and close oneself off into a sophisticated aesthetic is merely to justify a stifling exasperation in the name of a negative criticality. We can only hope that these exasperated architects can get beyond their bodies as inheritors of modernism, since no future memories are going to arise from the impasse of two bodies locked in a stalemate. And we must think of a new body image that will help us out of this deadlock. It would not be an unnatural body, but one accustomed to a new nature, and one which would yet be able to accept the old. It is only when these two natures come together that houses seeking new bodies will begin to speak in a positive language.

奥戈曼的"里维拉和卡洛之家"是在当意识沉迷于机器时代之时，找寻主体的一种尝试。但是，当它被另一类有着土地情结的强大的集体记忆拒绝之时，这尝试便告失败。(让我们把分析拉)回到他本人，奥戈曼试图让自己回归乡土的记忆，结果以失败告终。他无法同时兼容两种主体。但是，因为我们还活着，至今这两个主体依然伴随着我们的生活，我们城市空间的杂乱无序，可以被认为正是我们与之抗争的结果。许多建筑师继承着现代主义的传统并且用其语言来表现着他们的作品，他们却左右彷徨，无法找到一个落脚点。而被认为是点燃了我们激情的乡土力量，则已经失去其对于现代化的抵抗力，并且发现其主体被晾晒在当地那已经萎缩的世界。也许，上面所提到的那群年青的建筑师们，无法与本世纪初爆发革命的墨西哥相提并论，但是对我而言，这些人似乎象征了一个业已滑过现代化的顶峰且迷失其方向的日本。看到这些人含糊其辞，既没有信心去继承现代主义又无力与社会对话，长谷川润没有了任何感觉和言辞。失去大众语言并将自身封闭于诡辩的美学中，只是籍否定的"临界"之名，为一种令人窒息的恼怒而进行的辩解。既然无法从两个主体都已陷入困境的僵局中获得有关未来的记忆，我们唯一能够希望的就是，这些恼怒的建筑师们能够超越他们作为现代主义继承人的主体。而且，我们必须找到一个能够帮助我们走出僵局的崭新的主体意象，它不会是一种非自然的主体，而是一种纳新却不吐故的主体。只有当这两个新旧主体和谐相处时，探寻新主体的住宅方能传达出一种积极的语言。

第 4 章　专业英语课外阅读

4.1　佛光寺[1]

Fo-kuang Ssu

The oldest wooden structure known today is the Main Hall of Fo-kuang Ssu, in the Wu-tai Mountains, Shanxi province. Built in 857, twelve years after the last nationwide persecution of Buddhism, it replaced a seven-bayed, three-storied, ninety-five-feet-high hall, which had housed a colossal statue of Mi-le (Maitreya), also destroyed. The existing structure is a single-storied hall of seven bays. It is extremely impressive with its rigorous and robust proportions. The enormous tou-kung of four tiers of cantilevers—two tiers of hua-kung and two tiers of ang—measuring about half the height of the columns, with every piece if timber in the ensemble doing its share as a structural member, give the building an overwhelming dignity that is not found in later structures.

截至目前所知木构建筑中，最古老的实例是山西五台山佛光寺大殿。该建筑建于公元857年，即会昌灭法之后十二年，原址有一座七间、三层、九十五尺高的大殿，供奉弥勒菩萨巨像，后来被毁。现存建筑为重建而成，单层、七间，其严谨而雄壮的比例令人印象深刻。巨大的斗栱有四层出跳——两层华栱、两层昂（双抄双下昂），斗高度约等于柱高的一半，其中每一构件都在体系中分担结构功能，从而使建筑整体极其庄重，这在后来建筑中未曾有过（图4-1～图4-3）。

Elevation of Fo-kuang Ssu

● 图 4-1　佛光寺立面图

Interior of Fo-kuang Ssu

● 图 4-2　佛光寺室内

（图片来源：图 4-1，图 4-3 中国科学院自然科学史研究所主编，中国古代建筑技术史．北京：科学技术出版社 1990：70-73；图 4-2 来自网络 picasaweb.google.com）

---

[1] 资料来源：费慰梅编．梁从诫译．梁思成英文原著，图像中国建筑史．天津：百花文艺出版社，2001年：166-171．编者摘选、校对．

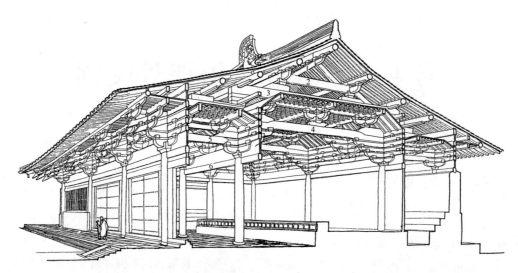

Fo-kuang Ssu

图 4-3 山西五台县佛光寺东大殿梁架剖视示意图
1—叉手；2—平梁；3—四椽草栿；4—四椽明栿；5—乳栿；6—内额

The interior manifests grace and elegance. Spanning the hypostyle columns are "crescent-moon beams", supported at either end by four tiers of hua-kung that transmit their load to the columns. In contrast to the severity of the exterior, every surface of the beams is curved. The sides are pulvinated. and the top and bottom are gently arched, giving an illusion of strength that would otherwise be lacking in a simple straight horizontal member.

大殿内部十分典雅端庄。月梁横跨内柱间，两端各由四跳华栱支承，将其荷载传递到柱上。殿内梁的每个面都呈曲线形，与大殿庄严的外观恰成对照。月梁的两侧微凸，上下则略呈弓形，使人产生一种强劲有力的观感，而这是直梁所不具备的。

The building's most significant feature, from the point of view of dating structural evolution, is the formation of the "truss" immediately under, and therefore supporting, the ridge. On the top tier of beams are placed a pair of ch'a-shou ("abutting arms") butting against each other to carry the ridge pole, while the "king post" is missing altogether. This is a rare survival of early construction practice. Similar construction is indicated in the Stone shrine at the Tomb of Chu Wei (first century A. D.) Chin-hsiang, Shantung province, and also in one of the Tun-tuang paintings. In actual specimens, it is employed in the eolonnade around the courtyard of Horyuji (seventh century), Nara, Japan. The Fo-kuang Ssu example is the only one of its kind preserved in China and is never seen in later structures.

从结构演变阶段的观点看，这座大殿的最有意义的特点就在于有着直接支承屋脊的人字形构架。在最高一层梁的上面，有互相抵靠着的一对人字形叉手以撑托脊，而侏儒柱则没有同时使用。这是早期构架实践的稀有实例。过去只在山东金乡县朱鲔墓石室（公元 1 世纪）雕刻和敦煌的一幅壁画中见到过类似的结构。其他实例，还可见于日本奈良法隆寺（7 世纪）庭院周围的柱廊。佛光寺是国内现存此类结构的惟一遗例，在以后的结构中从未见过。

What makes the Main Hall even more of a treasure is the presence within of sculpture, painting, and calligraphy, all of the same date. On the large platform is a pantheon of nearly three dozen Buddhas and Bodhisattvas of colossal and heroic size. Of even more interest are the two humble, life-sized portrait statues, one of a woman, Ning Kung-yu, donor of the Hall, and the other of a monk, Ynan-ch'eng, the abbot who rebuilt the temple after the destruction of 845. On the undersides of the beams are inscriptions written with brush and ink, giving the names of the civil and military officials of the district at the time of the completion of the Hall, and also that of the donor. On one frieze a fresco of moderate dimensions, unmistakably T'ang in style is preserved. In comparison the Sung painting in the next bay, dated 1122, itself a great treasure, is eclipsed. Thus in a single building are found examples of all four of the plastic arts of the T'ang dynasty. Any one of them would be proclaimed a national treasure; and the assemblage of all four is an unimaginable extravagance.

使大殿更为珍贵的是，它保存了同时期的塑像、壁画和题字。在巨大的须弥座上，有30多尊巨型佛像和菩萨像。但最引人注目的，却是两尊神情谦卑的等身人像，其一为本殿女施主宁公遇像，另一为本寺住持愿诚和尚像，他在弥勒大阁845年被毁后主持重修。梁的下面有墨笔书写的大殿重修时本地区文武官员及施主姓名。在一处栱眼壁上留有一幅大小适中的壁画，为唐风无疑。与之相比，旁边内额上绘于1122年的宋代壁画，虽然也十分珍贵，却不免逊色了。这样，在单体建筑内竟保存了中国唐代所有的四种造型艺术，其中任何一件都足以被视为国宝。四美荟于一殿，真是奇迹。

The next one hundred and twenty years is a blank period from which not a single existing wooden structure is known. Then there are two wooden structures in the Tun-huang caves, dated 976 and 980. Although they hardly deserve the name of real buildings, for they are merely porches screening the entrances of the caves, nevertheless they are rare examples of the architecture of the early Sung dynasty.

此后的120年是一段空白，其间竟无一处木构建筑被发现。在这以后敦煌石窟中有两座年代可考的木建筑，分别建于976年和980年，但它们几乎难以被称之为真正的建筑，而仅仅是石窟入口处的窟廊，然而毕竟是罕见的宋初遗物。

4.2　滨水区设计标准[1]

WATERFRONTS

滨水区

Current interest in the water's edge and the flourishing of public spaces on waterfronts across the United States is the result of a process going back for decades. Once places of trade, military, or industrial advantage, or even places of neglect, waterfronts are increasingly seen as economic and social assets to their communities.

时下全美对滨水区研究的广泛兴趣以及滨水公共空间的繁荣发展是过去几十年来不断发展的结果。那些滨水区域，曾经被用于贸易、军事或作为工业预留用地，甚至一度被忽视，如今日益被人们当作其社区的经济和社会资产。

STANDARDS AND REGULATIONS

When contemplating new waterfront projects, take into account the specific standards enforced by federal and state regulatory systems. The following agencies have a role in the regulation of our coastal ecosystems.

标准和规则

在设计新的滨水项目时，必须要考虑到由联邦和各州的监管机构所规定的特殊标准。下述的机构在负责有关滨水生态系统的管理中扮演了重要角色。

Federal Agencies (for Navigable Waterways and Connected Wetlands)

U.S. Environmental Protection Agency (EPA)

U.S. Army Corps of Engineers

National Oceanic and Atmosphere Administration (NOAA)

The Department of Homeland Security (especially the Federal Emergency Management Agency (FEMA)

---

[1] 资料来源：American Planning Association. *Planning and Urban Design Standards*. New Jersy: John Wiley & Sons, Inc., 2006.

and the U. S. Coast Guard)

 U. S. Fish and Wildlife Service

联邦政府机构(管理航道及其所连接的湿地)

 全美环境保护组织(EPA)

 全美陆军工程兵部队

 美国国家海洋和大气管理局(NOAA)

 国土安全部(特别是联邦紧急管理署和全美海岸警备队)

 全美鱼类和野生物种服务部

State and Local Authorities

 Coastal commissions

 Special waterfront agencies

 Port authorities

 Waterfront transportation authorities

 Planning departments and redevelopment agencies

 State or local public trust managers

州政府和地方当局

 海岸专门调查委员会

 特殊滨水管理机构

 港口当局

 港区交通主管部门

 规划部门和重建机构

 州或地方政府公共信托管理机构

MORPHOLOGICAL ANALYSIS

 To understand a waterfront, study its evolution. Consider the shoreline's various stages of development. Create a series of diagrams analyzing the historic and current conditions of the water edge, which will be critical in designing its future uses. In addition, understanding the sectional analysis of a coastline is important when planning a new use on the water and its connections to the built fabric of the city.

形态分析

 要了解一个滨水区,首先就要研究它的演变进程。要研究在各个不同的发展阶段,海岸线的各种变化。创建一系列的图表,用以分析对比该滨水区历史及当前的状况,这对该区域的未来规划十分重要。另外,对滨水区进行某种新的规划以及考虑它和城市建成区结构的关联时,分析了解海岸线的截面(形态),就显得异常重要了。

Natural Edge

 A natural edge diagram describes the undisturbed conditions of the shoreline's ecosystem and its often rich variety of species. Such natural conditions might be used as a benchmark for waterfront restoration.

自然边界

 一张自然边界示意图描绘的是滨海生态系统未经外界干扰时的状况,它通常都拥有高度的物种多样性。这样的自然状况往往可以用作滨水生态复原区建设的基准。

Productive Edge

 A diagram of the waterfront's historic productive uses can be helpful when planning new uses on the water. Maintaining productive waterfront uses is often a priority. Elsewhere, historic artifacts might be incorporated in a new design as cultural and perhaps functional features, such as old gantries, working piers, and cranes. Historic interpretation can be important for the new design by creating a strong identity of a place rooted in the region's past.

人工边界

 对滨水区进行新规划时,一张有关该区域生产历史的图表能够起到帮助作用。维持滨水区现有的生产正常进行常常是需要优先考虑的事。其他的一些历史文物则可以作为文化要素或功能特征融入新的设计中,比如那些老式铁路跨线桥、防洪堤、升降起重机。在新的设计中,对该地区的历史诠释举足轻重,因为这种诠释可以创造出一种扎根于地域历史的浓烈的地域特征。

Public Life: Placemaking on the Water

 Renewed interest in waterfronts has resulted in the conversion of major areas of industrial, shipping, and transportation uses to more public uses. Identify on a diagram potential economic anchors such as large civic or commercial buildings, which can attract more uses over time.

大众生活：滨水区的场所营造

人们重新关注滨水区使得它从单纯为工业、航运、运输服务转化为更多的大众服务。从滨水区结构图上找出那些具有经济发展潜能的区域，比如大片的民用或商业建筑区，这些区域随着时间的推移能有更多的用途。

ANALYSIS OF ENVIRONMENTAL AND ECOLOGICAL WATERFRONT CONDITIONS

Pollution and deterioration of the coastal environment often requires major investment in its restoration, considerably increasing a project's total cost. Pollution mitigation, remediation, stormwater management, stream and wetland restoration, and habitat protection are some of the basic aspects of waterfront restoration and development.

Environmental education is a key component in successful waterfront revitalization. Include design elements and signage that provide information about the historic uses of tile waterfront area and its current environmental status. Consider alliances that involve local citizens and institutions in long-term restoration efforts. Inform the local community about the health hazards of activities along the new waterfront, such as fishing and swimming, if there is potential for danger.

滨水环境和生态现状分析

因为滨水环境的污染与恶化，需要对其生态的复原予以大量的投资，这样一来，在很大程度上增加了项目的总投资。滨水区的复原与发展一般有以下几个基本内容：污染的减排与整治，雨水管理，溪流和湿地的生态复原以及生态栖息地的保护。

要成功复原滨水区，环境教育是一个关键因素。教育应当包含各种设计要素和各类标志，它们提供有关该滨水区历史上的利用及其目前的环境状况。应考虑将当地居民和政府公共机构长期有效地联合起来，共同致力于滨水区的复原。同时应告知当地公众在新建滨水区活动时要注意的事项，例如在捕鱼、游泳时可能存在的危险。

Ecology of the Water Edge

Investigate ecological conditions at the shoreline to determine the type of cleanup and tile subsequent appropriate ecological system when designing the waterfront. Often, this process can inspire the designer to incorporate ecological elements, both aquatic and terrestrial, into the new design, turning them into opportunities to educate and inform the public about the natural history of the shoreline.

滨水生态

在对滨水区进行设计时，需要研究水岸线的生态状况，用以确定该区域的清理模式和最合适的生态系统类型。通常，这一过程能够激发设计师将各种水体的和陆地的生态学要素融入新的设计中。这样又能让公众有机会了解该区域的自然历史。

Transportation and Connections

Abandoned or active rail lines, freeway structures, neglected culverts, chain-link fences, walls, or even private gates can be obstructions to accessing the waterfront. Take into account their presence and potential for relocation when redesigning new waterfront destinations.

运输和交通

废弃的或现行的铁路、高速公路、已经被忽视了的各类管道、链式围栏、墙体，甚至私人住宅的大门都可能成为滨水区通道上的障碍。在为滨水区做新规划时，需要考虑这些障碍物的存在及其潜在的搬迁处。

Land Use

Many kind uses can be found on the waterfront, depending on its economic and social function. Land uses can include industrial production, commercial development, transportation nodes, recreational uses, public infrastructure, institutional and educational structures, and new residential areas. Successful waterfront development will include several coexisting uses, providing urban vitality and activity at the water's edge.

土地使用

滨水区的土地由于其经济和社会作用有着各种各样

的用途。土地利用涵盖了工业生产、商业发展、交通集散、休憩旅游、公共基础设施配置、公共机构和教育机构,以及新的居住区。要成功地发展一个滨水区,就需使各种不同的土地利用模式能够完美地共存,这样才能为滨水区注入长久的生命力与活力。

Environmental Factors

Given the heavy industrial uses that occurred on the shorelines in the past, cleanup processes and programs play a fundamental role and are a key step in the redevelopment process of sites along the waterfronts. Soil analysis is a basic step in the challenging process of cleanup and restoration of a waterfront area. Cleanup costs can be substantial and can add to the total cost of a waterfront redevelopment project.

Because of contamination in the ground, in buildings and other structures, and possibly in groundwater or adjacent surface water, state and federal environmental agencies and financial institutions often require considerable remediation or cleanup before redevelopment can occur, or as part of the redevelopment process. Of particular concern are any anticipated changes to a structure's configuration. A brownfield, as defined by U.S. EPA, is a polluted property that in order to be redeveloped needs to undergo such cleanup process. Also, many jurisdictions prohibit additional fill or require mitigation measures to replace open water.

环境因素

如果某片滨水区曾经承载了过度的工业利用,其清理的过程将发挥基础性作用,同时也是滨水区生态复原过程中一个关键步骤。在滨水区的清理与生态复原过程中,土壤分析是基础性的一步。值得一提的是清理工作的耗费很大,会增加整个滨水区复原项目的总投资。

如果某滨水区土地、建筑、其他建筑物、地下水或者是相邻地表水已经受到污染,联邦和州环境组织以及财政机构会因此要求其在开发项目之前进行大规模的整治与清理,或者将此类清理作为再发展的一部分。他们会特别关注任何在外形结构上可以预见的变化。例如,"棕色土地"(根据全美环境保护组织的定义),就是一种被污染了的土地类型,为了生态复原,它就需要经历这种清理过程。同时,许多司法机构禁止另行的填充或要求采取(污染)减排等措施改善公共水域(的质量)。

WATERFRONT DESIGN PROCESS

Because of the often controversial and political nature of waterfront projects, their development is a complex process involving many different state and federal authorities as well as grassroots organizations and community stakeholders.

滨水区设计过程

由于滨水区的建设项目常常都极具争议性,并牵扯到政治因素,它们的发展是一个复杂的过程,不仅涉及各类基层组织和投资资金持有人,还涉及联邦和各州政府。

Community Involvement

Involve the community from the beginning in waterfront redevelopment projects. Educating and informing the community about the challenges ahead will create a strong foundation on which to draft a long-term vision for a new, inclusive waterfront. Environmental monitoring and education are effective tools to build a large community constituency, together with effective visioning tools such as community workshops and charrettes.

社会参与

在滨水区生态复原项目开始之初就应引入社会的参与。在项目开始之际就让社会公众了解将来可能会遇到的问题,这样就为一个大范围的滨水区开发新的长远规划打下了坚实基础。环境监测与教育是获得大批公众拥护者的有效手段,其他的有效的远景规划手段还包括社区讲习班和专家研讨会等。

Remediation Plan

A remediation plan is necessary when high toxicity levels are found on-site. The intensity and thoroughness of the cleanup process differs with the specific uses planned for the site: a residential area, for example, requires a much higher level of remediation than an area for a parking structure.

Conceptual Framework Design

When designing a waterfront, issues of scale play a major role. A framework plan often builds on previous studies and has the overall planning of the area as a main goal. A comprehensive framework plan allows flexibility and leaves room for future land-use decisions regarding the waterfront. This type of plan ensures a cohesive allocation of investments, connects the new sites to the rest of the urban or rural developments, and supports appropriate uses on the water.

Detailed Design

A detailed plan finds its place within a strong framework and usually focuses on the appropriate specific program for an area. A detailed plan for a waterfront calls for new and reinterpreted uses and creates new places and destinations through the implementation of solid design guidelines.

整治规划

一旦在滨水区检测到高毒性的污染，便需要立即采取整治措施。规划中，由于不同区域的预定使用功能，它们的清理过程的强度和完整性也随之而异。例如，一片用于居住的区域，其整治的强度就远远大于用于停车的区域。

概念规划

滨水区规划中，规模与尺度是一个关键问题。概念规划常建立在充分的前期调研之上，其主要目标是对该地区做出总体规划。一个综合性的概念规划必须具备一定的灵活性，它能为滨水区长远的土地利用预留出用地发展空间。此类规划能保证有一个持续连贯的投资部署，可使新地块与周边城市市域规划或乡村规划保持紧密联系，也使得整个滨水区处于最佳利用状态。

细部设计

细部设计是概念规划的组成部分，它通常注重于一块适当的特定区域的专项规划。滨水区的细部设计要求规划出新的功能，并根据严谨的总体规划方针创造出新的使用空间，达到规划目的。

WATERFRONT TYPES

Different waterfronts encourage different types of activities. River waterfronts promote activities enhancing connections across the two riverbanks: physical and visual connections are equally important in this kind of waterfront. Waterfronts by the ocean or the bay connect the urban fabric to activity nodes along the water and promote the use of piers for recreational activities. Finally, a body of water such as a lake or a reservoir promotes activities around the edge, invites points of activity along the shore, and is a great setting for water-related sports.

滨水区类型

不同的滨水区激发出不同类型的活动。沿河滨水带倾向那些能将河岸两边有机关联起来的活动行为。在此种类型的滨水区中，实体联系和视觉联系显得同样重要。滨海区和海湾地带就应将各种滨水活动与城市结构有效地联系起来，并且需要推广运用人工码头（即由岸上伸向海中的支架长堤）用于度假游人的娱乐活动。而那种沿湖或水库的滨水区则适合环水的活动行为，可沿湖岸设置活动点，此类滨水区还非常适合开展水上休闲运动。

WATERFRONT DESIGN COMPONENTS

Waterfront projects can have different scales, from a plaza to a greenway, and different character, from container port to wetland. Waterfront components can be a series of open-space elements, a system of connections to the inner core of the city, a new development on the water, or a strategy for sustainability.

滨水区设计的构成元素

滨水区建设项目有各种不同的规模，小型的如亲水广场，大型的如滨水绿道；也有各种不同的特性，有的是集装箱港口，有的则是生态湿地。滨水区设计的构成元素可以是一系列的开放空间要素，可以是一个与城区中心相连接的系统，也可以是全新的发展规划，或者是一个在现状基础上的可持续发展战略。

Design Strategies

Consider the following overall strategies for the design of a successful waterfront area.

Continuity: A continuous waterfront system for walking, jogging, biking, and rollerblading.

Sequence: A sequence of recurring open spaces at significant points along the water. Such places might have a special view or might be directly aligned with major city streets.

Variety: Multiple uses along the water create successful synergies and accommodate different users.

Connection: Visually and physically connect spaces along the waterfront and from the new waterfront to the bay (with views and piers) and to the city (through access points and pedestrian circulation links).

设计策略

一个成功的滨水区设计，应全面考虑下述的所有策略。

连贯性：要有一个连贯的滨水系统，用以步行、慢跑、骑车和轮滑。

有序性：沿水岸在重要地段有顺序地布置开放空间。这些开放空间一般会有标志性景观，或者与城市主要干道位于同一轴线上。

多样性：滨水区的多重使用能为其带来巨大的合作优势，能使各种不同的使用模式更加和谐共存。

关联性：通过各种有形的实体关系和无形的视觉关系将各种滨水空间联系起来。可以通过景点和码头将滨水区与海湾联系在一起，而那些易于通达的地段和环步道系统则可以成功地将滨水区与城市联系起来。

Design Elements

Open Space

Plazas: Waterfront plazas are often part of larger waterfront developments, such as commercial and recreational buildings along the water. They are often hard-surfaced areas with seating, shaded areas, and prime views of the water. In larger developments, plazas can be designed to allow for large recreational gathering structures such as amphitheaters or stage areas where local civic events can be held. They also offer great opportunity for displaying the historic memory of the waterfront through interpretive features or art installations.

Parks: Along the water, parks can be hardpaved areas or more natural soft areas. A new park can also be connected to a local ecosystem, such as a wetland, and to larger natural areas, such as greenways along the shoreline.

Piers: Piers can be interesting components in the redesign of waterfronts. They can reinterpret history, provide views, and promote recreation such as fishing. Incorporate safety elements such as lighting and railings, as well as sitting areas with benches to rest and enjoy the view. Focal elements such as art installations or small commercial buildings can be included at the end of a pier to make walking and strolling along its length a more exciting activity.

设计要素

开放空间

广场：滨水广场通常是大型滨水区如滨水的商用建筑和休憩性建筑的组成部分，它们一般拥有休息区、林荫区以及良好的观景视线。其地面多为人工铺地。在发展大型的滨水区时，广场往往会被设计成可以举办大型休闲聚会的场所，例如那种能够承办当地市民集会、庆典的圆形剧场或露天舞台。在广场上设置解说性建筑或艺术品可以向市民展示该滨水区的历史。

公园：滨水区公园可以是人工铺地也可以是较为自然的"软"地面，新建的公园不仅能够与原有的生态系统有效结合，如原有的生态湿地，也可以与诸如滨水绿道之类的大片自然地域相通。

人工码头❶：在重新设计滨水区时，人工码头是一个引人关注的要素。它们可用于重现历史、提供观景场所、促进垂钓等休闲活动。设计中在安排坐椅休息区以便游人休息和欣赏景色的同时，必须要考虑到诸如照明、栏杆等安全因素。在人工码头的尽头布置一些能够

---

❶ 也可翻成"栈桥"，这种人工码头或栈桥，在英国、美国、加拿大的海滨城市极为普及，其上是一个非常宽广的观光休息处。

引起游人注意的艺术品设施或小型商业建筑,则能使滨水漫步显得更加活泼有趣。

Connections

Paths: Biking and jogging are among the more iconic uses of a recreational waterfront. Water views and linear, often unobstructed, connections along the water make these activities especially pleasant. Design paths to accommodate these activities. Use smooth paving materials in areas for bikes, and ensure that path widths accommodate bikers and walkers alike, possibly with separate rights-of-way.

交通

人行道:骑车和慢跑是滨水休闲活动中最常见的。水景和沿途通畅的视线使得此类活动更加放松、愉悦,因此,需要为这类活动设计适宜的道路。在车行区采用平稳的铺路材质,并且确保道路宽度能够满足车行者与步行者的同时使用,尽可能做到人车分行。

Promenades: A promenade can connect spaces along the water or be a destination in itself, offering recreational opportunities for strollers, joggers, bikers, and in-line skaters. Depending on the specific character of the waterfront, promenades can be constructed and sophisticated urban places or natural and understated linear connections. Design elements such as paving materials or light fixtures can vary according to such character. Accommodate biking and jogging activities with materials that can withstand the effects of the moist microclimate.

观光长廊:观光长廊可连接不同的滨水空间,而其本身又为散步、慢跑、骑车、滑轮等休闲活动提供了场地。基于滨水区的不同特性,观光长廊可以建成优雅的规则式样也可以是自然朴实的非直线型构造。而铺砖材质、照明装置等设计要素因其特性要尽量多样化。活动区的设施、用材则必须能承受由潮湿性小气候所带来的不利影响。

Water connections for tourists: Tourism can be an economic engine driving the waterfront redevelopment process. Water taxis and ferries can be tourist attractions, as well as interpretive tools of an area's productive past.

Water connections as mode of transportation: When waterfronts are more developed and can support a high number of residential buildings, water connections can become an effective mode of transportation, making the link between residence and work place an easy and interesting transit alternative.

满足游人需要的水上交通:旅游业对滨水区的发展起到经济推动作用。水上游轮和渡船在默默述说滨水区过往历史的同时,也对游人具有很大的吸引力。

作为交通方式的水上交通:当滨水区发展得较为完善,能够承受建造一定数量的休憩性建筑时,此时水上交通就成为一种有效的交通方式。它的存在使得居住地与工作地之间的交通更为便捷,也为居民的出行交通提供了更多的选择。

Development

Working waterfronts: In the past, waterfronts were the exclusive realm of harbors, fishing fleets, shipbuilding, warehouses, and manufacturing plants. Changing technology made some of these uses obsolete, and rising land prices connected to the rediscovery of the water edge have endangered many local maritime enterprises. These enterprises can add to the local economy and to the city's character. Consider retaining and promoting existing maritime uses when possible, and integrate their needs with the overall plan of the new waterfront.

For large working ports, container handling, shoreline configuration, updated equipment, regional distribution networks, and environmental impacts are key planning issues. Planning efforts at many ports seek to designate safe and inviting locations for the public to view port activities.

开发

开发中的滨水区:过去,滨水区是海港、鱼湾、船厂、仓库、机械化工厂的专用区域。随着科技的飞速发展，上述的一些用途遭到废弃。滨水区的复兴带来的土地价格的飙升则危及许多本地滨水企业。而这些企业是当地的经济支柱也是其特色。规划时应尽可能地保留与促进滨水区原有的各种用途，并将它们的需求与滨水区的总体规划有效结合起来。

对于大型的港口，集装箱的管理、海岸线的结构处理、现代化的设备、区域性的配给网络以及对环境的影响都是规划需要考虑的关键问题。很多港口都致力于寻求安全、适宜的地理位置以吸引大众参与港口的各项活动。

Infill and adaptive use: Infill development can be a catalyst for change in forgotten areas of a waterfront. Adaptive use of historic buildings can be a powerful redevelopment strategy to create new destinations and to reinterpret the waterfront's past in new ways. Successful renovations can generate dynamic synergies that can boost local economies and provide a sense of place.

填充利用和适应性利用：在一些被忽视的滨水区域，填充式发展是寻求变革的催化剂。对历史性建筑的适应性利用是一种强有力的再发展战略，能发展新的用途，也可以从新的方面阐释滨水区的过去。成功的革新能够给该地区带来合作优势，既可以发展地区经济又可以保持地方特色。

Recreation and tourist destinations: The number of tourists it attracts is often the measure of a waterfront's success. Promote tourism in the early phases of waterfront redevelopment to encourage investment. Educational, recreational, and interpretive features and activities are often found in fire public areas of a waterfront, where visitors exploring the character of the region can readily appreciate a new identity anchored in the past.

休憩和旅游目的地：对游人吸引力的大小常常成为衡量滨水区建设成功与否的标准。在滨水区再发展过程的初期推广旅游活动可以吸引对滨水区建设的投资。在滨水区里随处可见的教育性、消费性以及标志性的建筑与设计促使游客在新的环境中感受古老文明的气息。

New mixed-use development: After the initial success of a waterfront redevelopment, larger developments often follow. All uses benefit from the prime location and the recreational opportunities a new waterfront offers. Some jurisdictions invite residential uses along the water, to bring density and vitality to the area. Be sensitive when locating residential uses at the edge, to ensure public access is maintained.

全新的综合发展：在滨水区的建设取得初步成功后，随之而来的是更大规模的再发展。新的滨水区会因其优越的地理位置和休闲项目的设置而为大众提供各种服务。为了赋予整个滨水区以新的生机与活力，某些管辖部门会沿水设置住宅区。对这些居住用地的规划要特别注意，从而确保滨水区对公众开放的通道畅通无阻。

Art: Public areas along waterfronts offer great opportunities for education and art appreciation. In particular, the rich social and cultural heritage of these sites encourages artists and a municipality to collaborate in often striking public art projects that foster a sense of place. Allow flexibility in waterfront plans to ensure that art interventions and programs can be incorporated.

艺术：滨水区的公众区域为大众提供了绝佳的教育和观赏机会。尤其是该地区丰富的艺术和文化遗产能鼓励艺术家和当地政府通力合作而创造出吸引大众的艺术作品，并形成当地的特色。滨水区规划要具备灵活性，能够确保艺术的融入。

Sustainability

Ecological preservation: Every waterfront is part of a watershed. Consider sensitive habitats and floodplains during the design process.

Ecological design: Natural conditions of waterbodies and the edge conditions are increasingly seen as opportunities to inspire design and suggest uses along the water. Many new developments incorporate ecological design principles as powerful elements of the design concept. Ideas such as wetland restoration, native vegetation preservation, and stormwater management have created a new design vocabulary in waterfront planning.

可持续性

生态保护:每一个滨水区都是水域的一部分。在设计过程中应考虑到敏感的物种栖息地和洪泛区。

生态设计:水体及其边界的生态状况日益受到重视,因为它们能激发滨水区新功能的设计。许多新的发展项目都将生态设计原则作为设计的关键要素,将其融入到整个设计之中。例如湿地复原、天然植被的保护、雨水管理等理念,都已成为滨水区规划中新的设计语汇。

4.3 街道设计标准和规则[1]

MAIN STREETS

Main Street is often thought of as the heart of the community, occupying an iconic position within the typical American small town. The form of a main street is typically a local commercial corridor along the main thoroughfare through town, with buildings organized in storefront blocks and parking on the street.

During the 1960s, as cities expanded outward, automobile use increased, and retail stores were reconfigured to depend almost exclusively on automobile access, main streets declined.

In the late-1970s, many older main streets began to reemerge as vital centers and, today, many communities across the United States have seen significant revitalization of their main streets In addition, many suburban communities that never had a traditional main street are seeking to create one by developing a new greenfield town center or redesigning a commercial strip.

主要街道

主要街道常常被看作社区的中心,它在传统的美国小城镇中占据了标志性的地位。主要街道的典型模式一般为,沿着城市的主干道布置一条商业走廊,走廊两边为店面式建筑,并配有街道停车区。

20世纪60年代,城市急剧向外扩张,汽车的使用大幅度增加,零售商店发生巨大变化,它们几乎全部布置在汽车通道的两侧,而不再位于主要街道上。这导致主要街道衰微。

70年代后期,许多历史悠久的主要街道再度作为城市重要中心而被重现。至今,全美许多社区的主要街道都已得到巨大的振兴。另外,那些从来都没有形成一条传统的主要街道的郊外社区,也正在寻求机遇,通过建立一个新的城镇中心绿地或重新设计现有的商业地段,为社区开创一条主要街道。

IMPORTANCE OF MAIN STREETS

A successful main street helps define a unique identity for a community within tile larger regional context, while providing opportunities for small businesses to become established. A walkable main street can also help decrease the number of single-purpose automobile trips.

主要街道的重要性

一条成功的主要街道有助于社区形成独特的个性,并且能为小型商业活动提供发展机遇。适于步行的主要街道同时有助于减少单功能车行道的数量。

MAIN STREET FEATURES

Main streets flourish when they provide a variety of goods and services, a pleasant community environment, and convenient access for their users. Design and physical appearance contribute directly to livability and economic success. Main street should be a visually stimulating area that encourages people to linger and explore. The following components should be addressed when designing a new main street or revitalizing an existing one:

- Building form
- Streetscape design
- Parking
- Traffic
- Pedestrians
- Bicycles
- Transit

---

[1] 资料来源:American Planning Association. Planning and Urban Design Standards. New Jersy: John Wiley & Sons, Inc., 2006.

主要街道特征

如果街道拥有多样化的商品及服务项目、社区环境优越、并且能为使用者提供便捷通道，那么主要街道就会繁荣发展起来。街道的设计及其外观会直接影响到社区的可居住性和经济效益。主要街道应当是一处视觉冲击力强的区域，能够刺激行人停留、游玩。在设计一条新的主要街道或者对现有街道进行重新规划时，下述的要素需要充分考虑：

- 建筑形式
- 街景设计
- 停车
- 交通
- 步行区
- 自行车
- 中转运送

Building Form

Along main streets, the impact of the built environment is influenced by several elements, such as storefronts, height and bulk, setbacks, door and window openings, and roof shape and profile.

建筑形式

在主要街道沿线，建筑环境的作用受到诸多因素的影响，例如店面、高度与体积、建筑后退部位、门窗以及屋顶形状和轮廓。

Storefront Buildings

Traditional storefront buildings, with large display windows on the ground floor and one or more stories above, are the basic units of main streets. Storefront buildings are designed to facilitate retail activity. Large expanses of glass in the ground-floor facade allow pedestrians to look into shops and see displayed merchandise.

The long, narrow shapes of storefront buildings make it possible to group a large number of shops on one block. In turn, these stores can display a wide variety of goods and services to shoppers as they walk down the street. Storage spaces in the rear of the buildings allow delivery of goods from alleys and secondary streets.

Storefront buildings were designed for commercial activity, and their physical shape and characteristics reinforce this purpose. The rhythm of storefront openings along the street creates a powerful visual image that consumers recognize and associate with commercial activity.

New buildings should be compatible with surrounding buildings and the entire block. The patterns of storefronts, upper facades, and cornices and their repetition from one building to the next along a street give the whole streetscape visual cohesiveness and generate a physical rhythm that provides orientation to pedestrians and motorists. Building improvements that take place on a main street should be compatible with the design characteristics of the overall streetscape, as well as with those of tile specific building.

店面式建筑

传统的店面式建筑的底层通常都配有大型展示性橱窗，这些都是主要街道的基本组成。店面式建筑能促进零售业的发展，底层外墙上安置大块的玻璃使得行人能够看清展示窗内的商品，并能透过橱窗了解商店内部的情况。

长且窄的店面式建筑能够将街区内大量的商店集结在一起。反过来，这些商店又能陈列大量的各式各样的商品，以供行人在路过时观摩。建筑后方的存储区域能满足货物在小径和次级街道之间的传递。

店面式建筑为商业活动而设计，而其外观形式和独特个性能够大力促进商业的发展。沿街店面的门窗形式能带来强有力的视觉冲击，使得消费者更全面地了解商业活动。

新建的建筑物应当与周围的建筑以及整个街区保持一致。店面、建筑外立面、檐口的形式以及沿街建筑群的重复性，都会影响到整个街区在视觉上的连贯性，并且能为步行者和驾车者指明方向。主要街道上的建筑的改进在满足特定功能的同时，应当与街景的整个风格保持一致。

Height and Bulk

The height of most buildings within a main street

should be relatively constant, although maintaining tile typical minimum height of two or three stories is more critical than establishing a maximum height. Building scale and proportions should also be consistent. Wide buildings should usually be divided into separate bays consistent with the prevailing storefront rhythm.

高度与体积

主要街道的多数建筑其高度是相对恒定的，尽管保持二至三层建筑的最低高度远远重要于限定其高度上限。建筑物的规模和比例也需要保持一致。较宽的建筑物应当分隔成与店面韵律模式相一致的独立开间。

Setback

Buildings should be flush with the sidewalk, except for small setbacks for entries, courtyards, or outdoor seating areas, to engage pedestrian activity and encourage drivers to slow down and watch for pedestrians and parking cars.

建筑外墙的后退

建筑应与人行道齐平，除了入口通道、庭院、户外休息区等后退区域。这些区域可以促进活动行为，帮助司机放慢行驶速度，有利于看清行人和车辆。

Door and Window Openings

Tile typical storefront has a high proportion of transparency from ground-level display windows and doors, and this should be maintained in newer buildings. The proportions of dot)r and window openings in traditional main street buildings tend to be relatively constant. Keep proportions and height of upper-floor window placement consistent with the existing pattern, to reinforce a strong horizontal relationship between upper-story, windows along the block.

门窗开口

一般店面的外观有很高的透明度，采用落地式以展示橱窗和大门，这种做法在新式建筑中应当予以保留。那些位于主要街道上的、传统式样的建筑，其门窗比例往往是相对恒定的。保持位于建筑物上层的窗子的比例与高度与现行模式相一致，增强各层窗子之间的横向联系。

Roof Shape or Profile

Roof profiles are usually consistent throughout the main street. Whether most buildings have the typical flat roofs, mansard roofs, or another shape, maintain consistent profiles.

Streetscape Design

There are numerous streetscape elements and design details that are desirable for main streets. These elements create a visually rich and inviting environment and provide visual cues and signals for motorists that they are entering it pedestrian-dominated district.

屋顶的形状或轮廓

同一条街道上的屋顶形状要保持一致。不管是最常见的平屋顶，还是坡屋顶，或者其他的屋顶形状，都要保持外形的一致性。

街景设计

大量的街景元素和设计细节可以应用在主要街道上。这些元素可以创造一个视觉丰富、吸引力强的景观环境，同时为驾车者提供视觉信号，提醒他们已经进入一个以行人为主的区域。

Street Trees

Street trees are effective visual signals. Along with the overall building density and scale, they can help define the main street district. As they mature, they create a canopy over the street, providing shade and aesthetic appeal.

Lighting

Lighting along the corridor should be geared toward pedestrians, to encourage main street activity into the evening hours. To have a significant effect on the appearance and sense of safety of the area at night, lampposts should be between 10 and 12 feet high. They can be installed in addition to, or in place of taller road-illuminating fixtures.

行道树

行道树是有效的视觉标志。它连同街道的整体建筑密度和规模一起，能帮助确定主要街道区域范围。在树木长成之后，他们巨大的树冠为行人提供树阴，带来美的享受。

照明

街道照明应重点布置在街道的步行区域，这样可以促进晚间的活动行为。将街灯柱的高度控制在10~12ft之间，可以在增强夜间步行区域的外观及安全感等方面起到有效作用。这些街灯柱可以是那些较高的道路照明灯具的附加物，或（干脆）替代那些照明灯具。

Wayfinding Systems

Wayfinding signs can be used to direct visitors to the main street from regional highways and assist them in navigating within the district and other parts of the community. Such signs also promote the area's identity and sense of place. Businesses can use this identification system for cooperative district advertising and event sponsorship.

Open Spaces

Public or semipublic spaces such as plazas and pocket parks are important main street elements. Relatively small areas adjacent to a sidewalk can bring life to the street and nearby businesses. Open spaces should be highly visible, adjacent to or bisected by the main stream of pedestrian flow; provide ample seating, shade, and weather protection; and offer a focal point, such as a fountain or gazebo.

Other Elements

Other visual signals that may be used in a main street area include hanging planters and window boxes. Space should be provided on sidewalks for display boards, benches, trash receptacles, drinking fountains, and bike racks.

指路系统

指路标志可以为旅行者提供帮助，指引他们从地域性的高速公路到达城市街道，并帮助他们在社区的各个区域顺利通行。这类标志可以增进该区域的识别度和场所感。商业组织也可以利用这些标志进行区域合作的广告活动和赛事赞助。

开放空间

诸如广场、小型公园之类的公共或半公共空间是街道的重要组成部分。一些毗邻人行道的小型活动区域也能为街道和附近的商业区注入活力。开放空间要具有较高的可见性，应当布置在人流密集的地方，这些开放空间可供行人休息、纳凉、避雨；而且它们通常都具有一个焦点景观，如喷泉、凉亭。

其他元素

其他可用于主要街道上的视觉要素还有悬挂的植栽和窗框。人行道需要为展示板、长椅、垃圾箱、喷泉以及自行车架的安置提供空间。

Parking

Main street parking must meet the needs of customers, merchants, employees, visitors, and residents. It should be regulated, to encourage turnover of customer spaces and to discourage abuse by long-term parkers, and it should be accessible to handicapped visitors.

There are many ways to create parking areas that meet these objectives without adversely impacting the character of the main street.

On-Street Parking

On-street parking spaces usually turn over most rapidly. Parking in these spaces is generally limited to two hours or less, as they are intended for use by customers making short trips. These spaces can be angled or parallel. The traffic movements involved in on-street parking help to calm traffic, while the parking itself creates the perception of a narrower street.

停车

街道停车必须满足顾客、商家、员工、游客和居民的需要。应对此类型停车加以管制，增快顾客停车空间的周转率，并且阻止长时间停车的不文明行为，同时停车区的设置应当便于残疾人使用。

许多途径可以在不对街道特性产生不利影响的前提下，为大家提供更多的停车区域。

路边停车

路边停车区的周转速度特别快。此区域的停车时间一般都在两小时以内,是为那些进行短时间活动的顾客所准备的。这些停车位有的与道路平行,有的则与道路成一定角度。尽管在路边停车本身会使得街道显得更加狭窄,但它仍然是一种缓解交通压力的有效手段。

Parking Lots

Parking lots tend to accommodate long-term parkers, such as employees, more effectively than on-street spaces. Shared parking in a convenient location can also create a "park once" environment for the visitor. Parking lots can be located behind the main street storefronts with alley access, on an adjacent block near the main street core, or, in the busiest locations, in satellite locations served by shuttles. In general, parking lots should not be located in the typical commercial strip configuration, between the street and a building's front door. Small parking lots between buildings may be acceptable if no alternatives exist, but should continue the street wall by means of an attractive fence, masonry wall, or hedge.

露天停车场

露天停车场可以为那些需要长时间停车的人提供便利,如上班族,其有效性高于路边停车区域。在交通便利的位置停车也能为游人创造一个高效率的停车环境。停车场可以布置在带有快速通道的商店的后面,也可以布置在与主要街道相毗邻的街区里,或者布置在有短程穿梭运输交通工具连接的交通极繁忙的"卫星城"地段。一般来说,停车场不能布置在街道与建筑物正门之间的商业地带。在没有其他更好的位置选择时,可以在建筑物之间的空地上布置小型停车场,但是要采用一些有吸引力的栅栏、石墙、灌木篱将街道连接起来,保持其连贯性。

Structured Parking

Structured parking may be publicly or privately owned and operated. Constructing a parking structure is significantly more expensive than surface parking spaces. In main street areas that have a parking shortage, however, constructing a parking structure in an unobtrusive location is often preferable to demolishing buildings to create new surface lots. Parking structures can be combined with "liner" store, fronts around their perimeter, and even with residential uses on upper floors.

车库式停车场

车库式停车场可以是公共设施,也可以是私人拥有并经营。车库式停车场的建造费用远高于地面停车场。在主要街道上,停车位总是非常紧缺,然而,在一个不唐突的位置建造车库式停车场,始终比拆毁现有建筑物然后在其上修建露天停车场更为科学更可取。车库式停车场可以与周边的商店有效结合起来,甚至停车场的顶楼还可以用于居住。

Traffic

Traffic is a critical element of a busy, vital main street, and should be managed so that it is an asset. This can be done through controlling the speed through the corridor and the nature of the trip.

Many urban main streets are designed to accommodate traffic at 25 mph, but many suburban main streets are on arterials designed for 45 mph traffic. Sometimes, the main street is also a state highway, carrying a heavy volume of regional traffic. The on-street parking and streetscape improvements mentioned above, as well as physical traffic-calming devices such as curb extension, can be used to slow traffic and improve pedestrian safety.

交通

对于人流量大的主要街道而言,交通是一个关键因素,应对其进行有效管理,使其成为一个利于街道发展的因素。可以通过控制车辆通行速度和限制活动类型等手段达到管理目的。

许多城市主要街道其规定的交通限速是25mile/h,但是,许多位于交通干线上的郊区主要街道所规定的交通限速则是45mile/h。在有些地方,主要街道也是州级的高速公路,它承载了高负荷的区域交通。在使用一些缓解交通压力的设备如拓展路缘的同时,也要充分利用路边停车的手段和街景改良措施,共同作用达到缓解交通、提高步行区的安全性的目的。

Pedestrian Connections

Sidewalks are a common element in older or urban main streets, but are lacking or appear only sporadically in many newer suburban districts. Sidewalks should always be provided, to define a pedestrian space where there is no threat from moving cars; they should ideally be at least 10 feet wide to provide room for intense pedestrian activity as well as streetscape elements.

Pedestrian connections among uses can be as important as the traditional sidewalk route along the street. Walkways from rear parking areas are important for pedestrian wayfinding and safety. In suburban settings where some buildings may be set back from the street, a secondary pedestrian system between parking lots and in front of buildings can improve pedestrian circulation.

步行区联系

无论是古老的、还是城市主要的街道，人行道都是一个必不可少的要素。但是在许多新建的郊区，只是零星地布置了少量的人行道，有些甚至就没有布置人行道。人行道是必须要设置的，它可以使步行区远离来往车辆的威胁。理想的人行道至少需要10ft宽，它在作为街景要素的同时，也为行人的活动提供了空间。

步行区的连接与传统的人行道路线安排同样重要。与停车区相通的步行道在指示道路和保障行人安全方面都起到重要的作用。在郊区，有些建筑物缩在街道的后面，此时在停车区和建筑正门之间设置次级步行道系统有助于改善步行区的流通状况。

Bicycles

Cyclists are often overlooked as potential customers. Provide bicycle parking and dedicated bike routes to make the main street safe and convenient for cyclists, thus encouraging people to mix errands and exercise and expanding the customer base.

Transit

Many main street areas are served by transit systems. Comfortable accommodations for transit riders, including seating, transit shelters, and signage for transit stops, will encourage them to linger and shop.

自行车

骑单车者往往是被忽略了的潜在客户。提供自行车停车区和自行车专用路线可以提高街道安全性，也使骑车者更为便利。鼓励人们将自己的工作和骑单车锻炼结合起来，这样还可以扩大顾客量。

中转

许多主要街道都布置了运输系统。为驾车者提供了包括座椅休息区、庇护物等在内的舒适区域，并为交通停靠处做出了醒目的标志，这些安排都刺激了驾车者较长时间的停留和购物。

PUBLIC/PRIVATE PARTNERSHIPS

When considering main street enhancements or improvements, public and private investments need to be linked. A key public investment often will attract additional private investment. Joint facilities, such as public parking lots, may allow private lots to be turned into buildings or open space. Street improvements, when combined with pedestrian improvements, can improve both traffic and pedestrian activity within the main street area. It is essential to involve all public and private partners when developing and maintaining a successful main street.

公共/私人合作关系

当考虑对街道进行改建时，需要将公共投资和私人投资有效结合起来，一个关键的公共投资常常吸引到更多额外的私人投资。例如，如果设置了公共停车场，那私人停车场就可以改建成建筑或开放空间。将街道的改进与步行区的改进有效结合起来，就可以同时改善街道区域内的交通和步行活动状况。一个街道的成功发展并长期维持，公共和私人投资的合作是至关重要的。

STREETSCAPE

Streetscape design in the broadest sense refers to the design of a street, including the roadbed, sidewalks, landscape planting, and character of the adjacent building facade or planted setback. Each of these individual parts is important in successful streetscape design. Information on streets and street design is included in Part 3 of this book; this section focuses primarily on the pedestrian realm of the sidewalk.

Memorable sidewalks and streets that are oriented toward the pedestrian experience characterize excellence in streetscape design. Special attention to streetscape with a consistent focus on implementation can establish a new and welcoming character for a whole city or neighborhood.

Several individual elements can be used to shape the character of sidewalks and overall street elements, including street furniture, landscape planting, lighting, and other amenities. Successful streetscape design balances the desire for pedestrian amenities, such as benches and street trees, with an understanding of the functional aspects of streets and sidewalks.

Planners, designers, and developers can design and implement Streetscapes at a variety of scales:

- The sidewalk in front of an individual property
- Individual streets
- Larger street networks in neighborhoods and districts
- Entire communities and municipalities

街景

从广义上说，街景设计指的是街道设计，包括路床、人行道、景观植栽以及相邻建筑立面的特征或种植平台的特征。在成功的街景设计中，上述各个独立部分都是非常重要的。关于街道和街道设计的内容在本书第3部分中；本章节主要介绍人行道的步行区。

那些让人们印象深刻的人行道和街道在街景设计方面都十分出色。对于街景营建的持续关注能够为整个城市及其相邻区域创造出全新的、大受欢迎的特征。

一些独立的要素能够用于塑造人行道的特征乃至主要的街景，这包括街道设施、景观植栽、照明以及其他各种设备。成功的街景设计在充分考虑街道和人行道的各种功能的情况下，合理地协调了行人对各类设施的需求，如坐椅、行道树等。

规划师、设计师以及开发商应能够对各种不同规模的街景进行设计与营建：

- 私有房产前面的人行道
- 独立的街道
- 邻里和街区内的大型街道网络
- 整个社区和城市

SIDEWALK ZONES AND DIMENSIONS

An important characteristic of sidewalks is the pedestrian "path of travel". A typical sidewalk has three zones: the building zone, the path of travel, and the curb zone. Successful streetscape designs accommodate a clear path of travel, typically in the center of the sidewalk. The curb zone, on the outer edge of the sidewalk, is typically the location of streetscape amenities.

All sidewalks should comply with the Americans with Disabilities Act (ADA) requirements to accommodate a clear path of travel. When including streetscape amenities, such as street furniture or landscape planting, provide increased sidewalk width in addition to the path of travel. For example, sidewalks with street trees typically require a 10-foot-wide sidewalk, to accommodate a six-foot pedestrian path and the four-foot-wide tree bed.

人行道区域及其尺度

人行道的一个显著特征就是其步行区域——"步行道"。典型的人行道由3个区域组成：建筑区域、步行道、路缘区。成功的街景设计必须拥有一条清晰完整的步行道，它基本上都位于人行道的中央。路缘区位于人行道的外围边缘，大体说来，各种街道设施都布置于此。

所有的人行道设置都须遵守《全美残疾人公约》所提出的必须具备一条清晰完整的步行道的要求。当街道内含有各类设施如街道装饰品或景观植栽时，除步行道外，还必须增加人行道的宽度。举例来说，栽有行道树的人行道一般为10ft宽，其中分为6ft宽的步行道和4ft宽的植栽区。

PEDESTRIAN LEVELS OF SERVICE

Similar to traffic levels of service on roads and freeways, pedestrian levels of service (LOS) classifications exist for sidewalks. These range from A (completely unimpeded movement) to F (complete congestion). The LOS calculation is based on average sidewalk width and the total volume of pedestrians in a given period of time. Wide sidewalks in conjunction with a high pedestrian LOS can seem empty and uninviting; narrow sidewalks with several streetscape elements can result in both physical and visual clutter and a low pedestrian LOS.

Identify the current pedestrian level of service and the level the community, would like as a basis for determining the amount of pedestrian amenities that can be accommodated comfortably on any given sidewalk.

LOCATION OF STREETSCAPE AMENITIES

The majority of public streetscape amenities are located in the curb zone of the sidewalk, often clustered at intersections. In some communities, the sidewalk is enlarged at the intersection, referred to as a "bulb-out." Bulb-outs can accommodate more streetscape elements, such as trees and benches, and can serve as a traffic-calming measure.

步行服务等级

类似于城市干道和高速公路有不同的服务等级一样，人行道也有不同的步行服务等级，从A级（可以完全无障碍地行进）划分到F级（极易引起堵塞）。人行道的平均宽度和一定时间段内的行人容量是确定人行道服务等级的基础。一条较宽的、又同时具备较高服务等级的人行道看上去显得空旷，其吸引力就低；而拥有一系列街景要素且又较窄的人行道就会引起行人心理和生理上双重的喧闹感，这样的人行道其服务等级也相应较低。

确定当前的人行道服务等级和社区等级是确定步行道上设施数量的基础，只有这样才能确保人行道的舒适度。

街景设施的位置

大多数的街景设施都位于人行道的路缘区，且常常大量布置于道路交叉口处。在一些社区，道路交叉口处的人行道会被扩大，就如一个弧状的"球茎凸出"处，这里往往拥有更多的街景要素，如树木、坐椅，并且是一种舒缓交通的手段。

STANDARDS AND REGULATIONS

Streetscape design and implementation is regulated at the local level. Specific requirements and regulations likely will vary for each community. Consult local regulations before planning streetscape improvements or modifications. Consult applicable local codes and ordinances for appropriate plant material and buffer guidelines, which are often contained within landscape regulations.

Typically, within each community there are multiple agencies that govern specific aspects of streetscape design and implementation. These agencies can include planning departments for planning and design; public works departments for utilities, road maintenance, and dimensions requirements; park and recreation departments or forestry departments for recommended street trees and plantings; and economic development agencies for working with the owners of private properties to control tile location of private street furniture and displays.

On the federal level, the ADA requirements with regard to streetscapes focus on the width of a clear path of travel on sidewalks, to allow two wheelchairs to pass each other unimpeded, and the slope and location of special curb treatments.

标准和条例

街景的设计与营建受到当地情况的控制。不同的社区有各自特殊的需求和规定。在制定街景的改良方案或修正方案前需要了解并考虑当地的各类条例。在选择适当的种植材料及确定种植方针时，要考虑当地各类景观条例中可适用的规则与条例。

一般来说，在每个社区中都有多重机构分管街景的设计与营建过程中的特定方面。这些机构中有负责规划设计的部门；负责公用设施、道路维护以及尺度需求的部门；公园和旅游地管理部门或负责培育行道树和其他植物的森林部门；以及与私有资产持有者共同协作以控制街道范围内私有物品的摆放与展示的经济发展部门。

从联邦政府层面上，《全美残疾人公约》对于街道的要求主要是关于人行道内清晰完整的步行道的宽度（必须确保两个轮椅能毫无障碍地并排通过），以及道路的倾斜度和特殊路缘物的位置。

STREETSCAPE ELEMENTS

The following section provides an overview of five key categories of streetscape elements:

- Paving
- Landscape planting
- Street lighting
- Street furniture
- Public facilities and private streetscape amenities

This section provides a brief introduction to each element, its typical placement on sidewalks, and the available types of design and construction. Specific street furniture design and vendors can be found in trade publications and on the Internet.

街景要素

下述的部分提供了关于街景要素的5个关键类型的概述：

- 铺地
- 景观植栽
- 街道照明
- 城市街具
- 公共设施和私人街景设施

这一部分为每个要素做出了简洁的介绍，重点是关于人行道的位置以及设计和营建的类型。有关特殊的街道装饰物设计及其销售商的资料均能在各种贸易类出版物和互联网上找到。

Paving

Paving material is perhaps the most visually prominent streetscape element. Choice of paving material often depends on the scale of the sidewalk, the overall character and design intent of the street, and local climate conditions. For cities in colder weather climates, use more durable materials that allow for expansion and contraction in extreme temperatures and that can withstand the use of salt and other melting agents. For locations that receive higher levels of rainfall throughout the year, use materials with more surface texture, as they will provide greater traction. In some extreme cold weather climates, communities have added electric heating coils embedded beneath the paving to melt snow and ice. Long-term maintenance and replacement should be considered throughout the design process.

铺地

铺地材质可能是视觉上最突出的街景要素。决定如何选择铺地材质的因素有：人行道的规模、街道的整体特征与设计意图以及当地的气候状况。在那些气候较寒冷的城市需选用更为耐用的材质，以适应在极端温度条件下，材质可能会出现的膨胀和收缩，并且还必须能承受住路面上使用工业盐或其他的融雪物质。而在那些全年都有大雨量降水的城市，就需使用纹理更明显的材质，它能提供较大的摩擦力，防止行人滑倒。在气候极端寒冷的地方，需要在铺地下方埋置电热线圈，用以融化冰雪。另外在设计过程中需考虑到铺地的长期维护与更新。

The most common and economical choice of material is scored concrete. Dyes can be added to concrete to add color and character to the pavement and retain its cost and maintenance benefits. Stone or brick pavers are a more expensive paving material, hence are often reserved for more ceremonial or special streets, such as a main street. Some harder stones, such as granite, which can hold up under the pressures of everyday use of the sidewalks, can be used as curbs. Because special paving materials are often more expensive, economical solutions can be derived by combining concrete and special pavers in a variety of interesting patterns along the sidewalk.

Special paving can also be used in crosswalks or entire intersections as a design element or a traffic-calming measure. Colored concrete or pavers in a crosswalk provide a visual clue to changes in the character of the street, and raised crosswalks make drivers more cognizant of driving through a pedestrian zone.

最常见、也是最经济的铺地材质就是混凝土。给铺地着色能够丰富其色彩，使其带有鲜明的特点，且能保持其价值。石料或砖料是较为昂贵的铺地材质，所以它们常常被用于那些更为正式以及特殊的街道，如主街。而一些如花岗岩之类的更为坚硬的石料，由于它们能够承受住每日使用所带来的巨大受压力，所以可将其用作路缘石。另外，由于特殊的铺地材质都较为昂贵，经济的使用方法就是在人行道上采用各种模式将混凝土和其他材质混合使用。

特殊的铺地材质可作为设计要素或降低交通流量的措施应用于人行横道处或道路交叉口处。在人行横道处使用有颜色的混凝土或其他材质能够给行人以醒目的提示，告知他们道路已经发生变化，同时使得司机在通过步行区时提高注意力。

Landscape Planting

Street trees and other plant material add four-season color, visual interest, and living and ever-changing texture to a streetscape. Landscape planting can soften the hard surfaces of sidewalks and help improve air quality. Unlike most streetscape elements, street trees and plantings change over time, require continual maintenance, and can cause problems such as roots cracking sidewalks and leaves clogging sewer grates. Even with the potential problems, street landscape planting is often a first choice for many communities when seeking to improve street character. This section describes a variety of street planting types, general planting and location guidelines, and a few roles of thumb to consider when selecting and installing landscape planting along streets.

景观植栽

行道树及其他植物给街道带来了四季色彩，给人们以视觉上的享受，使得街景更为活泼、富于变化。景观植栽能够弱化人行道给人的僵硬感，并且改善空气质量。与其他街景要素不同的是，行道树和其他植物会随着时间而不断变化，并且还会带来一系列的问题，比如导致路面开裂，大量落叶堵塞住下水道的格栅等等，因此它们需要持续不间断的养护。尽管存在许多潜在的问题，许多社区在大力寻求如何改变街道特征的时候，景观植栽仍是首选。这一部分描述了各种种植类型、大众化种植、栽种位置指南以及在选择和栽种植物时需遵循的一系列规则要点。

Street Trees

The most visually prominent of all street planting is the street tree. Street tree selection should include consideration of numerous factors, including the community's recommended tree list, its overall aesthetic desire, climatic concerns, potential for disease and pests, maintenance requirements, the space available for root growth, and the size of a mature tree crown and canopy.

The total volume of soil in which trees are planted will affect the size of the mature tree. Greater room for roots to grow allows for larger trees with more expansive tree canopies.

Residential Streets

Street trees on residential streets are typically located in a planted strip between the sidewalk and the curb. When selecting a tree species, consider the size of the individual mature tree canopy and root system, so that trees will not compete for light and nutrients.

行道树

所有街道植物中最突出的就是行道树。行道树的选择必须考虑多种因素，这包括社区推荐的树种名目、整体的审美需求、当地气候条件、潜在的疾病和虫害、管理维护的需求、可供树木生长的空间大小、成熟树木的树冠尺寸等等。

树木栽植处的土壤状况将会影响到成熟树木的尺寸。若为树根提供更大的生长空间，其成熟树木的冠幅就会越大。

居住区街道

居住区街道上的行道树一般种植在人行道与路缘区

之间的带状种植池内。选择树种时需考虑成熟树木的树冠尺寸和其根部生长状况，以免树木之间相互争夺阳光和营养。

Commercial Streets

Street trees on more commercial streets are often in containers or in linear planting strips in the sidewalk. The tree species selected may depend on the desires of adjacent business and property owners, because they are often concerned about trees blocking their storefront windows. Smaller, more ornamental trees or trees with higher or lighter canopies are often chosen for commercial streets.

On many commercial streets, especially in more recent developments, street trees often compete with underground utilities for space, which can limit the number and location of trees. Wider commercial sidewalks often provide enough room to accommodate both underground utilities in the pedestrian path of travel and street trees in the curb zone. Narrower commercial sidewalks can be more limited in their capability to do so.

商业街

商业街上的行道树通常栽植在树池内或呈线性种植在人行道上。树种的选择主要由商业街上的商店和私有财产的持有者决定，因为他们会比较在意这些树木是否会遮挡住店面的橱窗。商业街上一般采用那些体型较小且带有装饰性的树木或者那些树冠较高的树木作为行道树。

在大多数商业街，尤其是近期发展起来的商业街，其上的行道树常常要与地下设施争夺生存空间，使得树木生长的位置和数量受到限制。较宽的商业街一般都能提供充足的空间而同时满足步行道的地下设施和路缘区的行道树对空间的需求。而较窄的商业街在这方面就会有诸多的限制。

Trees in Medians

On commercial and larger residential streets, trees can be planted in medians, either in the center of the street or in the area separating through-lanes from local traffic and parking lanes, which are found on many boulevards. Medians typically need to be at least 6 to 10 feet wide (excluding the curb dimension), depending upon local regulations, to accommodate a mature street tree. Medians wider than 10 feet can also include strips of special paving along the curb, to provide maintenance access. Also of note are median planting programs that install ornamental plantings and perennial garden planting, which require yearly maintenance.

中心带的树木

在商业街和大型的居住区街道上，树木能栽植在中心带。它们既可以栽植在街道的中心带，又可以栽植在交通停车区与步行通道区的隔离地带。许多城市干道上都能见到这种做法。一般说，中心带至少应具备6～10ft的宽度（不包括路缘的宽度），根据当地的标准，可以在其上栽植成熟的行道树。宽度超过10ft的中心带可以沿路缘配置一条特殊的铺地带，作为专用维护通道。另外值得注意的是，中心带的种植工程包括栽植装饰性植物和四季常绿的植物，需要长年的维护。

Distance Standards

Most communities have established standards for the distance between street trees and intersections, alleys, and curb-cuts, to avoid obstructing the view of cross traffic and pedestrians waiting at the corners. Check with the governing agency (typically the city or state department of transportation) to determine local requirements. Many communities seek a 25- to 30-foot distance between street trees on urban residential or mixed-use streets.

距离标准

大多数社区都制定了相关标准，用以规定行道树与道路交叉口、巷口、路缘的距离，避免行道树遮挡住交通视线以及在转角处等待通过的行人的视线。需要与当地政府部门（一般是城市或州交通管理部门）相协商，以确定当地的要求。许多社区在城市居住区街道和具有多重使用功能的街道上采用25～30ft的树间距。

Tree Crown

On streets with buildings located adjacent to the

property line, regardless of the type of land use, when selecting the tree species to plant, consider the mature shape of the tree crown, to prevent the tree canopy from growing into tile building wall and potentially requiring severe pruning over time.

Tree Base Covers

When trees are located within the sidewalk, the base of the tree is typically covered by some form of water-permeable materials, which can range from metal tree grates to stone or brick pavers, decomposed granite, or other crushed stones. The selected covering should be stable enough for pedestrians to walk on it. In some cases, metal tree grates can be acceptable for use within the ADA-accessible path of travel. Most types of tree base covering are designed to allow for the continual growth of the tree trunk. Brick or stone pavers can often be removed; some metal tree grates include radial links that can also be removed; and materials such as decomposed granite can be moved aside as the tree trunk grows.

树冠

在建筑毗邻土地边线的街道上，无论该土地是何种使用类型，在选择树种时都必须考虑成熟的树冠形状与大小。以避免成熟的树冠伸入建筑外墙内而需要花费大量人力物力进行修剪。

树基覆盖物

栽植在人行道上的树木，树的基部通常都会覆盖各种形式的可渗水的材料，可以是金属格栅、石质或砖质的铺地，或者是风化了的花岗岩，又或者是碎石。所选用的覆盖物必须坚固到足以供行人在其上行走。在遵循《全美残疾人公约》关于步行道要求的前提下，许多地方广泛使用金属格栅作为覆盖物。各种树基覆盖物的设计都必须充分考虑树体的持续生长。石质或砖质的铺地材料是可以移动的；一些呈放射状布置的金属格栅也可以移动；而一些像风化了的花岗岩之类的材料也会随着树木的生长而移动。

Tree Guards

Most street trees are fairly small when planted and require wooden stakes or more elaborate metal tree guards to help support and or protect them as they become established. Wooden stakes are a temporary solution; metal tree guards are more permanent and should be sized to accommodate the diameter of the mature tree trunk to avoid hindering the growth of the tree.

树的保护

大多数的行道树都是在它们还很小的时候就栽植在道路边，这就需要用木质的树桩或特制的金属护架帮助它们固定，直至树木足够强壮。木质的树桩是暂时的解决方式，金属护架则能持久使用。但金属护架必须能够根据树木的大小调整自身的尺寸，从而避免护架阻碍树木的生长。

Small-Scale Landscape Planting

Other landscape elements of the streetscape include planted beds in the ground or raised planters, hanging planters attached to light fixtures or buildings, and plantings in medians. Any landscape planting within the sidewalk needs to allow a clear path of pedestrian travel, and as such is typically found in the curb zone or in private planters within the building zone, if the width of the sidewalk permits.

Medians between 2 and 6 feet wide, excluding curb dimensions, can easily accommodate small-scale planting, such as grasses and bushes.

Borrowed Landscapes

Though not located within the public right-of way, planting on adjacent private property often plays an integral role in the overall landscape character of a street. These landscape elements are referred to as "borrowed" landscapes. Take into account the type, scale, and location of private landscape planting when designing an overall street planting plan.

In addition, private landscape planting can provide a visual buffer and natural transition between a street and adjacent land uses, or between different land uses. Also, depending on plant types and density, they may provide physical barriers and noise reduction from street traffic.

小型景观植栽

其他植物景观要素还包括地面上的植床或被垫高了的种植带、与照明装置或建筑物相结合的悬挂性植坛，以及道路中心带上的植物。人行道范围内的所有植栽都不能阻碍步行区内的步行道。如果人行道的宽度允许，植物一般栽植在路缘区，或者在建筑区域的私人领地内。

中心带的宽度一般在 2～6ft 之间（不包括路缘），所以它非常适合进行小型的景观种植，如栽植草坪和灌木。

借景

树木即使不种植在公共区域，而只是栽植在与公共区域毗邻的私人领地内，它仍然在形成街景总体风格的过程中扮演了重要角色。这些景观要素就类似于"借景"。在制定街道的种植规划时，需要充分考虑私人植栽的类型、规模和位置。

另外，私人植栽可以在街道和相邻土地之间或者利用类型不同的土地之间为行人提供视觉上的缓冲，并使得两者的过渡更为自然。同时，根据植栽的类型和功能，它们可以起到有形隔离、降低噪声的功用。

Preparation and Planting

Time the implementation of planting and landscape plans so that landscape materials are planted in the appropriate season for the species. In general, transplanting is not recommended during tine summer and winter months, unless climate conditions allow.

Prepare the soil or planting bed for the specific type of plant material. If more than one type of plant material is to be installed, address proper planting conditions for all plants. Many newer streets also include irrigation systems planned as an integral part of the streetscape, to facilitate ongoing watering.

If required, topsoil in planters and in the ground can be improved through special soil and fertilizer mixtures to provide optimum growing conditions for the specific plant species. Minimum soil depth in a planter varies with the plant type: for large trees, the soil should be 36 inches deep, or 6 inches deeper than the root ball; for small trees, 30 inches deep; for shrubs, 24 inches deep; and for lawns, 12 inches deep (10 inches if irrigated).

准备和种植

为植物的栽植制定合理的时间，从而确保各种种植材料都能在其最佳种植时节栽种。除非气候条件允许，一般不提倡在夏季和冬季进行树木移植。

为特定类型的植物准备相应的土壤或植床。如果要混合栽植多种类型的植物，就需要为所有植物都提供合适的种植环境。许多新建的街道已经将灌溉系统作为街景营造的一个重要组成部分，这样使得灌溉更为便利。

如果需要，植床和种植地的最上层土壤可以采用特殊的土壤和肥料的混合物，为树木提供最佳生长条件。植床的最小土壤厚度视树种类型而各有要求：大树至少需要 36in 厚的土壤，或者比树木的球根处深 6in；小树需要 30in 厚的土壤；灌木需要 24in；草坪只需 12in（灌溉条件下为 10in）。

Choose plant species carefully. Consider the ultimate maturity of the plant species when determining the size of the plant bed or planter. Different species require different volumes of soil to reach maturity. Sources for determining the appropriate species for the volume of soil available to support landscaping on the street include the community's arborist, landscape maintenance staff, the parks department, or private nurseries.

As mentioned above, avoid underground utilities, if possible. If utilities are located where root interference may be an issue, especially for street trees, implement special planting procedures or root barriers that control root growth.

谨慎地选择植物种类。在确定植床或种植带的尺寸时，必须充分考虑到该树种成熟时期的最大尺寸。不同的树种需要不同尺寸的土壤才能达到完全成熟。决定街道上的树木正常生长所需的最佳土壤尺寸的人士或部门包括：社区的树木栽培专家、景观维护人员、公园管理部门、私人苗圃等。

如前所述，要尽可能地避免树木接触到地下设施。如果地下设施位于植物根系极可能会蔓延到的地方，就必须采用特殊种植方法或者安放根系阻碍物来控制根系的蔓延与生长。

Planter materials such as wood or concrete can affect soil temperatures in planters, so they should be considered when specifying appropriate planting species. Cold or heat can cause severe root damage in certain plant species. Proper drainage helps alleviate this condition. Irrigation, mulches, and moisture-holding soil help reduce moisture loss from the wind and sun. Most planters do not require insulation, but in colder climates, planters with small soil volumes located over heated structures may require insulation. Consult local sources for a list of cold-hardy plants, and select planter materials that best suit local conditions.

种植容器的材料（如木头或混凝土）会影响到容器内土壤的温度，所以在选择植物种类时必须充分考虑这一点。对于某些树种而言，冷或热都会导致严重的根系损害。适当排水能缓解这种情况。灌溉、覆盖植物根部、使用能保持水分的土壤都能帮助减少由阳光和强风造成的水分流失。多数种植容器不要求有保温隔热功能，但是在比较寒冷的气候里，容积较小的种植容器就需要能够保温。了解当地有哪些耐寒的植物，选择最适合当地气候的材料做种植容器。

Street Lighting

Exterior street lighting provides general illumination for safety and wayfinding proposes for both pedestrians and motorists. Lighting is used to illuminate buildings, landscapes, roadways, parking areas, signs, and other outdoor areas, as well as advertising in certain instances. In addition to being a practical consideration, the choice of light fixtures, type of lighting source, and illumination patterns are also design elements.

街道照明

街道的照明设备为步行者和驾车者起到安全警示和道路指示的作用。灯光照亮了建筑、景观、道路、公园、标识物以及其他的户外区域。在一些情况下，灯光还起到广告的作用。除了实用的考虑，灯具支架的选择、光源类型、照明模式等都是设计的要素。

Illumination Levels

Most communities have requirements for minimum levels of illumination on their streets. Lighting should be designed to attain the recommended light level, distribution, and glare control, and should also address the aesthetic impact of the illumination.

Illumination levels are measured in footcandles (lumens per square foot) and lux (lumens per square meter). A footcandle is the unit of illumination lighting a surface, all points of which are 1 foot from a uniform light source, equivalent to one candle in brightness or illumination. Recommended illumination levels may be found in the Illumination Engineering Society of North America (IESNA) Lighting Handbook and other IESNA publications.

Most street-lighting manufacturers can provide photometric studies to determine the resulting illumination levels for specific designs and applications. Computerized point-by-point calculations are recommended for more accurate results.

Luminaires or lamps for street and parking lot lighting are categorized according to the lighting patterns they create on the ground, ranging from Type I to V. While many communities have requirements for roadway illumination levels, fewer communities have requirements for sidewalks and other pedestrian areas. A general rule of thumb for sidewalks and bikeways is 0.2 footcandles in residential areas, 1.0 footcandles in commercial areas, and 5.0 footcandles near building entrances.

照明等级

关于街道的最低照明等级，大多数社区都有各自的要求。照明设计必须符合关于照明等级、光源分布以及强光控制的要求，同时还要使得照明更具美感。

照明等级由尺烛光（每平方英尺的流明）和米烛光

（每平方米的流明）来量度。尺烛光可解释为：约等于一根标准蜡烛烛光亮度的点光源，在距其1ft距离的地方，1ft^{2}面积所接受的光照为1"尺烛光"（fc）。推荐的照明等级在北美照明工程协会（IESNA）的《照明手册》和其他IESNA的出版物上均有记载。

绝大多数照明设备制造商都能提供光度测定报告，用以确定在某个设计和应用中最终需要的照明等级。如果需要更精确的测定结果，我们推荐采用计算机进行点对点的计算。

用于街道和停车场照明的泛光灯或照明灯需要根据它们自身的照明模式进行分类，可以从Ⅰ型划分到Ⅴ型。尽管大多数社区对车道的照明等级有相关要求，然而只有极少数社区对人行道和其他步行区也有照明要求。根据经验，一般居住区内、商业区内、靠近建筑入口处的人行道和自行车道的光通量分别是0.2fc、1.0fc、5.0fc。

Location of Streetlights

Streetlights are typically located in the curb zone of the sidewalk. Spacing of streetlights should be uniform, with the distance depending on the minimum illumination levels required. Regular spacing is often broken by curb-cuts along the street, so the placement of light fixtures requires some level of flexibility. If the sidewalk includes street trees, locate streetlights between the trees so that the tree canopy does not interfere with illumination coverage. Average distance of shade trees from streetlights is 40 feet on center and 15 feet on center for smaller ornamental trees. Pedestrian lighting fixtures may be required to supplement the street lighting or in plazas and parks. Additional lighting for security purposes is often located near building entrances and in parking garages. Require such lighting to be placed to control glare.

街灯的布置

街灯通常布置在人行道的路缘区。根据所需最低照明等级的相关要求，街灯的间隔必须是统一的。但是固定的间隔常常会被路缘打断，所以灯具支架的位置安排需要一定程度的灵活性。如果人行道上栽有行道树，街灯就会位于树与树之间，此时必须保证树冠不影响街灯的照明范围。一般而言，大树中心处距街灯的距离是40ft，装饰性小树距街灯的距离是15ft。有时，也在步行区安置照明灯用来辅助街灯或公园和广场的照明。出于安全目的而增设的照明设备一般布置在建筑入口处和停车场服务区，此种类型的灯光布置必须对光的强度加以控制。

Streetlight Types

There are three broad classes of lights on streets: those that illuminate the roadway, those that light the sidewalk and the pedestrian realm, and other ancillary light fixtures such as bollards and fixtures mounted on the facades of buildings and security lighting. Standard roadway lights, often called cobraheads, are usually mounted to a mast arm and suspended over the roadway at heights of 25 to 40 feet. Cobrahead lights are typically mounted on simple aluminum poles and are frequently used on highways and other major traffic thoroughfares. They may not always control glare.

On more important or intimate streets, many communities opt for more ornamental street poles and lighting fixtures, often with a particular theme or design that the community has selected. These lights fixtures are usually mounted on ornate poles less than 25 feet high. Many of these types of light fixtures also include the option of a pedestrian-scale light fixture, usually mounted around 12 to 15 feet above the sidewalk. Note that with light fixtures mounted at this level, it is difficult to control glare and achieve proper illumination levels. Light fixtures often inclnde an option for brackets (either single- or double-sided) to attach banners and other temporary graphic elements between the pedestrian fixture and the street-level fixture.

Private street lighting comes in a variety of shapes and sizes and is typically mounted to the facade of the building or located on smaller-scale poles in private landscape planted buffers，

街灯类型

街灯可分为三大类：一种是对车道进行照明的街灯；第二种是对人行道和步行区域进行照明的街灯；第三种是辅助性的照明街灯，如护栏上的灯具、建筑外立面上装饰性的灯具以及安全照明灯具。标准的街道照明灯，也常常被称为"蛇头灯"。它通常有一个杆臂立于车道上，高度在25～40ft之间，蛇头灯被安置在铝制灯杆上。这种灯常被用在高速公路及其他交通干道上，它们不需要控制光强。

对于较为重要或私密性较强的街道，许多社区会选择更富于美感的灯杆和照明装置，并往往带有该社区所选定的特定主题或设计风格。这些灯具通常安装在低于25ft的华丽的灯杆上。灯具支架的类型中也包括步行区的灯具支架，它们位于人行道上，高度在12～15ft之间。需要指出的是，这种高度上的灯具，往往很难控制光强，难以达到最佳照明等级。灯具支架也有单边或双边的选择，在特定情况下，可以在步行区的灯具支架与街道的灯具支架之间系上彩旗结合其他的临时性装饰物。

私有街道的照明灯有各种各样的形状和大小，它们一般安置在建筑的外立面上，或是在私人花园中的小型灯柱上。

Lighting as Security

Sufficient lighting increases security and decreases opportunities for criminal activity. The overall perception of safety is greatly affected by lighting. Both sufficient lighting levels and proper glare control are critical to preserving visibility and helping pedestrians and drivers see potential dangerous situations. Streetlight levels should permit faces to be identified at 50 feet. The use of multiple light sources is preferable to fewer brighter light fixtures. Insufficient or uneven lighting can cast shadows where an assailant might hide. Too much light can also be a problem, creating an unattractive image or a nuisance to residents.

Lighting fixtures require maintenance. Lamps diminish in brightness as they age, trees may block illumination, and broken fixtures create dark areas. Select light fixtures that are durable and easily maintained. Consider any special conditions that may affect lighting. For example, a senior citizen's residential complex may require increased illumination for night lighting.

Increased lighting levels at outdoor uses such as gas stations and car lots often serves a combination of security and advertising purposes, as the lights are used to both draw in customers and illuminate the products for sale. Excessive lighting in such instances, however, can cause nearby areas to seem "dark" even if properly illuminated.

安全照明

充足的照明可以增加安全性、降低犯罪率。安全感在很大程度上受到灯光的影响。充足的照明灯光和恰当地控制强光在维持可见度和帮助行人和驾车者看清潜在的危险状况两方面起到关键作用。街道的照明等级要满足行人在50ft的距离内可以看清他人的脸部。复合式光源比那些数目少而光线强烈的光源更为可取。不充足或分布不均匀的灯光会为犯罪者提供用以隐藏的阴影。灯光过多的话也会带来问题，比如会使得景观不具有吸引力，或给当地居民造成光污染。

灯具需要维护。灯具的亮度会随着使用时间的增长而减弱，树木可能会阻挡住了灯光，而破损了的灯具就无法再照明。最好选用那些耐用的、易维护的灯具。充分考虑到任何会影响照明的特殊状况。比如，一个老年人居住区就需要延长夜间照明的时间。

在诸如加油站和停车场等户外区域增大照明等级，可以起到安全和广告的双重作用，因为，灯光同时还可以吸引顾客、照亮待售的商品。然而，此处过度的照明会使附近的区域显得阴暗，即使这些区域已经有合适的灯光。

Lighting Considerations

The color of the light that is cast is often an important consideration in streetscape design. Light sources such as high-pressure sodium that have poor color retention can create a yellowish glow on the street, which should be avoided. White-light sources such as metal halide, fluorescent, and compact fluorescent luminaries are recommended for sidewalks and other pedestrian areas and situations requiring color discrimination.

Choose fixtures that are physically strong and resistant to vandals, weather, and the environment. Also, choose light sources that have a longer lamp life to minimize repeated replacement of lamps. Fixtures should be able to start and operate at the lowest anticipated temperature on a site. Consult an individual fixture's specifications to determine if the color rendering, lamp life, and starting temperatures are appropriate for the street being designed.

照明需考虑的因素

在街景设计中，灯光的颜色是需要重点考虑的因素。高压钠灯之类的光源由于其色彩维持力低，产生的灯光微黄，不利于照明，应避免使用此类灯源。在人行道、其他步行区域以及需要区分灯光颜色的地方，我们推荐使用诸如金属卤化灯、荧光灯、高压荧光灯之类的白色光源。

选用那些牢固的、能抵抗蓄意破坏、恶劣天气与环境的灯具。并且选用有较长使用寿命的照明灯具，将灯具的更新率降至最低。在当地可能存在的最低温度条件下，照明灯必须能够正常启动与工作。决定灯具的灯光颜色、使用寿命、启动温度是否达到设计要求之前，请详细阅读灯具的使用说明书。

Light Pollution

Light pollution is light with no useful purpose. Inefficient light sources and certain types of light fixtures cause this energy waste. Some communities have developed outdoor lighting ordinances that regulate a variety of types of light pollution. When specifying the type and location of street light fixtures, address the different types of light pollution and available design and manufacturing solutions.

The International Dark Sky Association (IDA) in Tucson, Arizona, has developed a model outdoor lighting ordinance. The ordinance addresses the reasonable use of outdoor lighting for general illumination and safety purposes, to minimize light pollution, conserve energy, and protect the natural nighttime visual environment. Lighting zones have been established to identify different uses and characteristics, from very dark to high light-level applications.

光污染

光污染是指那些没有正当用途的灯光。低效率的光源和不恰当的灯具类型造成这种能源浪费。一些社区颁布了户外照明法令，用以整治各种类型的光污染。在确定街道照明灯具的类型与安放位置时，需要了解各种类型的光污染、可行性设计以及制造上的解决办法。

位于亚利桑那州图斯干的国际夜空联合会（IDA）已经颁布了一则户外照明条例。该条例阐述了户外普通照明和安全照明的合理使用模式，如何将光污染降至最低、节约能源、保护自然状态下的夜晚光环境。该条例还确立了不同的照明区域，用以确定不同的照明类型和特性，比如，从非常暗的区域到高照明等级区域。

Street Furniture

Street furniture includes the smaller-scale amenities located on sidewalks that add scale, functionality, and a human element to the streetscape. Types of street furniture include benches, tables and chairs, trash receptacles, bicycle racks, drinking fountains, and other items as desired. Street furniture is typically fixed in place, with removable elements as required, such as trash receptacle liners. Durability and ease of maintenance are important factor is the selection of permanent street furniture.

The placement of street furniture is based on function and need and may be included as part of community-wide streetscape requirements. The most common location for street furniture is within the curb zone of the sidewalk. Street furniture is often clustered near intersections, where pedestrians wait while crossing the street. An area of at least 10 feet immediately adjacent to the intersection should be kept clear.

城市街具

城市街具指的是人行道上小型的设施，它们扩大了街景的规模，为街景注入功能性和人文特色。城市街具包括了长椅、休憩坐椅、垃圾箱、自行车架、喷水池以及其他必备的设施。城市街具一般都有其固定的位置，并且在应用中会充分考虑到易于移动这一因素，比如装有滑轮的垃圾箱。耐用和易于维护是在选择永久性城市街具时需要考虑的重要因素。

城市街具的布置基于其功能和需求，也可能作为全社区对街景的需求的一部分。城市街具最常见的位置是人行道的路缘区。考虑到行人一般在此等待穿越道路，因此它们通常还会大量布置于道路交叉口附近。但是，在距道路交叉口至少 10ft 的范围内，不能布置任何器具。

When selecting street furniture, create a palette of materials and pieces that work together in color, style, and character. Some communities have developed and implemented a palette of appropriate streetscape elements, including street furniture, which provides an easy first step in selecting pieces for a project. Coordination of city services is required, especially for items such as fountains and features requiring electrical power. Review local codes and ordinances for any street furniture location requirements or restrictions.

The most common elements of street furniture include the following:

- Benches
- Trash receptacles
- Newspaper racks
- Bike racks
- Bollards
- Kiosks
- Transit shelters
- Signage
- Public utilities and other public amenities
- Private amenities

选择城市街具时，要创建一块在色彩、风格、特征上均能搭配协调的材质"调色板"。一些社区已经建立了合适的街景"调色板"，它为选择城市街具的材料和部件完成了关键性的第一步。城市各个服务部门的通力合作也是必需的，特别是负责喷泉等设施所需电力的电力部门。再次深入了解当地关于城市街具的条例与法令，对其中的要求和限制有充分认识。

最常见的城市街具有下述几种：

- 长椅
- 垃圾箱
- 报刊架
- 自行车架
- 护栏
- 亭子
- 交通服务设施
- 标识物
- 公用事业设施及其他公共设施
- 私人设施

Benches

Benches are essential to making a sidewalk pedestrian-friendly. Benches are available in a wide array of shapes, materials, and styles, including those with arms and backs and those that are simply a seat bottom. Benches can include a center or intermediate arm that can discourage loitering or sleeping on the bench. Benches are often located in high-use or high-pedestrian traffic areas and are typically fastened to the pavement for security purposes. Benches are typically placed parallel to the sidewalk and may face in either direction. Typically, if located in the curb zone, they face either a building or the street; if placed in the building zone, they face the street. Benches may also be placed perpendicular to the sidewalk when placed in bulb-outs at intersections. Bench location should be coordinated with transit services to be compatible with stops and waiting areas.

长椅

长椅的存在使得人行道步行区更加怡人。由于形状、材料及风格的不同，长椅的种类繁多，比如有些长椅有手扶杆和后背，而有些只有一个简易的坐凳。在长椅的中间或其他位置应设置手扶杆，可避免行人在长椅上长时间逗留或睡觉。长椅通常布置在行人众多、交通密集的步行区域，出于安全考虑，它们一般都被牢牢固定于地面。长椅的布置一般平行于人行道，朝向任意。一般来说，如果长椅位于路缘区，它们既可以朝向建筑，也可以朝向街道；如果长椅位于建筑区，它们就朝向街道。当位于靠近道路交叉口处时，长椅会与人行道成直角布置。长椅的布置应与交通服务设施结合起来，如在交通停靠站和候车区均应该安置长椅。

Trash Receptacles

Trash receptacles are among the most ubiquitous elements of a streetscape. They come in a variety of types and materials, ranging from more modern concrete square containers to more traditional metal or wood-slatted round containers. Many styles can also include an attached receptacle, often on the top of the container for recyclable materials. Some communities are starting to include separate receptacles for recyclable materials.

Provide trash receptacles at frequent-enough intervals so that their use is convenient and that they are well-maintained. Publicly maintained trash receptacles are typically located in the curb zone; privately maintained receptacles are located in the building zone, often adjacent to building entrances.

垃圾箱

垃圾箱是最常见的街景要素。它们有各种各样的类型和制作材料，有的是由混凝土材料制作而成的方形垃圾箱，有的是由传统的金属或木头制成的圆形垃圾箱。在许多垃圾箱的顶部会设置一个回收容器，用以回收那些可以再利用的垃圾。有些社区已经为可以再利用的垃圾准备了专门的垃圾箱。

保证相邻垃圾箱之间的间隔适中，这样使用起来会更为便利，也易于维护。公共垃圾箱一般布置在路缘区，而私有垃圾箱一般布置在邻近建筑入口处。

Bike Racks

As more communities seek to make their streets bicycle-friendly, it is critical to provide adequate bike racks throughout major activity centers. Bike racks can be modern in their styling, ranging from vertical metal slats on a flat base to continuous sinuous curving pieces of metal, or more artistic shapes. In addition to formal bike racks, many bicycle riders often lock their bikes to street sign poles when there is no formal bike rack available.

Newspaper Racks

Newspaper racks serve an important function in the community, and are protected by the First Amendment, but improperly placed newspaper racks and too many different newspaper racks crammed onto small sidewalks can be both an eyesore and a safety hazard. To control the design aesthetic of newspaper racks, many communities are installing larger-scale, single newspaper racks with multiple containers inside. Although these multiple containers are an increased expense to the municipality (individual racks are paid for by the individual publication), they establish a cleaner and more coherent streetscape environment. Some communities are exploring the use of a single structure that includes both multiple newspaper racks and a space for utility boxes, further streamlining the sidewalk character.

自行车架

许多社区在寻求途径使得街道能够更好地容纳自行车，在主要中心活动区设置合适的自行车架就是一种重要的解决方法。自行车架的设计可以很现代，可以是安置在地面上的竖直金属板条，或是弯曲的曲线形的金属板条，也可以是更具艺术美感的形式。在已经没有多余的自行车架可用的情况下，许多自行车主将自行车锁在街道标牌的立杆上。

报刊架

报刊架在社区中发挥了重要作用，属于一级维护设施。但是如果在不恰当的位置安放报刊架以及在人行道上设置过多的报刊架会让人厌烦，并带来安全隐患。为了让报刊架的设计更科学更具美感。许多社区采用了那种体积较大而形式简单的报刊架,此种报刊架内部有多个储存格,利于存放更多的报刊。尽管这种多功能的报刊架的采用会增加政府的财政投入(单功能的报刊架由出版商承担费用),它们的使用会使得街道环境更为清洁、更具条理。一些社区正在开发使用那种可同时容纳报刊架和公共事业设施的城市街具,如此,人行道更加现代化、一体化。

Bollards

Bollards are streetscape elements of concrete or steel that typically prevent traffic from encroaching in pedestrian areas. Besides being a necessary functional element, bollards can be an attractive, well-designed component of the overall streetscape. They are typically located along the curb edge of a sidewalk, but bollards can also be used to protect pedestrians on traffic islands and medians and to protect standpipes, streetlights, street trees, public art, and other sidewalk elements. Bollards have been used as a security element around sensitive buildings and important sites. They come in a multitude of styles, from fixtures reminiscent of hitching posts to sleek steel posts.

护栏

护栏多由混凝土或钢铁制成,布置它们是为了阻止车行交通侵入到步行区域。它不仅是必备的功能性要素,而且也可以是整个街景中极具吸引力的设计要素。护栏通常布置在人行道的路缘区,但是它们也可以用来保护交通岛和道路中心带上的行人,还能保护竖管、街灯、行道树、公共艺术品及其他街道设施。护栏还可以布置在敏感性建筑和重要场所的外围,起到安全保护作用。护栏的风格也很多样,有的是怀旧风格的护栏,有的是光亮的金属护栏,等等。

Kiosks

Kiosks provide a central location for information on community events and other announcements. Well-designed and -located sidewalk kiosks can help establish the design tone for an individual street or even a larger community. Kiosks can be designed to include amenities such as newspaper racks, maps, public phones, and signage. When deciding whether kiosks may be appropriate, consider sidewalk width, pedestrian volume, the proposed design, and long-term maintenance, to ensure that the kiosk provides a benefit to the community. Kiosk design can range from more elaborate or traditional types to more modern or contemporary concrete, wooden, or metal designs. Often, kiosk design can be incorporated into a public art program, resulting in a collection of unique artistic pieces throughout a community. Like most street furniture, kiosks, especially due to their size, should be located within the curb zone and only in sidewalks with sufficient width. Sidewalk bulb-outs at intersections are prime locations for kiosks.

亭子

亭子为公布社区重要事件的相关信息以及其他通告提供了一个重要的集聚地。设计优秀并且位置恰当的亭子能够帮助街道甚至整个社区确定其独有的设计风格。设计亭子时可以适当地加入报刊架、地图、公用电话、标识物等公共设施。在确定亭子是否合适时,需考虑人行道宽度、步行区域大小、推荐的设计形式、长期维护等因素,并要确保亭子能够为社区带来益处。亭子的设计形式多种多样,有的设计很复杂很精细,有的设计走传统路线,有的又是现代的混凝土、仿木或金属设计。亭子的设计要融入公共艺术品设计之中,使得整个社区有着别具一格的艺术魅力。和大多数城市街具一样,由于其自身大小的限制,亭子一般只设置在路缘区或有足够宽度的人行道上。道路交叉口处是亭子落位的优先选择。

Transit Stops and Shelters

Integrate transit stops and associated transit amenities into the overall streetscape plan. Transit stops can range from a sign identifying the stop and route number or name to a bench or to a partially enclosed transit shelter that protects waiting passengers from the elements. Other elements often included are route maps, route schedules, and, more recently, electronic tracking displays to show the time of the next arrival. Transit shelters may include benches or individual seats that need to be flipped down to sit on, to prevent sleeping in the shelters.

Transit shelters come in a variety of shapes and designs. Basic shelters have a roof and a panel on the back side, for wind protection. In colder climates, shelters may be enclosed on three or four sides, with an opening for ingress and egress. Also in colder climates, shelters can include heating lamps that can be turned on by waiting passengers or lighting that is sensitive to light levels, turning on at sundown. Designs can range from traditionally detailed shelters to sleeker and more modern structures. Materials are typically steel or some other metal for the frame, with strengthened glass for the side panels. Often, the surface of the glass includes etching or other graphic elements to visually identify the glass and prevent people from walking into the glass. The glass needs to be shatterproof to prevent injury if the glass is broken or vandalized.

Transit stops are typically located adjacent to intersections, either before or after the stoplight. Buses have flexibility in changing lanes, so stops can be accommodated on sidewalks by having the bus pull into the parking or curb lane. Consider the location of street trees and other street furniture when locating transit stops, to ensure that there are no obstructions to the front and back doors for passengers entering and disembarking.

Some communities have implemented cutouts into wider sidewalks to allow buses to pull out of the traffic flow. Buses in dedicated transit lanes and rail transit have less flexibility. Many of these types of transit run in center lanes, which require transit islands in the middle of the road. Special care should be taken to ensure that these traffic islands are comfortable and safe. See Transporation in Part 3 of this book for more information on planning for various forms of transit.

交通停靠站和中途候车亭

将交通停靠站和其他相关的交通服务设施融入到整个街景规划中来。交通停靠站可以是停靠处的一个站牌、标明交通路线的编号或名称，也可以是长椅，或者是一个用以保护候车的行人的半封闭的候车亭。其他的组成要素还有路线图、交通时刻表以及能够显示下一趟班车到站时间的电子公告牌。同时，在候车亭内可以布置长椅或单个的座椅，椅面向下倾斜一定的角度，有效防止行人在坐椅上睡觉。

候车亭可有各种各样的设计形式，其基本形式就是上部有一个顶棚，后方有一块隔板，防止强风灌入庇护物。在较寒冷的气候条件下，庇护物的三边甚至四边都全部围起，只在正面留一个入口让行人进出。另外，候车亭内要配有供暖灯，它们可以由候车的行人自行打开，或者使用对照明等级敏感度高的灯具，能够在日落后自动打开。庇护物可以是传统的、结构较为复杂的设计形式，也可以是金属材料的、造型现代的设计形式。候车亭通常采用钢铁或其他金属材料作骨架，隔板采用强化玻璃。在玻璃的表面一般会刻有蚀刻画或其他类型的图画，利于行人看清玻璃，以免撞向玻璃。此种玻璃必须是防碎玻璃，才能尽可能地避免由于玻璃破裂或遭受蓄意破坏后给行人造成的伤害。

交通停靠站一般布置在靠近道路交叉口处的位置，既可以在红色尾灯之前也可以在红色尾灯之后。在转线时，巴士在转换行车道时，有一定的灵活性。所以停靠站可以设置在人行道上，让巴士转进停车区和路缘带。确定停靠站的位置时，要考虑到行道树和其他城市街具的位置，确保乘客在前后门上下车时不会受到任何阻碍。

一些社区已经采取措施在较宽的人行道上设置了断点，允许巴士暂时离开交通带。行驶在专用车道和城市轨道上的巴士转换行车道的灵活性相应较低，而此类巴士大多行驶在中心道路上，此时，就需要在道路的中央设置交通岛。也就必须采取措施，确保交通岛的安全与舒适。欲了解更多关于运输设计的知识，可参阅本书第三部分关于"运输"的章节。

Signage

The shape, color, and graphic design of most traffic and directional signage are federally controlled. Community-oriented signs can be designed as an integral part of the streetscape plan. Street signs can be designed as simple, flat metal panel faces attached to aluminum or other metal poles or more elaborate signs with two legs and multiple spots for removable signs. These signs can include gateway features, monument signs, directional signage to public parking locations, and other community-focused signs. Most street signs are located in the curb zone of the sidewalk.

标识物

大多数交通和指示性标识物的外形、颜色、轮廓都是由联邦政府统一制定的。而社区性的标识物就可以作为街景规划的一个重要组成部分。街道标识物可以设计成简易的、平滑的金属面板，且下部装有铝制的或其他金属制成的立杆；也可以设计成较复杂的、立杆可以移动的形式。这些标识物包含了入口指示牌、纪念性物体指示牌、标明公共停车场方向的指示牌及其他的社区性标识物。大多数街道标识物都位于人行道的路缘区。

Public Utilities and Private Streetscape Amenities

There are four main types of secondary streetscape elements that a community has slightly less control over than street furniture: utility-related structures, ATMs and public phones, parking meters, and private streetscape amenities.

Utility-Related Structures

Utilities are the often-hidden systems that keep our cities running smoothly. The most visually prominent element on many streets are overhead electrical and telecommunication wires. Although telecommunication wires do not pose any serious danger, live electrical wires, even those that are coated, need to be kept clear of all obstructions, which typically means street trees. Trees located below electrical lines will need to be pruned to allow a clear space around the wires. Many newer communities have located these wires in utility corridors underneath the sidewalk, and some older communities have followed suit, undergrounding wires as part of redevelopment plans and streetscape improvements.

Utility cabinets, a necessary element in most city streets, house equipment to operate traffic signals, light rail systems, and telecommunications or utility company systems. For existing streets, there is little that can be done to move the existing cabinets unless major utility work is being done. For newly planned streets, the challenge is to locate these components in a manner that meets operational requirements while making the sidewalk more inviting and safe for pedestrians. This typically means placing utility cabinets in the curb zone.

公共事业设施和私人街景设施

有4种非主要的街景要素不受社区管理，它们是：公共事业设施、自动取款机和公用电话、汽车停放收费器、私人街景设施。

公共事业设施

公共事业设施系统是维持我们的城市正常运转的关键部分。街道上最常见的公共事业设施就是高处的电线和电信用线。电信用线一般不会带来危险，但是输电线，即使是那些已经包裹了绝缘材料的输电线都会有潜在的危险，所以其周围不应该有任何障碍物，尤其是行道树。输电线下方的行道树必须加以修剪，确保其与输电线之间有一段安全距离。许多新型社区已经将这些城市用线布置在人行道路面下的地下设施走廊中，其他一些社区也在纷纷效仿这一做法。地下线路已成为城市再发展规划和街景改良规划的重要组成部分。

在多数街道中，公共事业设施设备箱是必备的要素，箱内安放了启动交通标识物、交通灯系统和电信用线系统或公共设施系统的设备。对于现有的街道而言，除非公共设施的工作使命已圆满完成，否则不能移动这些公共事业设施设备箱。对于新近规划的街道，其面临的最大挑战就是在使得人行道更具吸引力更安全的同时，如何以一种更有效的方式布置这些设施，满足实际需求。典型做法就是将公共事业设施设备箱安放在路缘区。

ATMS and Public Phones

Public phones are becoming less common, and ATMs are gradually being added to the streetscape environment; nevertheless, it is useful to plan for and locate these elements accordingly. Pay phones are often located in either the curb zone or the building zone, whereas ATMs are almost always located in the building zone and are often recessed into the facade of the building.

Parking Meters

On most commercial streets, parking meters are a common site. Located within the curb zone of the sidewalk, parking meters range from the more traditional manually operated meters to more modern and elaborate electric meters that work with debit card systems. Multiple meters are rapidly replacing single-space or double-space meters.

自动取款机和公用电话

如今公用电话已不太常见，自动取款机的普及却丰富了街道环境；找到相应的方法利用这些要素也就非常有益。付费电话可以布置在路缘区，也可以布置在建筑区，而自动取款机总是布置在建筑区，且嵌在建筑外墙的凹进处。

汽车停放收费器(咪表)

在大多数商业街，汽车停放收费器是非常普遍的。它一般布置在人行道的路缘区，汽车停放收费器的形式也很多样，从传统的、手动操作的汽车停放收费器到现代复杂的、与银行卡系统联网的电子汽车停放收费器，种类繁多。多功能汽车停放收费器将很快取代单一功能或双功能的汽车停放收费器。

Private Streetscape Amenities

On many commercial streets, private business owners want to use the space outside their stores to place tables and chairs, display wares, or place temporary signs. The cost and maintenance for these private amenities are covered by the individual property owners, but the community has a stake in controlling the type and location of these amenities, to ensure a clear and safe path of travel. Communities typically control the placement of private amenities through zoning permits, specifying the height of elements and how far they can extend into the sidewalk, which depends on the overall sidewalk width.

私人街景设施

在很多商业街上，私人店主会利用他们店外的空间布置小桌椅、展示商品或安放临时性的标志物。这些私人设施的安置费用和后期维护由私人店主自行承担，但是社区有权利规定这些设施的类型和安放位置，以确保步行道的完整与安全。为了控制私人设施的布置，社区一般会根据人行道的宽度来划定这些私人设施的高度，可以摆放在哪些区域、能够占用多大的人行道空间等。

IMPLEMENTATION

Streetscape plans can be implemented at one time or phased in. For one-time construction projects, streetscape plans require a set of construction drawings, typically prepared by an urban designer or licensed landscape architect. Phased approaches or streetscape plans that rely on private implementation on an incremental basis typically require both construction drawings and streetscape design guidelines/summary charts of the allowable streetscape elements.

In many communities, the local government funds some of the cost through a business improvement fee paid by businesses along the street. Funding for streetscape improvements in conjunction with other street improvements is sometimes available through the National Main Streets Center of the National Trust for Historic Preservation or federal legislation such as ISTEA.

实施

街景规划的实施可以同时进行也可以分阶段进行。对于那些同时进行的建设项目，就需要大量的由城市规划师或注册景观规划师绘制的图纸。而那些依靠私人力量，逐渐增大工作量的街景规划或分阶段进行的街景规划，就同时需要建设图纸和关于允许使用的街景要素的概览性图表或指导方针。

在许多社区，当地政府通过向沿街的商业主征收商业改良税来资助街景项目的实施。此类经费有时候可以从(美国)历史保护国家信托基金会所属的(全美)主要街道中心或联邦立法(如ISTEA)等部门获得。

第5章 第七届 OISTAT[①] 国际剧场建筑竞赛

7th OISTAT THEATRE ARCHITECTURE COMPETITION 2007

Introduction

The OISTAT Theatre Architecture Competition is an international ideas competition, aimed at students and emerging practitioners, which is organised every four years by the Architecture Commission of OISTAT.

Selected entries are exhibited and cash prizes awarded at the Prague Quadrennial (PQ), the major international exhibition of scenography and theatre architecture, which takes place in Prague in the Czech Republic. The next PQ is due to take place in June 2007.

第七届 OISTAT 国际剧场建筑竞赛 2007年

简介

OISTAT 剧场建筑竞赛是一个面向全世界建筑专业学生和年轻建筑师的国际性的概念设计竞赛。由 OISTAT 的建筑委员会每四年举办一次。

在布拉格四年展（PQ）中展出入选作品并颁发奖金。PQ，舞台美术和剧场建筑的重要国际展，在捷克的布拉格举行。下一期布拉格四年展将于 2007 年 6 月举行。

Competition Theme

The aim of this competition is to pose a design problem for a new performance building with approximately 500 seats and to encourage a detailed exploration of this building type and the way in which it responds to a particular set of needs, which will be defined by the competitor. This may be a conventional performance or something more experimental. In this way it is hoped to encourage innovative thinking based on a deeper understanding of the relationship between the performance itself and the architecture, which facilitates it.

Collaborations between architects and other theatre practitioners such as directors, designers, technicians, actors, dancers, musicians, or students in those fields, will be welcomed, although it is not an essential requirement. As well as being a place for performances, a theatre is also a public building and its relationship to its setting and the design of its public circulation spaces will be of equal importance to the performance space itself.

竞赛主题

本届竞赛的主题为"500 座的水畔剧场"，鼓励参赛者详细探讨这一类型的建筑形式来满足它特定的需求。这将由参赛者界定。可以是传统的表演形式，也可以是实验性的。通过竞赛的方式，鼓励在创新思维的基础上，更深刻地理解剧场建筑的表演功能及建筑本身的关系。

虽然不是一项基本要求，但是本次竞赛欢迎建筑师与其他从业人员（如剧场导演、设计师、技术人员、演员、舞蹈家、音乐家，或与这些领域相关的学生）之间的协作。除了作为一处演出场所外，剧场还是一个公共建筑，因此剧院与其环境的关系、公共流线空间的设计与表演空间（的设计）同样重要。

The Site

As in the previous competition in 2003, competitors will be able to choose their own site in a location they are familiar with. This is intended to encourage a response

---

[①] OISTAT（Organisation Internationale des Scénografes, Techniciens et Architectes de Théâtre，简称 OISTAT），国际剧场组织，全称为国际舞台美术、剧场建筑师、剧场技术师组织。1968 年成立于捷克布拉格，创立之初是东欧地区剧场设计交流平台，原为联合国教科文组织（UNESCO）的外围组织，目前是全球性的国际组织。

which is rooted in a particular culture and setting, anywhere in the world. There is however a specific requirement that the site is located close to water, be it the sea, a river, canal or lake. The way in which the building looks outwards to its setting will be of equal importance to the way it looks inwards to the performance space. Many performance buildings around the world enjoy waterfront settings and the competition is intended to encourage innovative thinking about how these can be exploited.

位置

与2003年举办的竞赛一样，参赛者可自行选择自己所熟悉的基地位置。它可以在世界任何地方，但鼓励充分体现本土文化。特定的要求就是基地要位于水畔，可以是海边、河边或者湖边，建筑物的外部表现与完美的内部空间同等重要。世界上许多观演类建筑以水畔为基地，本次竞赛鼓励对此类作品开发的创造性思考。

Key Issues

Successful performance spaces have some very particular requirements, which competitors are expected to understand and explore in order to create an environment in which the unique interaction between audience, artists and technology, which constitutes a live performance, can flourish.

Key issues to be considered are as follows:

关键议题

成功的表演空间有一些特殊需求，参赛者应了解并探究这些需求，从而创造出使观众、艺术家和技术之间以独特形式交流的环境，构成有生气的表演空间。

需要考虑的关键议题如下：

Audience Cohesion

The way in which an audience is arranged, in relation to the performance area, plays a key role in creating a successful atmosphere where audiences feel engaged by the performance and performers can communicate well with them. How does this chemistry work and what factors are at play in a successful performance space? This can take many different forms but the key is maintaining an appropriate human scale where a single performer can command a whole audience. To achieve this the audience must be as close as possible to the performance and be able to see and hear well.

与观众的互动

为了创造一个观众被演出吸引并且表演者与观众有良好沟通的成功氛围，观众席的排布方式、与表演区的关系就很重要。如何擦出火花❶？成功的演出空间有赖于哪些因素？可以选用不同的形式，但最主要的是让单个表演者控制整个观众席的同时，仍保持适合于人的尺度。为了达到这一目的，观众必须尽可能靠近表演区，这样才能看得见、听得清。

Sightlines

To see well the audience must be arranged so they can all see the performance. Not only must their view be free of obstructions, but they must also be sufficiently close to the performers to distinguish their gestures and appreciate the scenic or architectural space they occupy. There are many different ways in which this can be achieved, depending upon the type of performance and the configuration of the space, but the essential principles are constant.

视线

安排好观众的位置，这样观众都能看见表演。不仅仅观众的视野中不能有障碍，而且他们要能充分地接近表演者，以看清表演者的手势、欣赏其舞台场景或建筑空间。要做到这一点可以有不同的方法，这取决于演出的类型和空间结构，但最重要的原则是不变的。

Acoustics

Good hearing is as important as good seeing. Different performance types require different acoustic conditions to be best appreciated. Speech, for instance, requires a less reverberant environment than that required for un-

---

❶ 西方人喜欢用Chemistry表示男女之间的吸引力，这里的Chemistry应该指表演区对观众的吸引力。因而采用了意译。

amplified music. Where a space is to be used for a range of different performance types some means of varying the acoustic may be necessary. The acoustic of a room is determined by its shape, volume and materials. Good hearing is also promoted by the exclusion of unwanted background noise caused by external breakin (traffic/trains/aircraft) or noise generated by building services. Competitors are not expected to carry out detailed acoustic studies but should demonstrate an understanding of the factors, which contribute to a successful acoustic environment.

声学

听得清与看得见同样重要。不同的表演形式需要不同的音响效果。举例来说，演讲所需的反射声就比音乐少。一个空间被用于不同的演出类型，就需要考虑不同的声学需求。一个房间的声学效果由房间的形状、体积和材料所决定。好的音质效果取决于排除不必要的、由外部噪声（交通/火车/飞机）或建筑设备所产生的噪声。参赛者不需详细说明对声学的研究，但应显示其对成功声学因素的考虑。

Technical Requirements

Most performances rely upon some form of stage technology to facilitate them. This includes stage lighting, projection, sound systems and mechanical systems, which are used to move scenery or reconfigure the room. Provision for these systems needs to be integrated into the architecture and must be accessible and safe to use. Safe access, particularly to high-level lighting positions, is of increasing concern in the theatre, particularly where technical set-ups have to be changed quickly between performances.

技术需求

大多数的演出都依赖舞台技术设备。这包括舞台照明、投影、音响系统和移动舞台布景或者重新装配房间的机械装配系统。这些内容要在建筑中综合考虑，使其可接近和安全使用。安全通道，特别是高处的照明设施，在剧场中是特别需要关注的，尤其是那些技术装备不得不在演出之间快速更换的地方。

The Brief

The issues above are some of the key factors to be considered in the design of any performance venue but they will vary considerably depending upon the performance type and pattern of use. It is for each competitor or team to define the type of building they are designing, how it will be used and its location.

Each entry must include the following information:

摘要

以上议题是在设计任何演出类建筑时都应考虑的主要因素，他们很大程度上取决于演出的类型和使用方式。参赛者或参赛团队应确定他们所设计的建筑的类型，将如何使用该建筑及建筑的位置。

每位参赛者都必须提供以下资料：

The Site/Location

This must be a real location, anywhere in the world, with a waterfront setting, selected by the competitor. Competitors must explain why they have chosen it and give details of its context and the community in which it is located. Information about the location in the form of drawings, photographs and a written description must be provided to allow the design to be understood in relation to its setting.

位置

必须是一个真实的场地，参赛者可以在全球的任何地方选择一个水畔，参赛者要解释为什么选择该场所并且给出基地所处社区的文脉细节。必须提供有关基地的图纸、照片和文字描述，以便于人们理解设计与场地的关系。

The Purpose

Competitors must state what type of performance(s) the design will be used for. Establishing a clear link between the performance and the architecture is a key aim of the competition. The design may be specific to a single performance, a particular performance type or a range of different uses. Drawings of the theatre space should show it in use for a performance.

目的

参赛者必须说明其设计适用于何种类型演出。在演出与建筑之间建立一种清晰的联系是本竞赛的基本目标。所设计的建筑可具体到某个单一性演出，某种特定的表演类型或各种不同的用途。剧场空间表现图应表现出具体表演类型的使用情况。

Accommodation

Having defined the location and purpose of the project, competitors must design a proposal for a new building, which provides for the following general requirements:

- A space for a live performance with an audience of 500 people.
- Facilities for the audience, including toilets and the sale of tickets, food and drink.
- Provision for technical installations for the performance (lighting, sound, mechanical systems).
- Backstage accommodation for up to 40 performers.
- Provision for delivery and setting up of scenery and equipment.
- Other facilities appropriate to the type of venue or performance proposed (workshops, rehearsal space, offices, plant).
- Provision for safe evacuation of all occupants in an emergency.
- Good access for people with disabilities.

设施

在确定了基地和工程项目的目标之后，参赛者要为新建筑提出方案，以满足以下需求：

- 一个可容纳 500 个观众和现场表演空间的观众厅。
- 观众服务设施，包括厕所和售票处、餐饮处。
- 表演所需的技术设备（照明、音响、机械系统）。
- 后台设施应满足至少 40 个演员使用。
- 设备的传送和舞台布景、器材的安放。
- 其他设备用房以及设施（工作室、排练室、办公室、绿化）。
- 发生紧急状况时的安全疏散通道。
- 残疾人通道。

5.1 Competition Rules and Conditions

The Architecture Commission of OISTAT is promoting an international ideas competition in a single stage, open to architects and students of schools of architecture.

Architects or students associated with members of the jury are not permitted to enter.

5.1 竞赛规则和条件

OISTAT 发起的国际竞赛，面向全世界年轻建筑师及相关科系的学生。

与评审团成员有关联的建筑师或学生不得参赛。

5.2 Documents to be Submitted

5.2.1 Drawing requirements

a. Plans of each level, at least two sections and important elevations to a scale of not less than 1/200.

b. Three-dimensional images of the building and the auditorium.

c. Auditorium studies showing it in use for a performance or performances.

d. Site plan to a scale of 1/1000

e. Description of the existing site (drawings, photographs)

f. Models cannot be accepted, although photographs of models can be included.

g. Drawings must not carry any means of identifying the entrant(s) apart from the code number referred to in para 5.2.2 (d) below.

5.2 需要提交的文件

5.2.1 图纸要求

a. 各层平面图，至少两个剖面图和一个重要的立面图，比例不小于 1/200。

b. 建筑物以及观众厅的三维空间表现图。

c. 不同演出时的观众厅研究。

d. 基地平面图比例 1/1000。

e. 基地现状描述(图纸、照片)。

f. 不接受模型,但可附模型照片。

g. 除 5.2.2(d)中提到的代码,不得在图纸及文件上附加任何表明身份的标记。

5.2.2 Every entry shall compromise:

a. A maximum of 6 panels at A2 size (594mm×420mm) mounted on card or suitable lightweight backing. If an image will not fit on one A2 panel it may be continued on an adjacent panel. Please provide a diagram indicating how panels should be assembled.

b. A CD containing electronic copies of the panels (in. pdf format). Entries in electronic format only will not be considered.

c. A short written description of the performance(s) to be housed, the site and an explanation of the design concept (maximum 200 words). The text will be incorporated on the panels but will also be provided separately on A4 size paper in an unsealed envelope.

d. All the documents and the CD are to be identified by a code of six numbers to be chosen by the competitor(s), 10mm high, written or printed in the top right hand corner of each document.

e. A letter with the name(s), address, telephone no. and email address of the competitor(s) in a sealed envelope, marked with the same code no. as in para 5.2.2 (d) above.

f. Colour techniques are permitted but competitors are reminded that if their drawings are selected for publication, they may be reproduced in black and white, and reduced to A4 size or smaller.

g. All text is to be in English.

5.2.2 每个参赛作品需提供:

a. 6张 A2(594mm×420mm)大小、衬以适当的轻质材料的图纸。如果图像的尺寸超过A2,可在相邻的面板继续。但请提供一张简图表明如何贴图。

b. 一张刻录电子文档(以 pdf 格式)的CD。只有电子文档的参赛作品不予考虑。

c. 一份关于表演类型、基地以及设计构思的简短文字说明(最多200字)。文字应结合到图面,同时需单独打印在一张A4纸上,放入一个未封口的信封中。

d. 参赛者自行设定一个由6位数组成的代码,手写或者打印(数字的高度为10mm)在每份文件的右上角,用于鉴别所有的文件和CD(也指代参赛者)。

e. 在一个密封的信封中放入写有参赛者姓名、地址、电话号码和电子邮箱的信件,并附上如 5.2.2(d)所提的代码。

f. 可用彩色,需要提醒的是,如果参赛作品被选定出版,则以黑白制作,并减至A4或者更小的尺寸。

g. 所有的文本需用英文表述。

5.2.3 This is an ideas competition and there is no intention that the winning entry will be built.

5.2.4 Entries will not be returned or insured by OISTAT. Competitors should retain copies of their work.

5.2.3 这是一次概念设计竞赛,没有创意就不能赢得竞赛。

5.2.4 OISTAT将不予退还或保留参赛者的作品,所有参赛者要自行保存副本。

5.3 Competition Schedule

5.3.1 The competition documents and conditions will be available from 1 June 2006 on the OISTAT Website: www.oistat.org/archcomp2007.

5.3.2 Questions can be sent by email to archcom@oistat.org Questions should be written in English and must be received no later than 1 October 2006.

5.3.3 The answers to the questions will be posted on the Website from 1 November 2006.

5.3 竞赛时间表

5.3.1 竞赛的文本和要求自2006年6月1日起发布于 OISTAT 网站。网址 www.oistat.org/archcomp2007。

5.3.2 有关询问的问题可发送电子邮件到:archcom@oistat.org，相关问题应该用英文书写，并于 2006 年 10 月 1 日前必须送达。

5.3.3 将从 2006 年 11 月 1 日起，在 OISTAT 网站上回答相关的问题。

5.3.4 Competition entries are to be sent to:
OISTAT-Architecture Competition
c/o Beneke Daberto
BDP Muenchen GmbH
AugustenstraBe 59
D-80333 Muenchen
Germany

5.3.4 参赛作品交至：
OISTAT 建筑竞赛
贝内克（达伯托　转）
BDP 慕尼黑有限公司
奥古斯藤街，59 号
D-80333 慕尼黑
德国

Entries must be despatched on or before 16 February 2007. Entries will be disqualified if:
- the postmark is a date after 16 February 2007.
- the entry is received after 16 March 2007.

参赛作品应于 2007 年 2 月 16 号或 2 月 16 号之前寄出。以下情况取消竞赛资格：
- 邮戳在 2007 年 2 月 16 号之后。
- 收件日期在 2007 年 3 月 16 之后。

5.3.5 The entry fee for the competition is €50 per entry. Competitors can pay via PayPal❶ on the website, or via bank transfer with their code number❷ as described in 5.2.2(d) above to:
ABN-AMRO Bank
Dam 2，1012 NP Amsterdam
The Netherlands
STICHTING OISTAT
BIC：ABNANL2A
ACCOUNT NUMBER：59.34.16.732
IBAN：NL62ABNA0593416732

All entries will be handled by a third party, and there will be no way for the jury to know the origin of the entry.

5.3.5 参赛报名费为 50 欧元，可根据上述 5.2.2 (d)所提示的参赛者代码，通过 PayPal 网上付款或者银行转账至：
ABN-AMRO 银行
Dam 2，1012 NP 阿姆斯特丹
荷兰
STICHTING OISTAT
BIC：ABNANL2A
账号：59.34.16.732
IBAN：NL62ABNA0593416732
所有参赛者的背景资料将由第三方处理，评审团将匿名审理作品。❸

5.3.6 Entry fees must be received no later than 16 March 2007.
Entries submitted without an entry fee will not be considered.

5.3.6 参赛报名费应在 2007 年 3 月 16 号之前收到。
超过规定时间，所参赛的作品不予考虑。

5.4 Prizes

5.4.1 The first prize will be €5,000, the second prize will be €2,500 and the third prize will be €1,000. There will be three additional prizes of €500 each. In addition to these prizes, there will be honourable mentions. The jury reserves the right to modify the distribution of prize money, within the same total amount and number of prizes.

5.4.2 The prizes will be announced and awarded at the Prague Quadrennial in June 2007.
participants.

---

❶ PayPal 是 eBay 旗下的网上支付工具，帮助在线付款。
❷ 这里的 code number 指参赛者身份的代码。
❸ 此处我们将之"意译"。这里的意思是评审团不会知道参赛者的情况，主要是体现其公正性。

5.4 奖金

5.4.1 一等奖奖金 5000 欧元

二等奖奖金 2500 欧元

三等奖奖金 1000 欧元

三个优秀奖,奖金各 500 欧元。除这些奖项外,还有荣誉奖。评审团保留在相同的总数和奖项中,修正比赛奖金分配的权利。

5.4.2 奖项将在 2007 年 6 月布拉格四年展上宣布、颁发。

5.5 Publication

5.5.1 The competition entries will become the property of OISTAT and may be published and exhibited in any country at the discretion of OISTAT.

5.5.2 OISTAT will respect and acknowledge the copyright of the entries.

5.5 出版

5.5.1 竞赛作品版权归 OISTAT 所有,可在 OISTAT 组织的任何国家中出版和展出。

5.5.2 OISTAT 会尊重而且承认参赛者的版权。

5.6 Acceptance of Conditions

5.6.1 By submitting an entry, participants or participating teams will:

a. Agree to the rules and regulations as set out in this programme.

b. declare that the proposed design is their own work.

c. agree to accept the decisions of the jury as final.

d. Agree not disclose their identities or publicise their entry in any way before the jury have made their selection. Any breach of this rule will render the entry invalid.

5.6 比赛规则

5.6.1 无论个人或团队参赛者都将遵守以下规定:

a. 同意大赛规则并遵守。

b. 所参赛作品为本人或团队所有。

c. 同意接受评审团的评审结果。

d. 同意在评审团做出决定之前,不以任何方式泄露自己的身份或公开表明参赛,不遵守该规则者,将被取消参赛资格。

5.7 Jury

5.7.1 The international jury will consist of 4 architects from the following continents:

Europe, Russia, Asia, North America, plus one other experienced theatre practitioner.

5.7.2 In case of the absence of a juror, OISTAT will assign another qualified person as a member of the jury.

5.7.3 The jury will produce a report explaining the reasons for its decisions and commenting on the prize-winning and honourably mentioned entries.

5.7.4 The report of the jury will be published on the internet and distributed by the OISTAT Centres.

5.7.5 The jury will select entries for an exhibition at the Prague Quadrennial in June 2007.

5.7.6 A brochure illustrating at least 25 entries will be published and will be available at the Prague Quadrennial 2007, after which distribution will be by way of the OISTAT Centres or via the internet.

5.7.7 OISTAT will offer the results of the competition to the press (publications covering theatre design and architecture)

5.7 评审团

5.7.1 国际评审团将由来自欧洲、俄罗斯、亚洲、北美的四位建筑师和另一位有经验的从事剧场工作的人员组成。

5.7.2 如果有评审员缺席,OISTAT 将任命另一位有资格担当评审的人员。

5.7.3 评审团将发布书面报告,解释评审结果并对获奖作品及荣誉提名作品发表评论。

5.7.4 评审团的报告将在因特网上发布且由 OISTAT 中心分发。

5.7.5 评审团将挑选入围 2007 年 6 月布拉格四年展的作品。

5.7.6 由 OISTAT 中心分发或在因特网上发布至少包括 25 个作品的图册,这一图册也可用于 2007 布拉格四年展。

5.7.7 OISTAT将竞赛结果交给出版社（出版物包括剧场设计和建筑）。

5.8 Time schedule

1 June 2006

Brief and Conditions posted on the OISTAT Website and notification sent to OISTAT Centres and schools of architecture.

1 October 2006

Final date for questions.

Questions received after this date will not be considered. Answers to questions will be posted on the OISTAT website from 1 November 2006.

16 February 2007

Closing date for despatch of entries.

Postmark validates despatch date.

16 March 2007

Closing date for arrival of entries and entry fee at OISTAT.

30 March-13 April 2007

Jury meeting and report.

16 April 2007

Notification of the prize-winners.

14-24 June 2007

Exhibition of prize-winning and selected entries at the Prague Quadrennial.

15 June 2007

Official announcement and prize-giving at the Prague Quadrennial. The first prize-winner will also be recognised on June 18, 2007 at the PQ awards ceremony.

Copyright：OISTAT 2006

5.8 日程安排

2006年6月1日

竞赛简介和要求发布于OISTAT网站上，通知书送至OISTAT中心和建筑学院。

2006年10月1日

提问最后期限。

在此日期之后收到的所有问题都不予考虑。

从11月1日始，于OISTAT网站上回答相关问题。

2007年2月16日

参赛作品寄出截止日期。

以当地邮戳为准。

2007年3月16日

收到作品和报名费的最后日期。

2007年3月30～4月13日

评审团会议。

2007年4月16日

通知获奖者。

2007年6月14～24日

获奖作品展，并选择入围布拉格四年展的作品。

2007年6月15日

发布官方的公告，并在布拉格四年展上颁奖。一等奖获得者将亮相2007年6月18日举行的布拉格四年展颁奖典礼。

第6章 国外建筑设计图选译

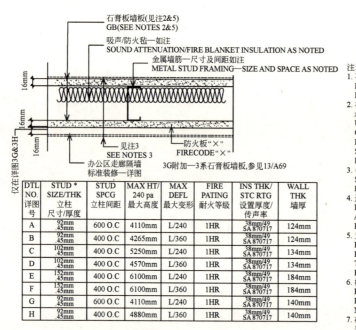

G3 1小时耐火等级干法施工墙板
G3 1 HOUR DRYWALL PARTITON

注:
1. 石膏板墙板体系总说明见图RA-440.
   REFER TO DRAWING A-440 FOR GYPSUM BOARD PARTITION SYSTEMS GENERAL NOTES.
2. 在高湿度部位采用防水石膏板或有薄面层的水泥板,如淋浴室,更衣室,游泳池或桑拿浴室等.
   USE WATERRESISTANT GYPSUM BOARD OR CEMENTITIOUS BOARD WITH THIN SET TILE FINISH OR IN AREAS OF HIGH HUMIDITY, SUCH AS SHOWER ROOMS, LOCKER ROOMS, POOL OR SAUNA ROOMS.
3. 各房间装修见装修表及立面图.
   SEE ROOM FINISH SCHEDULE AND ROOM ELEVATIONS FOR APPLIED FINISHES.
4. 适当的金属墙筋间距见图所注.
   PROVIDE METAL STUD SPACING AS APPROPRIATE TO ATTAIN RADIUS OF FINISH PARTITION AS SHOWN ON DRAWINGS.
5. 为达到所要求的耐火等级,采用耐火石膏板及水泥板
   PROVIDE FIRE RATED GYPSUM OR CEMENTITIOUS BOARD MATERIALS AS REQUIRED SO THAT THE PARTITION ASSEMBLY WILL ATTAIN THE FIRE RATING NOTED.
6. 标准隔墙说明见图所注,标准管道井壁说明见详图9.
   REFER TO DETAIL NO.3 FOR TYPICAL PARTITION NOTES. REFER TO DETAIL NO.9 FOR TYPICAL SHAFTWALL NOTES.
7. 在平面图上表示出需要耐火等级时,按要求采用耐火石膏板隔断.
   PROVIDE FIRE RATED GYPSUM BOARD AS REQUIRED TO PARTITION WHERE ARE SHOWN ON PLAN TO HAVE A FIRE RATING.

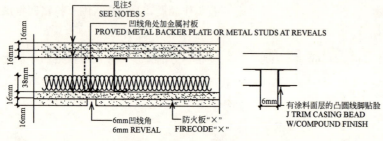

G4 干法施工墙板
G4 DRYWALL PARTITION

隔墙类型及详图
PARTITON TYPES AND
石膏板干法施工墙板体系
DETAJLS-GYPSUM
DRYWALL SYSTEMS

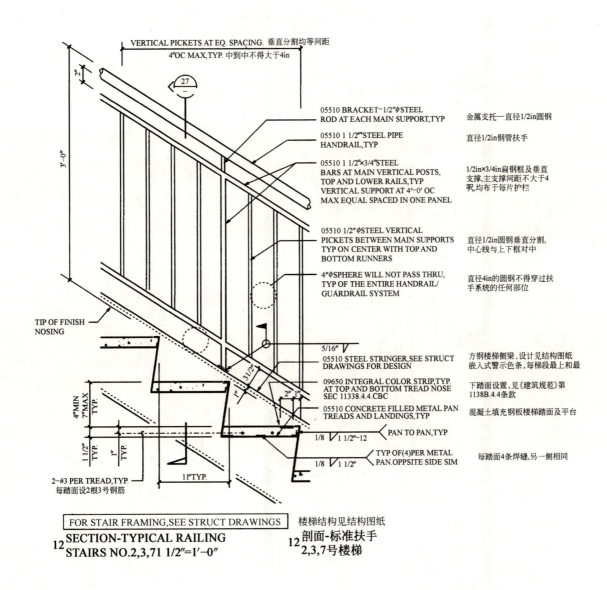

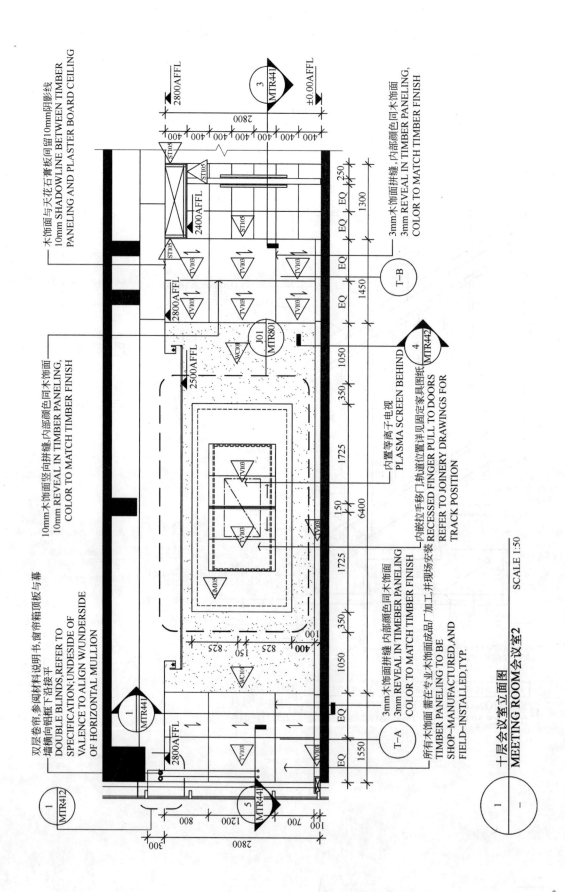